A CHAPTER OF FINGERPRINTS

'The Last Chapter'

A fingerprint is an impression left by the friction ridges of a human finger. The recovery of fingerprints from a crime scene is an important method of forensic science. Moisture and grease on a finger results in fingerprints being left on many different surfaces.

A CHAPTER OF LIFE IN FINGERPRINTS

'The Last Chapter'

Compiled by

Retired Chief Superintendent

BRIAN HUMPHREYS

© Copyright Brian Humphreys 2024

All rights reserved

No part of this publication may be reproduced,

Stored in a retrieval system,

or transmitted, in any form, or by any means,

electronical, mechanical, photocopying, rRecording or otherwise, without the prior written permission of the publisher.

	CONTENTS	Page
	Introduction	5
	Some Fingerprint Related Acronyms	6
	Common Fingerprint Terms	7
Chapter 1	Fingerprints – Their Origin in Crime Detection	8
Chapter 2	The Digital Explosion	12
Chapter 3	The 'Driving Force' and Early Days	15
Chapter 4	AFRC – Beginnings of the Interim Solution	24
Chapter 5	Trouble at Mill and an Office Move	29
Chapter 6	Goodbye IBM	35
Chapter 7	Operation Shakespeare	38
Chapter 8	Early Life After IBM	42
Chapter 9	EAS, Hubs and USA, Here We Come	47
Chapter 10	AFRC Progression and Life in the US	59
Chapter 11	Dealing with 'The Met' and 'Non-Members'	67
Chapter 12	2nd Generation AFIS – But PITO's on the Prowl	71
Chapter 13	Livescan and the Quality of Tenprints	77
Chapter 14	Visitors from America	86
Chapter 15	Livescan's Progress	90
Chapter 16	Promotion and Jo Pays a Visit	93
Chapter 17	The CMG Secretaryship	104
Chapter 18	The Red Team Review	107
Chapter 19	Interpol Calling?	115
Chapter 20	Onwards and Upwards Toward Interpol	122

Chapter 21	2001 Draws Nearer and Bermuda, Here I Come	129
Chapter 22	Flirting With SMI	141
Chapter 23	Antigua Here I Am!	145
Chapter 24	Meeting Interpol and off to Jamaica and Barbados	160
Chapter 25	CCLEC Meeting, Trinidad and Antigua Again	175
Chapter 26	Second Visits to Bermuda and the Bahamas	189
Chapter 27	It's 2001 and Only Six Months to Go	198
Chapter 28	We Catch the Jamaican 'Big Fish'	205
Chapter 29	The Dutch Caribbean	210
Chapter 30	Dominica and Guadelupe	216
Chapter 31	Barbados Again and Bermuda Stalls	223
Chapter 32	Turks and Caicos and on to Jamaica Again	228
Chapter 33	Bahamas Immigration and Jamaica Again	237
Chapter 34	The St Lucia ACCPO Conference	242
Chapter 35	My Alarm Call in Antigua	247
Chapter 36	What Now?	251
Chapter 37	Letting Sleeping Dogs Lie	257
Chapter 38	Goodbye Sir John & Nightmare in Seattle	261
Chapter 39	A 'Dude Ranch' and the Last Chapter	268
	About The Author and Thanks	278
	Reflective Notes	279

Cover
by
Google Images

Introduction

Writing my life story was a long, drawn-out affair which obviously followed a long, drawn-out life. If I was to die tomorrow, then it would be without complaint. I have been very lucky and handsomely rewarded.

When in a position to retire from the police service, I was asked if I would join a small team of others in the rolling out of the first computerised fingerprint system in England and Wales. This was to cater for all aspects of fingerprint identification used in the process of detecting crime. The organisation and deployment of the equipment wasn't anything to do with being able to identify fingerprints, that was a job for fingerprint experts who had received specialised training on a five-year program.

My fingerprints were the first to be scanned across the Atlantic Ocean and, additionally, to be received and searched in that process by British fingerprint experts situated on the West coast of America. I was also sent to numerous Caribbean Islands on an Interpol 'proof of concept' pilot to spread the gospel of modern fingerprint systems to police forces that lacked in such expertise. It included being embroiled in civil disputes by being employed as a 'para legal' by a top US firm of lawyers.

So, having written other books about my general policing experience, I thought that I could write a deeper and more interesting insight into my experience of working in the fingerprint world.

With that in mind, this book is the final chapter of my career life story and is not at all intended to be a reference book for those experts and others involved in the searching for fingerprints, storing them and identifying people by them. In that context, I have included in it, parts of my domestic life along the way. What I have said is what I believed and at the same time, whilst I have honestly provided an insight into various personal differences, with others, I have not set out to offend anyone.

SOME 'FINGERPRINT RELATED' ACRONYMS

ACCP		Association of Caribbean Chiefs of Police
ACPO		Association of Chief Police Officers (England, Wales & Northern Ireland)
AFIS	*	Automatic Fingerprint Identification System
AFR	*	Automatic Fingerprint Recognition
AFRC	*	Automatic Fingerprint Recognition Consortium
ANPR		Automatic Number Plate Recognition
CARICOM		Caribbean Community
CMA		Consortium Management Agreement
CMG		Consortium Management Group
DOD		Digital Optical Disc
EAS		Emergency AFR System
IAFIS		Impact Assessment on Fingerprint Identification System –(SINCE 1999 FBI's – Integrated Automated Fingerprint Identification Service)
IBM		International Business Machines
IMSI		International Mobile Subscriber Identity
LAN		Local Area Network
WAN		Wide Area Network
LSU		Litigation Support Unit
MIDCRO		Midland Criminal Record Office
NAFIS		National Automated Fingerprint Identification System
NAMSI		North American Systems Incorporated – later SMI
PCA		Police Complaints Authority
PITO		Police Information Technology Organisation
SEATAC		Seattle and Tacoma Airport
SMI		Sagem Morpho Incorporated. Often just 'Sagem'.
SOCO		Scenes of Crime Officer/s
TWOC		Taking Without Consent

*   Automatic sometimes quoted as 'Automated'

COMMON 'FINGERPRINT RELATED' TERMS

MARK

A fingerprint or part of a fingerprint found at the scene of a crime.

TENPRINT

The form used at police stations or prisons to record prisoners' fingerprints. (In the US – Tenprint Card or just Card)

MARK TO TENPRINT SEARCH

Launching of a mark to search the tenprints stored on a database in order to match with a suspect.

MARK TO MARK SEARCH

Launching of a mark to search a mark's database to ascertain if offences are linked with each other.

TENPRINT TO TENPRINT SEARCH

Launching of a Tenprint on a Tenprint Database to ascertain if other tenprints belong to the same person. This often detects people using false details.

TENPRINT TO MARK SEARCH

Launching a Tenprint to a Mark database to ascertain if those Tenprints match any Marks found at scenes of crime.

HIT OR MATCH

Those occasions when any of the above searches result in a match with the databases searched.

ACQUIRE OR ACQUISITION

Loading of a Mark or Tenprint onto the database.

Chapter 1 – Fingerprints – Their Origin in Crime Detection

Much has already been written by others on how the chapters of fingerprint identification have evolved. I do not intend to replicate those chapters in any depth. Suffice to say that in 1880, Dr Henry Faulds, a Scottish Physician wrote an article in the journal 'Nature' suggesting that fingerprints would be useful as a technique for the investigation of evidence left at a scene of crime.

The first fingerprint evidence involving a scene of crime fingerprint in England was heard at the Central Criminal Court on 13th September 1902. On 27th June 1902, Henry Jackson pleaded not guilty to a charge of burglary of a house at Denmark Hill, South London and stealing billiard balls. Detective Sergeant Collins examined the scene and an imprint of Jackson's left thumb was found in dirt on a newly painted window-sill.

A respected barrister of the time, Richard Muir, was appointed to conduct the prosecution case. Collins explained the system and produced photographic enlargements and tracings of both the fingerprint (termed 'mark') left at the scene and that of the suspects fingerprints. Jackson was found guilty and sentenced to seven years penal servitude.

Fingerprint evidence was first used in a case of murder in 1905 at the Central Criminal Court. Alfred and Albert Stratton pleaded not guilty to the murder of Mr and Mrs Farrow at their shop in Deptford. During examination of the scene an impression was found on a cash box. Inspector Collins gave evidence in this case and explained the identification system with the aid of a blackboard and photographic enlargements of the impression from the cash box and the right thumb of Alfred Stratton. The prosecution was again conducted by Richard Muir, and the jury found the Strattons guilty. They were later hanged.

As a young bobby, I quickly learned that taking the fingerprints of those arrested was a miserable and mucky affair. For one thing, it was necessary to hold the hands of prisoners who, on many occasions stank to high heaven of either alcohol, body odour or on most occasions, both. Also, it can be imagined how they were not at all wanting to ease the process for those recording them. The recording of their fingerprints would mean to them, that they were more likely to be caught in the future. This reluctance meant that they would often try to smudge their fingerprints to make them more difficult to view. However, there were some helpful ones who would almost do it themselves.

Three sets of fingerprint forms (tenprints) were to be completed. One each for Scotland Yard and the 'Midland Regional Criminal Record Office' (MIDCRO), Birmingham, and the other for our own Herefordshire Constabulary (later to become the West Mercia Constabulary). This was a job that could take around an hour or more. However, just one smudge meant that the whole form needed to be scrapped and started again.

 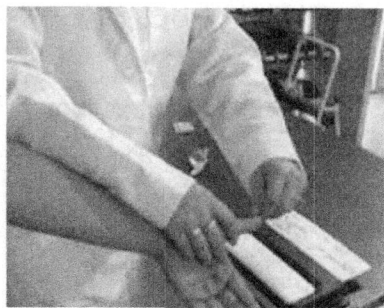

Photographs from Google Images

The other main disadvantage concerned the fact that black fingerprint ink stored in similar containers to toothpaste, was required to be coated across the whole area of each of the donor's finger tips by being rolled through tacky ink from nail edge to nail edge and across the whole area of each palm. This was achieved by squeezing the ink tube and 'spotting' the ink onto about a foot long brass plate which had been mounted on a block of wood. The ink would then be rolled furiously on the block by use of a small hand held roller until it became an even, 'tacky' film on it. It was more likely to have more black ink all over the prisoners and those taking the prints than was required on the forms. Impressions of the palms were achieved by rolling the ink directly over the palms. It can be imagined what sort of a mess ensued.

There were occasions, when donors were not even able to stand and deceased persons were obviously a good example. Such incidences were quite common but more often than not, this process applied when it was necessary for identification purposes. In those cases, ink pads enclosed in plastic boxes, similar to powder puff compacts, were available and it was the pad that would be revolved around the finger as opposed to the finger being rolled onto the ink pad. At the last resort in difficult cases, it has been known that fingers would be required to be separated from deceased's hands.

The whole process was finalised by the need to get the equipment and both prisoner and officer cleaned up and have signatures appended to the tenprints. Little did I know then, that I was to become involved in the digitisation of a procedure which hadn't changed for well over a century. Since then, systems needed to be introduced on how to categorise and store them in order to make them easier to search. Their digitisation now serves as a far more efficient system used in the detection of crime.

Having been formed during pregnancy, our criminal justice system has accepted that our fingerprints are unique. The friction ridges on our fingers develop patterns of whorls, loops or arches, or a combination of all three on our ten fingers. But those with the rare disease called 'Adermatoglyphia' or sometimes referred to as 'immigration delay disease' are born with finger pads that are smooth, apart from some possible creasing. However, it is fortunate that this is an extremely rare condition, with only four extended families in the world known to have it.

'Biometric' solutions are now involved in a plethora of systems, two of which I have used during the day when I actually wrote this chapter. (Opening my mobile phone and making an 'on line' bank transfer). Many airports now operate biometric 'fast track' fingerprint systems for local frequent flyer passengers and as my wife Jo discovered at Disneyland some many years ago, to gain entry into shorter queues for Disney amusements! It is this 'Biometric' term which is used when normally referring to the processes used in 'non-criminal' systems such as to permit either 'physical' or technologically based access to premises or systems. The term 'digitisation' seems to be the preferred collective noun when reference is being made to the conversion of what was hitherto manually documented data and so I suggested that this is applied when considering their conversion as described in this book.

I was by no means a fingerprint expert but working within this field of crime detection for fourteen years, I am able to say that in addition to the eight different patterns into which fingerprints were categorised, prior to digitisation, it was necessary for a very long time for experts to identify sixteen similar characteristics of a mark left at the scene of a crime with the fingerprints of a suspect before they could introduce their opinion and declare that those marks were or were not similar. For example, the characters of marks found might include the sudden ending of a 'ridge' or the splitting of a ridge and many other characteristics which could be identified with the expert's naked eye. That was a time consuming process.

Similar skills of identifying these characteristics are necessary during the digitised process except that now, the power of the computer could be used to attach minutiae by use of the software thrown up on the screen to those locations of the characters identified by the experts. The experts' workstations then ease the process by which distances and locations of the minutiae can be measured by the process which makes identifications being a far speedier affair.

Chapter 2 – The Digital Explosion

It wasn't long before my police retirement that improved methods and technology connected with crime investigations were on the horizon. This was the case due to the speed of progress in the digitisation of many forms and documents in other 'non-police' environments, such as in businesses and organisations. So far as I'm aware, the following wasn't available to improve crime detection during my days of being involved in the manual recording of fingerprints as described above.

1. Tracking by use of mobile phone technology. ('International Mobile Subscriber Identity' (IMSI).
2. The automatic recording of motor vehicle registration plates was another forensic break through not previously known by myself. This was ANPR – (Automatic Number Plate Recognition). What a tremendous tool this must be now. I can think of many cases where this would have solved major crimes committed in my day. The one that immediately springs to mind is the murder of Marie Wilks on the M50 Motorway on 18th June 1988.
3. The recording of prisoners' DNA was in my view, the greatest advancement in the forensic science aspects of serious crime detection. Launched in 1995, it became such a massive tool in the armoury of detecting crime.
4. The plethora of CCTV cameras in our cities and towns have appeared in no time at all. Yes, there were a few installed in my day but in such numbers that I cannot recall any case which depended on their images. Thankfully, they now cover vast areas in our urban areas.
5. Luminol is a chemical that has been in existence for many years but to my knowledge, it was never used in crime scene investigations. It is an organic compound which, when oxidized, emits light — a phenomenon known as chemiluminescence. This is similar to the reactions that fireflies use to emit light, and to those used in "glow-sticks" and some roadside emergency lights.

In practical terms, blood splashes can be cleaned most thoroughly and certainly beyond the power of human sight. Their enhancement through an application of luminal can therefore highlight the very useful indications of blood so as to indicate the point of attack etc.

The progress of forensic technology as listed above has appeared more or less since my 1994 retirement, so what makes us believe that that is the end of it? We are now to shortly expect facial recognition as an additional tool and with the computational power existing and improving as it is, progress is surely bound to continue.

In the early 1990s, the use of fingerprint technology had been experimented with and indeed used by some US agencies, including the FBI. In the Autumn of 1991, the FBI's IAFIS (Impact Assessment on Fingerprint Identification System) project was in its infancy. This was just an assessment concerning the subject of 'privacy' and was launched into what was intended to be the first generation of 'Biometric' fingerprint storage.

The British Home Office and many police forces were interested in its progress and an Assistant Under Secretary of State, Mr. Gordon Wasserman introduced a project which was to be named NAFIS. (The 'National Fingerprint Identification System). Indeed, since 1965, an American company, 'TRW' had been earmarked to introduce an electronic system to British police forces. A special meeting was convened at New Scotland Yard to discuss the idea that a future national fingerprint database for the United Kingdom might run in tandem with the US's IAFIS which now was an acronym converted from the privacy assessment mentioned above into the 'Integrated Automated Fingerprint Identification Service'. So, in order to meet the growing demand for automated fingerprint identification in the US, the FBI then developed and implemented the full 'joined up' IAFIS in 1999, some eight years after the Automatic Fingerprint Recognition Consortium (AFRC) commenced its fingerprint searching service in 1991 at Worcester.

I can't over-emphasise how more efficient such a digitised system was going to be. Whilst those 'ink and roller' fingerprints taken were sent to Scotland Yard and Birmingham, it can be imagined how long it would take to eventually be matched to a suspect's fingerprints already held, on 'Tenprint' forms stored in the databases. The long waits of months and sometimes years to discover matches, were to be reduced to seconds and minutes and the propensity of finding them, would be far in excess of that manual system. In the whole of my service and having taken probably hundreds of sets of fingerprints, I can only recall two occasions when a welcomed letter from Scotland Yard was received informing me of matches. In both cases, it was far too late to have been of any use.

In England and Wales, when repeat offenders for various crimes were prevalent, in order to speed up the process locally, fingerprint experts would compile 'bundles' of fingerprints stored separately into their various categories of the crimes committed. The two main ones were the common 'Burglary' and the 'Taking of Vehicles without Consent' (TWOC) bundles. This meant that when fresh marks were submitted by 'Scenes of Crime' officers (SOCOs) for those crime categories, the fingerprint experts would have a quick look through the relevant bundle before making a general search.

With such an antiquated system, thousands of prisoners lived under false identities or had simply given false details after their arrest. Many will have escaped the judicial system. Also, without a networked system, a burglar could commit numerous offences in a wide area of the country without it being apparent that those offences were linked. When I consider that the manual system existed for the whole of my police service, despite limited successes, I realise now, how futile it was. Police forces of England and Wales couldn't wait for a centralised and automated database to be built.

The Association of Chief Police Officers of England Wales and Northern Ireland, (ACPO) was an association just for Chief Officers of Police. Their members often work in collaboration with the College of Policing and the Association of Police and Crime Commissioners (APCC). However, ACPO has since been replaced by the National Police Chief's Council (NPCC). It is these bodies which can bring governmental pressure to produce such systems.

Being based on the progress of science, my story is bound to contain a mass of acronyms but although some have changed over the years, I shall stick with those that appertained at the time so, for the purposes of this book, I shall keep the reference to ACPO and not the NPCC which broadly have the same purposes.

Chapter 3 – The Driving Force and Early Days

Sir John Charles Hoddinott CBE

It was ACPO that was largely responsible for providing both an 'Interim Solution' and the first fully national digitised system in the UK. However, it was the 'Interim Solution' involving 37 of the 43 police forces in England and Wales in which I was involved. This was the Automatic Fingerprint Recognition Consortium (AFRC), which ran for ten years before NAFIS was finally ready to be introduced.

Having worked for HM Inspectorate of Constabulary, I was aware of most of the Chief Constables then in being, Sir John Hoddinott was among the most admired of them. We were to eventually work very closely together and it was because of his commanding presence, that I had always thought that he was a little older than myself. I was surprised when I eventually learned that I was in fact, almost exactly one month older than he and apart from our ranks, our service almost ran parallel with each other.

Unlike many Chiefs I had known; he was such a wonderful leader who sadly died way before his time. Although mentioning his death at this early stage of my book might seem unusual, I think it necessary to record here, what a great man he was and how successfully he was to lead the way forward in forming our fingerprint consortium. The following was just one of the many tributes paid to him upon his death and was published by the Hampshire Constabulary's History Society. I make no apology for using these pages to fully describe him.

"Both John's father and grandfather served with Hampshire Constabulary, but John joined the Metropolitan Police and served with them until he was made Assistant Chief Constable of Surrey Police. He came to Hampshire in 1983 as the Deputy Chief Constable and moved up to Chief Constable in 1988. He was a prominent Chief Constable who was President of the Association of Chief Police Officers in 1995. He played a major role in the development of Automated Fingerprint Recognition and the security inquiry after the bombing of the Grand Hotel in Brighton in 1984. He was awarded the CBE in 1994 and was knighted in 1998. He retired in 1999 and tragically died in 2001.

Sir John went to Barton Peveril Grammar School, Eastleigh, and joined the Metropolitan Police as a cadet in 1961. He became a constable in 1963 and was promoted sergeant in 1967 and inspector in 1969. Later that year he attended Trinity College, Cambridge, where he gained a second class honours degree in law and economics in 1972.

He returned to police duties in London's West End Central police station where he served for three years, and received three Commissioner's Commendations.

In 1975 Sir John was promoted to chief inspector when he transferred to the obscene publications squad. In 1977 he was promoted to superintendent and served at Paddington police station before transferring to the drug squad as Detective superintendent.

He was then promoted to chief superintendent and in January 1981 was appointed officer in charge of the CID at West End Central. In June 1981 Sir John became assistant chief constable (operations) with Surrey police. He was appointed deputy chief constable in Hampshire in September 1983 and became chief constable on September 1 1988, retiring in September 1999.

He was president of ACPO in 1994/5, and was knighted in the Queen's birthday honours of June 1998. Sir John was married to Avril, and they had two daughters, Louise and Rebecca.

He was to lead a major investigation into a police shooting in Sussex, where he condemned Sussex Chief Constable, Mr Whitehouse and other senior officers for attempting to justify the shooting. Sir John said he had found "prima facie evidence" of wilful neglect of duty by Mr Whitehouse.

In 2001, after his retirement he was helping develop a new police complaints system. He was using Operation Lancet, an inquiry into corruption in Cleveland police, as a blueprint for the work. He had been appointed to investigate the £7m Operation Lancet inquiry by Home Secretary, Jack Straw.

It was whilst on this enquiry Sir John sadly passed away whilst working in Middlesborough.

The Chief Constable of Hampshire Paul Kernaghan said: "Sir John's death has come as a shock to me personally and to everyone associated with Hampshire Constabulary.

Sir John was above all a husband and father but he was also an outstanding police officer. It would be fair comment to describe him as a giant professionally. As Chief Constable of Hampshire and president of the Association of Chief Police Officers, Sir John scaled all the professional heights and was recognised as the outstanding officer of his time. He retired in 1999 but continued his commitment to public service both as a Deputy Lieutenant of Hampshire and as a senior member of various government reviews. It says much for the man and his values that even whilst in retirement he was still ready and able to undertake work on behalf of the community.

Sir John will be missed. My thoughts and those of the entire force are with Lady Hoddinott and his girls."

As reported by The Southern Daily Echo on 24th August 2001 his funeral at Romsey Abbey was attended by eight hundred mourners. The following quotations uttered by many eminent people who knew him closely, says it all: -

"the man described as one of the country's finest officers"

" an outstanding officer and one of the most liked of his generation"

"John was the most outstanding police officer of his time"

"big in stature and huge in influence. He was that and so much more - he was truly inspirational."

"I worked with John for many years. He was the greatest man I ever knew, and certainly the best policeman I have ever come across or heard of."

"Sir John was a great copper and a tremendous family man. He was a great leader for the service in Hampshire and the Isle of Wight. That 800 people turned up to say goodbye shows the feelings people had for him, and he'll be sorely missed."

"He was a very rare breed of police officer. Even as a chief constable and president of the Association of Chief Police Officers, he was always able to relate to the bobby on the beat."

Later chapters will include how I had the honour of working closely with Sir John and how sadly, due to working in America, I was unable to attend his funeral.

I retired from the police service in 1994, which was the year that Sir John had been elected as the President of ACPO. He was already the Chief Constable of the Hampshire and Isle of Wight Constabulary. I add that presidents of ACPO were voted into office by their own colleague membership, therefore, that in itself, was a strong indication of their admiration and confidence in those elected into this office.

This temporary AFR solution was operating in its infancy when, as a self-employed contractor, I joined its staff. Indeed, it was much later when I was often alone with him, working in many of the Caribbean Islands. We had heart to heart discussions on occasions and I'm sure that later on, I shall be mentioning some humorous events concerning our relationship.

I am told that Sir John tried his level best to ensure that the Police Forces in England and Wales were to benefit from AFIS as soon as possible and to that end, he had paid many visits to the Home Office to discuss the situation with Mr Gordon Wasserman and others as mentioned in the previous chapter. His trials and tribulations at the Home Office had commenced way before my 1994 retirement when he was then, not only the Chief Constable of Hampshire and the President of ACPO but was also, the Chairman of the AFR Consortium which was formed in October 1991. The AFRC was therefore his baby and had stemmed from the procrastination of the Home Office. He was not at all happy with a projected delay until 30th June 2001, the date which the Home Office indicated when NAFIS, the national database of fingerprints would be launched. This was another decade away, because it was in 1991 that the seeds of the AFR Consortium were being sewn.

Sir John was leading the charge and heads of CID departments in all forces were already licking their lips in the knowledge that he was in the driving seat. It was after many keenly fought meetings, Home Office procrastinations and force frustrations, that he gained permission from the Home Office to launch a small consortium of mostly Hampshire's neighbouring forces to experiment with a localised AFIS. Money, was as ever, the stumbling block but eventually, although this was to cost a great deal of member forces' budgets, the Home Office agreed that the system would indeed, attract the Home Office Grant. (Two thirds of their budgets).

Initially, Surrey and the States of Jersey Police agreed to accompany Hampshire in this mini-project. But this little group had rapidly spread to seven forces and they were collectively known as the 'Southern Consortium'. These were the seeds of great things to come and it wasn't long before all England and Welsh forces met at the Hampshire based Bramshill Police College in March 1992 to discuss the enlargement of this consortium. This culminated in 37 of the 43 forces agreeing to join in the project. The remaining six, Avon & Somerset, Kent, Nottinghamshire, Sussex, South Yorkshire and Hertfordshire either thought it best to wait for the 10 years for NAFIS to arrive or that they were not in a financial position to contribute their share of the budget.

Speaking for myself, as always, fate showed Its hand in the part it played in my life because it was necessary to set up a project office at a centrally placed location. It was our Chief Constable of West Mercia of the day, David Blakey (another forward-thinking chief) who agreed to give up a large police house in 'The Drive' at Hindlip Hall, the headquarters of our West Mercia force. As it happened, I was the Chief Superintendent of the 'Operations' Department with my office very adjacent to that house which has since been demolished to make way for a brand-new CID headquarters. Had it not been for those decisions, I would not have become involved and my life post-retirement, would have taken on an entirely different path.

The whole of the fingerprint collections from all member forces had already been acquired to our database through a massive 'Back Record Conversion' process. The maintenance of the database was contracted to, and hosted by IBM at IBM's facility at Warwick and duplicate digital optical discs (DODs) were located in Scotland. These locations were classified 'secret' at that time and the project, so far as IBM's involvement was concerned, was code named 'BEAR'.

The other act of fate was, being informed that the Consortium's Project Office was on the lookout for a senior police officer to take up the position of 'Service Manager'. I was in a position to retire with a full pension and had already informed my Chief Constable who had earlier been Tony Mullett that I would not, for personal reasons which he was aware of, be applying to other forces to become an Assistant Chief Constable.

In addition to office clerical staff, there were only about five main employees working at the project office and I managed to privately speak to two of them separately but who had had the benefit of working with the Project Manager, Patrick Pitt (Pat). They were circumspect but not entirely happy concerning his management skills. They were of the view that his management style was difficult for some to operate under and leaned more towards being confrontational as opposed to diplomatic and measured. Some staff were said to have been treated with derision at times.

Pat was then, a serving Police Superintendent, who had been the head of Hampshire Constabulary's Computer Department and had been seconded to project manage the AFR Consortium at Worcester. I suppose 'confrontational' was probably the correct adjective. My experience however, became such that as much as I too disliked his style, he was at least a very hard-working individual who quickly got to grips with the strange language and world of computers and technology in general. As the leading project manager, there was no doubting that he threw everything he could muster into trying to achieve our objectives. The problem was, in my view, he appeared to favour confrontation as a means to achieve rather than diplomacy. Perhaps not being able to suffer fools gladly would have been a description, nearer the mark.

I was later to become aware of a fear that some held of him. It became clear to me before (and certainly after) I arrived, that there existed a division of loyalty with some who were to become his lieutenants of the day, earning his support and hence they remained silent. Some of those plus others would silently indicate their discontent but without wanting to upset their positions and the benefits they provided.

I had also been warned about a specific member of the team who was strongly suspected of 'tittle tattling' tales back to this man. This person's skills on the computer were such that he bragged that all he could do on them was to submit his invoices and use the email system which, as Pat had explained to me, was an integral part of our functions.

So, this wasn't the perfect picture I had hoped for and I couldn't understand how the staffing of such an office who were all involved in such an exciting project, could have fallen into this pickle. In all my service under many supervisors, I hadn't yet worked for anyone who I couldn't get along with. So, my attitude was, that if this was going to be the first exception, as a self-employed contractor drawing a handsome pension, I could pull out quite easily at any time.

The grape vine told me that this project manager was interested in taking me on board and I decided to write for an interview. It wasn't long before I was invited to meet him for dinner at the 'China City' restaurant on the main Kidderminster to Worcester Road. I had not seen him before and I must admit to being a little apprehensive due to him being a serving superintendent and me being a one rank higher, a retired chief superintendent. From my point of view, I had no bother with that situation at all but I wondered how might that affect him?

With only knowing his reputation and not his physical profile, I did what I was told years ago and that was to take the ground early. On my early arrival at the restaurant, I explained to the staff that I was to have a meeting with a gentleman I did not know. He was going to have to find me as opposed to the reverse. They understood and sat me at a table for two in a position where I could observe those entering. It wouldn't be many men who would be walking into a Chinese restaurant in the evening alone. That worked and as soon as he walked in, I indicated to him that he might be looking for me.

After all the horror stories I had heard about him, all I can say, was that I had a thoroughly enjoyable evening which included the polishing off of a very enjoyable meal. He had been particularly interested in my duties when I had been seconded to HM Inspectorate of Constabulary. I later learned that he was not that happy at writing formal letters or reports and that as a consequence, he was looking for me to use my so-called talent in writing. If only he knew that I have always to this day, had to struggle with my literacy. In times to come, he would often ask me to, in his words, "Give it your HMI speak Brian" to draft important letters and documents.

So, back to my so-called interview. The one thing that came as a complete surprise was that in his words again, "Of course, you will receive most of your work via email and respond to any projects given by email". It must be realised that in 1994, there were no personal computers to be seen in police offices other than the word processors used by secretaries, though the larger 'standalone' server type were now being used for large force systems.

Suspecting that emailing was something to do with personal computers, I replied, "Well that shouldn't be a problem Pat". I must have kept a straight face because he simply replied, "Good". The whole evening was such an enjoyable experience that I was left wondering what on earth his described reputation was all about. He was pleasant and very good company. The structure of our meeting was certainly not that of an interview. It appeared to me that he had already made up his mind and that he was simply verbally settling me down by describing the duties he was expecting me to perform as a 'Service Manager'. Being very much mystified, I returned home to immediately inform my wife Jo, that we were going shopping in the morning, for a computer.

It was my lack of confidence which made me ask the supplier if he would set it up for me and show me the fundamentals. This he did and I remember him telling me that apart from switching it off at the plug to allow the 'heads' (whatever they are) to close properly, it was almost impossible for me to break it no matter what buttons I pressed on the keyboard. I always bore that advice in my memory and it has served me well. I could experiment.

I was very fortunate because I was so interested in what these computers could do, I became fascinated and often stayed up in the early hours exploring the functions of the software, particularly 'Word' and 'Lotus 123's spread sheets. There was little or no 'wi-fi' in those days and I recall using email by having to 'dial up' through an ethernet connection which required me to plug into a BT telephone line. In short, unlike many others I know, I have always thoroughly enjoyed computing and emailing and am very thankful that every penny I have earned in my 'post-retirement' era has been due to the use of my computer. I had also been able to write my life story just for my grandchildren and many books which I subsequently published myself. All this was much to the concern of my wife, Jo, who, under no circumstance was willing to be taught or indeed, have anything to do with computers.

I had then been a member of the service club, 'Round Table' and later a Rotarian with about a forty membership. I mention this solely to say that in those early days, there was only one other member who possessed a computer and hence, an email address. He was a printer and used it in his business so we conspired together to have some fun with our other computer-less members. He designed a banner depicting a fictitious 'cyber' Rotary Club. This was circulated among our members and I recall addressing them to tell them about this new club. I especially dwelled on how we could earn an attendance tick by simply logging on to the club at a certain meeting time every Tuesday evening. The attendance register was then very important to Rotarians because members were persuaded to meet a certain high level of attendance unless they were given leave of absence.

The members fell for this hook, line and sinker but questions about how projects could be managed by its members etc. soon led us to show our hands. Such fun whilst it lasted!

Chapter 4 – AFRC – Beginnings of The Temporary Solution

By March 1992, Sir John's efforts resulted in those thirty seven police forces in England and Wales now constituting the active membership of the AFR Consortium. I was informed that It now possessed the largest database of fingerprints in the world and was capable of searching 1500 scenes of crime marks against 3.25 million tenprint stored at IBM's Warwick database. That takes some believing when considering that this was supposed to be a 'temporary solution'.

My duties as a 'Service Manager' entailed being responsible for regularly visiting the 'Fingerprint Bureau' of each of our 37 member forces to ensure that they were familiar with ever changing rules and regulations concerning the use of their fingerprint hardware and other matters. Indeed, there were two of us with the same title. Terry Smith a retired Superintendent from Nottinghamshire was my 'other half' and we divided the forces by those situated in the North or South of England and Wales. I was to serve the southern half initially, but in later years, we swopped over so that we became familiar with the staff in all fingerprint bureaux. As with statute law, this did not include the Scottish or Northern Ireland forces. The States of Jersey Police was however, included in the South section and I enjoyed many visits there.

I naturally needed to get very acquainted with what the system entailed before taking on these visits. My first visit was in company with Ian Maskerey, a retired Detective Superintendent from Merseyside who was the Consortium's security officer. Ian was to leave us some time later and his place was taken by a Detective Chief Inspector from Northumbria by the name of Ron Wright. The 'Security Officer' probably worked closer to Pat Pitt possibly due to the nature of the 'security' of our offices and all the fingerprints in our possession. His Northumbrian responsibilities included being the head of the fingerprint bureau, so he was a natural choice.

From a security aspect, whilst very unlikely, one couldn't discount the scenario involving professional criminals or terrorists considering blowing up buildings if they knew where such fingerprints were stored. This would ensure that any fingerprint evidence against them, would disappear. For the same reason, duplicate sets of prints acquired, were kept on digital optical discs (DODs) for use on an electric database in Glasgow.

In order to complete my induction to the Consortium, I was then to spend a short period of time alongside my partners, Terry Smith and Arthur Vickers, another retired Police Superintendent from Humberside living at Hull when it was their turn to be the Duty Officer.

Ron Wright

Being the 'Duty Officer' entailed being in constant communications with all fingerprint bureaux. It was indeed, quite a busy and responsible duty. The system might crash, BT engineers might require being called out, computer engineers might be required to fix their machines etc. All this, plus the many service notice directives to be compiled and distributed to the member bureaux, made it a responsible, though not difficult job. There was a constant two way communication requirement with bureaux staff, mostly, with their particular head of bureau. The email facility made light of what might a few years ago, have been an administrative nightmare.

Whilst our system was being operated by IBM in Warwick, the software company headquarters (Sagem) were located in Paris and their specialised software technicians were in America, but in any event, contact with them would be IBM's responsibility as they were our 'service providers'.

Terry also took me to the IBM facility at Warwick and introduced me to some of the staff responsible for our project. He also accompanied me down to the Hampshire Constabulary headquarters where their bureau was installed at Winchester. This was not only the force containing the Chief Constable Sir John Hoddinott, but a number of his staff, including the Head of Bureau Glyn Tyrell and Pat Pitt who had been seconded to the project to get it off the ground. That was not only a good reason for visiting the Hampshire force because, Hampshire was included in my Southern part of England and Wales responsibility.

The Project Office at Hindlip Hall was staffed by a small group of local people. The receptionist Kerry Wilde, was a young Worcester girl who eventually set off for Jersey to become the partner of the States of Jersey police's head of fingerprint bureau. A spark no doubt ignited during one of his visits for meetings at the project office. Also joining Kerry, was a general clerical assistant , a young single man, Ian Duggan who I recall was a good cricketer and captained Droitwich cricket team.

The office manager was another source of information to Pat, a local lady, Angela Gale who chain smoked in her scruffy office to such an extent that it continually stank of nicotine. Ash trays seemed continually full. I regarded her as Pat's lieutenant but at the same time, I grew to regard her as probably the most efficient of the office staff.

Although Pat spent a great deal of his time in Worcester, he was a serving Hampshire Constabulary Superintendent and his family remained in Hampshire. He had a young lady, Karen Dorans who was the wife of a serving West Mercia Officer and she I believe, served as Pat's PA. Rumours of their relationship with one another were very rife but I can only assume that there was an element of fear hanging over the staff concerning the wisdom of talking too much about that. In years to come, however, they both ended up living and working in Washington State, USA. Rumours didn't bother me.

Pat Off Duty with a Montana Steak   **Karen Dorans**

Those I have mentioned so far, were either full time employees or in the case of retired senior police officers, self-employed, 'sole-trader' contractors. However, many more experts in their field, some police and other consultants, were either seconded short term or if not 'borrowed' police officers, mostly from Hampshire, were taken on as short term consultants to the consortium. At the same time, office staff sometimes changed and were later added to or were employed on a short term basis.

At that time, I had been the last of a number of recently retired officers, most of whom were of the rank of Superintendent to work for the project. Unless my memory falters, I think I was the only Chief Superintendent. I was to become a self-employed contractor and when not operational 'on the road' most of my duties would be at the Project Office or at home. Indeed, my contract actually stipulated that I would be employed from home and that I would supply my own equipment.

Luckily, we had a very good office at home in the village of Crowle on the outskirts of Worcester and only a short distance from the project office. I was to become the contractor who lived closest to it, a situation which was later to prove beneficial to me. Arthur Vickers often had to drive down from Hull not only for 'Duty Officer' duties but to carry out short term projects, as did David Moffat, a retired Chief Inspector from Stockport in the Greater Manchester Police area. So, our operational retired police officer operatives were all 'sole trader' contractors resident all over England at Worcester, Nottingham, Liverpool, Manchester and Hull.

It was about now, that newspapers were carrying stories about how HM Revenue and Customs were clamping down on businesses employing personnel under the guise of being self-employed. Numerous companies were making their staff redundant and then re-employing them as self-employed sole-traders. Those businesses were said to be escaping the red tape, cost and all other responsibilities of employing others.

There was no doubting in my mind that we were genuine self-employed contractors although under a microscope, the mechanisms of our employment and duties were not too dissimilar to that of those described above. It wasn't surprising that HM Revenue and Customs were concentrating on the so called self-employed workforce who were only delivering invoices to one client / employer and to that end, it was necessary for me to connect the National Insurance Department with Pat Pitt so that he could describe better than I, what our working relationship was. It became necessary for Angela Gale, the Office Manager, to send them a copy of my contract. Although I had no problem in ever getting my contracts extended each year, they emphasised that we were only contracted to provide our services for a stipulated number of days which varied depending on what sort of employment status applied to us.

However, it seemed a long time before they could be appeased and national newspapers continued to carry details of how they were trying to eradicate their problem. This was also the time when businesses were cutting back and many laid off senior managers who were setting themselves up as consultants. Indeed, I also worked for no-one other than the AFR Consortium. I was also provided with a certain amount of equipment and I wrongly, but willingly, needed to submit annual leave applications. So, as far as I was concerned, although I was contracted for a minimum number of days, I was, for all intents and purposes, employed by the AFR Consortium or at least it would seem that way to the Inland Revenue.

Being cautious however, I eventually decided to include in my registered 'self-employed' status, the added vocation as being a 'Private Investigator'. This occurred after my last Chief Constable, David Blakey, forwarded me some information about a company of Insurance Claim Investigators who were looking for 'Field Agents' to investigate claims with regard to car thefts, 'Road Traffic Accident Locus' and statement taking. At the same time, a solicitor Rotary colleague asked me if I had spare capacity to serve legal papers on behalf of his clients. Jonathan Brew was then the senior partner in charge of the 'Family Law' division of Harrison Clarke, Solicitors in Worcester and he gave me some old affidavits. It didn't take me long to understand the process which wouldn't take but an hour or so to complete a service and that included the making of my affidavit at the local county court office. All I had to do was 'save' a proforma statement on my computer and then for each case, simply change the dates and the names of the complainants and respondents. I was now safe from the prying eyes of HM Customs and Revenue.

Chapter 5 – Trouble at Mill and an Office Move

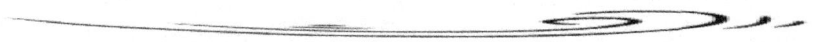

With our databases being located at IBM's facility on the outskirts of Warwick, fingerprint experts could search it by use of IBMs RS/6000 systems including workstations housed in each fingerprint bureau accessing an IBM super system at their facility. The software in use was that provided by the Defence Company, SAGEM.SA. (Mostly referenced as just Sagem).

I wasn't aware that the few fingerprint searching companies in the world were in the 'Defence' industry. I was told that this was because they were also involved in the software required to guide low flying fighter aircraft over hills and valleys. The correlation being, that fingerprints are also indeed, made up of hills and valleys, albeit on a far different scale. Indeed, it was Sagem, this company who, in their desire to spread the use of their fingerprint searching software, openly bragged that whichever US State first managed to capture a criminal by use of their software, that they would introduce a subsidiary company in that US location. They must have cursed that commitment because the particular state where that occurred happened to be Washington State located in the far north west corner of America, one of the furthest US states from their base in Paris.

However, unbeknown to me, I had arrived at just the right time to get embroiled in a huge dispute between the Consortium and IBM. Perhaps it was part of my learning curve that Pat took me along to our IBM system providers premises at Warwick where, at a high level conference, he was to attack the dismal service that we were suffering by them. The topic for discussion with their top level management, was concerning contractual issues about their maintenance and the need to increase capacity of both storage and speed in order to reach benchmark contractual levels. In short, the system was abysmal. It was strange that we were the only representatives of the consortium and of course, being in training, I took no part.

I have to say that although I was again impressed by Pat's knowledge of this strange equipment and the I.T. language surrounding it, his style of negotiation by confrontation came to the fore. The system was on crutches as far as we were concerned and although his frustration needed to be

29

displayed, any form of tactical diplomacy was absent. The system was limping along suffering many hours of 'down time'. I had often since wondered whether a different style of management might have succeeded though, in the climate that existed then, I had no doubts that that was ever going to work as we were too deep into the mire which then existed.

Hundreds of Fingerprint experts from all 37 member forces who had hitherto been using the old manual system, had been trained in the use of these new machines which would now help them work many times faster and be responsible for capturing many more criminals in England and Wales. It was still a giant leap forward. However, before delving too far into the vagaries of the system, I had better try my best to describe the organisation and structure of what was involved.

Through the will of the ACPO organisation under Sir John Hoddinott's chair, those 37 forces combined to contribute to the system as I say, which was then operating from a vacant police house in 'The Drive' Hindlip Hall. It would be funded by each member force contributing on a 'per record' held basis. Obviously small forces such as Gloucestershire and Warwickshire etc. would not be wanting to equally share the cost with those bigger metropolitan type forces – West Midlands, West Yorkshire, Greater Manchester etc. who would be storing many more records on the system and hence using it and receiving far more successes on it, compared with those smaller forces.

However, before the first fingerprint could be matched on the system, it was necessary to acquire (load) all of the forces tenprint forms which had been donated by prisoners, onto the database. Each form was required to have been lawfully held in accordance with the then, data protection legislation. For example, fingerprints held from those who had received just a caution for the offence committed had to be weeded by law, after a prescribed time, I think it was five years. This whole process involved a massive 'Back Record Conversion' (BRC) exercise which I thankfully, was not involved. At the same time, the process was used to weed out records which were or could be causing trouble with the system. Hence, it was called, a 'Preventive Measures' BRC.

So now we arrive at the other end of the system with force employed fingerprint experts who were based at each of their force's fingerprint bureau. These were people, by the way, which included the youngest of our two daughters, Sarah. They had all been trained at the National Training Centre for Scientific Support to Crime Investigation'. This was located within the Durham Constabulary Police Headquarters. Students were not classed as 'expert' witnesses until they had completed five years training and had passed their final examination. That is when they are permitted to give their opinion as an 'expert' witness. I'm proud to say that our Sarah gained 100% in her final examination, a feat not hitherto achieved.

Constant communication between the bureaux and importantly, the project office was vital and to that end, at each bureau, we installed a desk top computer equipped with email facilities. Rules, regulations and practices were continually sent out from the Project Office. Towards the end, due to the problems being experienced, it was necessary for us to regularly organise a system involving the staggered use of it so as not to overload it. This was when Terry Smith and I were required to pay additional visits to the bureaux under our supervision because as can be imagined, as 'Service Managers' we were at the brunt of numerous complaints concerning the system's 'down time'.

Bureaux staff were not, of course, directly employed by The AFRC, they were all employees of their respective police forces. However, so far as the operation of our system was concerned, the provision of their equipment and the management of them were 'sort of' under our control with and on behalf of the forces' hierarchy. This brings me to the management of the AFRC.

Pat was undoubtedly the manager of the AFRC so far as the Project Office and its staff were concerned. One of the bonuses in the setting up of the project was that the revenue received from all member forces was constant and by no means stinted. They would all be paying very substantial amounts of cash into 'The Pot'. We were therefore able to employ top class solicitors and barristers when the needs arose and would not be in a position to be financially 'bullied' by IBM or anyone else. With the consent of the consortium management group, (CMG) we were able to appoint other specialist companies required to keep the business efficient and rolling. Purchase Orders could be signed at Pat's level and as a result of my employment, I'm pretty sure that he had earned himself a promotion to Chief Superintendent on the back of him supervising an ex Chief Superintendent when he was 'merely' a Superintendent. If that was the case, it happened many months after I arrived.

Although Pat was the 'King Pin' at our level, he was far from that at a senior level. Just like any other large commercial organisation, we had the equivalent of a 'Chairman' and a board of directors. The Chairman being Sir John Hoddinott and his vice chairman being John Giffard, who subsequently became the Chief Constable of the Staffordshire Constabulary. This post holder was to change in years to come, but was always held by an officer of the ACPO rank of either Deputy or Assistant Chief Constable. The only dissimilar analogy with an ordinary business was that because this was going to be an amalgam of thirty seven individual constabularies, it was obviously necessary to have members on the board who each represented their own police force. These were invariably of the rank of Assistant Chief Constable. The collective noun for these people was the 'Consortium Management Group' It was from then on, always referred to by yet another acronym, the 'CMG'.

It was necessary for the CMG to meet at approximately quarterly intervals and on occasions, when necessary, even at shorter or longer intervals. The office manager, Angela Gale became the secretary of the group and I was later to take this over from her for a short period. It wasn't an easy task and involved quite a lot of preparation with not only the agenda and minutes of the last meeting but more often than not, the compilation of sometimes numerous appendices. With thirty seven (sometimes more) force representatives, visiting speakers, AFRC personnel etc., it can be imagined how much paper that generated with bundles of documents which were always contained with red cardboard top sheet covers. The production on a photocopier, of approximately fifty copies of each bundle was a huge task in itself performed by AFRC administrative staff.

It was necessary to find a venue for such large gatherings, the critical factor being the need for it to be large enough to hold the CMG meetings which more often than not, comprised Project Office staff and CMG members, but in some cases, their 'heads of bureau' plus lawyers and representatives of numerous companies involved, or seeking to become involved in any aspect of the process. In addition, the catering and comfort of attendees was also to be taken into consideration.

It was therefore necessary to invariably hold them in the Council Chamber of the Worcestershire County Council. A very posh room much like that of a modern day Crown Court. The meetings were always tape recorded and members had a microphone which could be turned on when anyone wanted to speak. All that was missing was a panel of interpreters and one could be forgiven for believing that we were at some NATO or other international conference.

An organisation as big and as important as this, required legal guidance and Mr. Ted Mason, a solicitor and Clerk to the Hampshire Police Authority, was instructed to work with Pat on the initial tendering processes and the formation of an eventual 'Consortium Management Agreement'. This was a form of a contract with each of the Police Authorities involved and the Home Office. A complicated process of 'Change Requests' was introduced to cater for any desired amendments to this initial contract and any other contract involving the AFRC.

The final version of this Consortium Agreement was signed on 14th April 1994, just seven months prior to my joining the team. It now included 38 Member Police Forces, though the Metropolitan Police was not to be an active participant. It had been in March 1992 that the AFR Consortium entered into a Contract with IBM. Sagem of Paris was a Sub-contractor to IBM so in effect; any problems with software were to be dealt with by them (IBM) who would deal with Sagem directly as their software contracted agents. This made it difficult for the consortium to deal with Sagem Direct.

My research indicated that they had grown through many buy outs, mergers of subsidiary companies and takeovers but their core identity for fingerprint technology alone was through the name they adopted, North American Morpho Systems Incorporated. (NAMSI)

The following has been taken from Wikipedia.

> *'French high-tech company SAGEM S.A. has carved out a commanding position for itself among the world's top electronics*

companies, despite its relatively modest size. France's second largest maker of telecommunications equipment, and one of the world leaders, SAGEM produces GSM and WAP mobile telephone handsets, a market in which SAGEM's products account for more than one-half of total market sales, fax machines, networking systems, and digital set-top boxes for Internet, cable, and satellite transmissions..........

Through its SAGEM Morpho subsidiary, the company is the world leader in automated fingerprint recognition systems, used by police forces and other agencies throughout the world.

Sagem introduced the Consortium to their wholly owned subsidiary in Tacoma. This was the company, 'North American Morpho Systems Incorporated' (NAMSI) which later became a major landmark in my life regarding the work I did for them in the USA and in many countries in the Caribbean. However, on 1st January 1998, NAMSI changed their name to 'Sagem Morpho Incorporated' (SMI).

The project at West Mercia's police house was beginning to grow and office staff were increasing accordingly. So much so, that we had outgrown our base and on 24th February 1995, we moved to rented office accommodation at 9, Roman Way Business Centre, Droitwich, a few miles away.

Terry Anley, another retired superintendent had an earlier involvement with the Consortium and following a short absence, later re-joined us at our new premises which, in typical Pat Pitt style had to be named as 'STAR BASE'!

Chapter 6 – Goodbye IBM

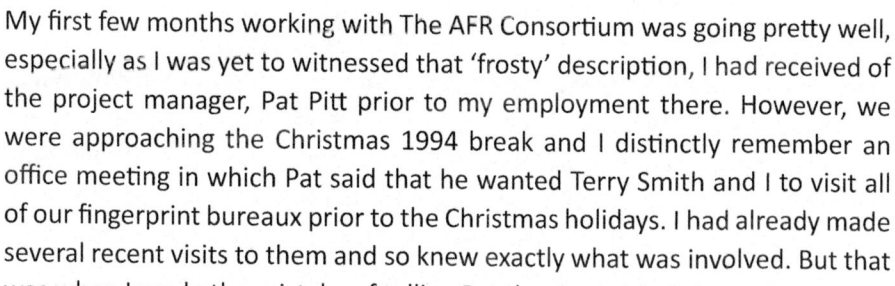

My first few months working with The AFR Consortium was going pretty well, especially as I was yet to witnessed that 'frosty' description, I had received of the project manager, Pat Pitt prior to my employment there. However, we were approaching the Christmas 1994 break and I distinctly remember an office meeting in which Pat said that he wanted Terry Smith and I to visit all of our fingerprint bureaux prior to the Christmas holidays. I had already made several recent visits to them and so knew exactly what was involved. But that was when I made the mistake of telling Pat that in my view, it was impossible to visit all of them again. I meant 'physically impossible' with that time constraint. I recall there were just a few days left before Christmas and Terry and I would need to visit just under twenty Police Headquarters in that time scale and hold meaningful dialogue with the heads of all bureaux. It was impossible.

Pat said nothing at the meeting but later made mention to me of his surprise about my 'negative attitude'! I was to be told, contrary to Terry's reputation as being Pat's informant, that Pat's instructions should always be concurred with, whether or not they were carried out. I recalled that I only visited the Hampshire Bureau at Winchester in addition to the West Mercia one, located almost 'next door'. He made no further comment.

I had earlier been informed of Terry's relationship with Pat and the subject of his 'snitching' to him had been repeated not only by those prior to my employment, but by others in the office. I was therefore always on guard and being handsomely rewarded for my toils, I wasn't going to be rocking any boats. I hadn't really thought of it at the time but I subsequently became very proud that as Terry and I were assistant project managers, we were small, but integral parts in the 'roll out' of the first computerised fingerprint recording and searching system in the UK. However, at this time, it was in a poor state and my term, 'Limping along' was very apt.

IBM were reluctant to spend more money on the system which continually crashed. Performing 'Duty Officer' duties became a nightmare as we were constantly fielding complaints from bureaux staff of the poor responses and service. The Code-name for IBM 'BEAR' was now in constant negative use and those meetings with them at Warwick appeared to be making no difference at all. It was like holding onto a Crocodile by its tail.

Christmas came and I had really warmed to the computer and was continually being surprised by what could be achieved on it. I had now taken on the full 'Microsoft Office' package and thus replaced my Lotus123 spreadsheets with Microsoft's Excel. I was now operating with my first Internet email service provider which was a 'Dial up' account with a company called 'CompuServe' I recall we had long numbers as our email addresses.

1995 started in the same vein and we were struggling to provide a satisfactory service through IBM, who seemed reluctant or incapable of putting things right. One of the lesser failures of them appeared when clear evidence was discovered that they were not honouring their side of the contract. There was a suspicion that they were charging us for making contractual maintenance visits to bureaux when they were not in fact, making them at all. Pat asked me to investigate. This resulted in me producing a spreadsheet which recorded exactly when these visits had been made so that I could compare the data with what they were charging us for.

So, it was just for a short period that I was to put my 'detective's hat' on again. This was just the sort of job I relished and IBM had forgotten, or were unaware that all visitors are recorded at police headquarters. It became quite clear that whoever was responsible for drafting our invoices had grossly over egged their pudding. Whether this was 'criminal' or administrative errors, I could not prove, but whatever, they had merely inserted all the dates when maintenance visits should have been made and these, by a long margin, were nothing like the reality which I discovered. Even at that early stage, a contingency plan was being hatched to pull out of the contract and to claim damages from IBM.

We had now taken on some extra help by the temporary secondment of Inspector Geoff Aston from Hampshire. Also, in addition to Terry Anley, the

Norfolk Constabulary agreed to temporarily release David Hosgood, their head of bureau who became a great help to us by bringing his knowledge of fingerprints and the practical procedures of using the technology concerned.

I loved working with spread sheets and so I was able to prepare some graphs and charts which not only depicted IBM's mistakes, whether they be mistakes or false accounting, but also the system's availability which very often dipped below 50%.

A contingency plan to retrieve our data from IBM was hatched. Blimey! What had I let myself in for? I hadn't been there two months and we were planning a massive withdrawal from the IBM contract which was to involve the 'cloak and dagger' operation of an unannounced visit to IBM with a High Court order directing them to hand over our data.

We were, however, maintaining our very best efforts to prop up the service but with the poor service being received, this wasn't an easy job. Although my contract as an 'Assistant Project Manager' (Service Manager) spelled out my duties, one clause stated that I would provide services in support of other tasks that may, from time to time, be required (The catch all). In short, I was hired as a 'Team Member' to help get the show on the road but to be specifically responsible for all aspects of 'Service Provision'. As mentioned earlier, it was just that Terry Smith and I split the job between us.

I was now able to produce some statistics on Lotus 123 and then on the Microsoft 'Excel' software. Pat took to this and, in his desire to use statistics to show off our progress, he came to enjoy the coloured statistical charts I was able to produce. I was to become the 'Consortium's Statistician' in addition to my 'service manager' role and later to produce a plethora of statistics and papers full of graphs of various kinds and bar charts. I was indeed, sometimes contracted to do this work separately, and in addition to my current AFRC contracted work. In practical terms, the number of contracted days was extended, as was the payments for them.

Chapter 7 – Operation Shakespeare

My old Vauxhall Carlton would soon be able to find its own way to just about every Force Fingerprint Bureau in England and Wales and wouldn't it be putting on some miles! The car refused to die but sadly, I eventually gave her away to my son in law after she had recorded well over 200,000 miles and of course, it wasn't depreciating at all. With not depreciating and earning me expenses to ride in her, she was massively adding to my income through my mileage expenses submitted each month.

As an example, at this time (February 1995) I made visits to Bedfordshire, Nothamptonshire, Surrey, Dorset, Dyfed Powys and Cheshire. By now I had found my feet but nevertheless I was very surprised to receive a Compuserve message from Pat. I have the original but it is too faint for reproduction here.

Dated 8th March 1995, it reads: -

Brian

A quick note of encouragement.
You have settled in very well and have gained a good grasp of the job.
I am impressed on how you have mastered the computer packages from a standing start.
The going is getting tough but hang in there and you will have a really interesting and exciting time.
I have been at this project for three / four years and have never ceased to be amazed at the diversity and unpredictability of it.
You're doing fine and have made the transition well.
Regards
Pat

I was surprised to receive this but my pleasure was tempered a little because I was becoming aware that my colleague, Terry Smith was unable to produce the computer work which I enjoyed and hence there was a danger of him becoming alienated or even jealous. I don't think the rest of the staff had noticed this because it was so obvious to them that Terry was Pat's pet 'side kick' and informant, so wouldn't be falling out with him. However, my computer literacy would continue to feature with our objectives and I suppose I was proud about that.

In addition to visiting fingerprint bureaux, there were 'Duty Officer' duties to perform at the Project Office where the battle with the poor service being provided by IBM continued. This culminated in an 'Emergency CMG meeting' held on 22nd March 1995. Having taken advice from a Queen's Counsel, it was decided that in view of IBM's continued failures, we would take steps to 'pull the plug' on the contract and sue them for damages.

Events happened very quickly and on the following day, I was instructed to prepare Service Notices 6 & 7 of 1995 to be sent to all our bureaux telling them not to acquire any further Tenprints or 'Scenes of Crime' marks to the system. This was in effect, the signal that we were pulling out of the contract.

This was such a serious move to make. We had acquired every prisoner's tenprint form onto the database for almost the whole of the country. Although this exercise meant that we retained the hard copy, the expense and effort of acquiring them to the system meant that we needed to retrieve the Digital Optical Discs (DODS) on which this data was recorded. In those days, large databases were operated by the searching of what looked like many very big record albums which were housed in 'Juke Boxes' and accessed in very similar ways to that of a musical juke box. It was the movement of a swinging arm causing the correct DOD to be attached to it and placed on a bed to be searched. It was in exactly the same concept as a music record juke box (if any reader can remember them) but of course, what it accessed was nothing like music. (Except that when that process resulted in a 'hit', it became music to our ears' – sorry, some music did become 'hits' didn't they?)

Our legal representatives had obtained an injunction directing IBM to hand over the 'DODS' containing our data. Our relationship with IBM was at such a low level that we were in effect, to operate a covert raid on IBM's Headquarters at Warwick armed with an injunction demanding them to return our DODs. This was to become known as 'Operation Shakespeare'.

I had taken part in many named operations during my police service but this was the first one on a civil dispute. I suppose we named operations as a matter of convenience for referral reasons which normally boiled down to personnel and financial subjects, though in later years a central database of names was kept. For a real example, instead of asking, "What's the budget looking like on that drugs job at Ludlow? You might say, "What's the 'Nightlight' budget looking like?

It so happens that as a Det. Superintendent, I once paid a supervisory visit to see how this 'Operation Nightlight' was proceeding. The small piece of a newspaper snippet below makes reference to it. On one occasion at an evening briefing, I happened to ask why the operation was called 'Nightlight'. The room burst into laughter.

men jailed

Five people were dealt with at Shrewsbury Crown Court — three of them jailed immediately —for their parts in a chain of cannabis use and supply centred on Market Drayton.

They were arrested after an 11-month vigil by police — nicknamed Operation Nightlight — which resulted in £5,000 worth of the drug being confiscated.

I was told that the DCI who was present, often reminded the officers concerned, not to forget the night lights. He was referring to special binoculars used in the dark called 'Light Intensifiers'. However, he could never remember the word 'Intensifiers' and so replaced it with 'Nightlights'!

Anyway, I prepared an 'Operational Order' and we were about to embark on what was called 'Operation Shakespeare' (Not exactly in Stratford but it was in Warwickshire). So, in possession of a personnel carrier I had hired, we made several trial runs. Blimey, I could hardly believe that we were about to raid and sue one of the biggest companies in the IT world, for 'Breach of Contract'.

The ambush on the Warwick IBM facility eventually took place on 7th April 1995, when, mob handed, we hit IBM's headquarters with injunction in hand. Despite all the precautions we had made, the staff appeared to acknowledge what was going on. There was no shouting and screaming and we achieved our objective with comparative ease and with the full cooperation of IBM staff.

I couldn't help feeling a little embarrassed and wondered whether this was all 'overboard' and could have been achieved in a different manner. I wasn't too proud and always felt that with more diplomacy and tact, we might have been able to improve our system without all this effort, expense and gung-ho! However, I was not in a position to know.

The Consortium was eventually awarded an undisclosed sum of damages from IBM. I had heard that it was £3m but none of us contractors were ever informed properly. It was after all an 'undisclosed' sum so I was content in really not wanting to know.

Chapter 8 – Early Life After IBM

The upshot was that we immediately searched for another provider. The thought was, that if we could find one, it wouldn't be too long before our fingerprint records could be transferred to a new system and off, we would go again.

My job was then, centred on winding down our member bureaux by removing all the AFRC kit that had been installed. This meant that I had little to do with negotiating with prospective service suppliers, though I do know that we almost immediately began negotiating with another American giant defence company, Lockheed Martin Corporation (LMC). Their approach was on a 'costs plus' principle which calculated to be more expensive than the IBM system. The other thing that really irritated was the fact that they had sent quite a large delegation over the Atlantic to present their proposal to us. We assumed that they had sent a sprat to catch a mackerel but to our horror, on their return, they sent us an invoice for all their expenses, including air fares.

All the headers on their PowerPoint overheads contained their slogan, 'WE CAN DO'. I thought, 'We can do without you!" But obviously that was no matter for me.

I think it was Nick Thornton from PA Consulting who joined Pat for the negotiations but I'm afraid I can't actually remember how, when and exactly under what circumstances, we parted ways but the CMG meeting held at the Bank House hotel near Worcester on 21st June 1995 must have been a 'Landmark' event when many important decisions on our future were made. The LMC representatives were called into that meeting to deliver their bid.

I've extracted the following selected bullet pointed subjects from that meeting: -

- The LMC proposal was thoroughly aired and discussed. Members to decide on their vote prior to 7th July 1995.

- The Hub System had commenced. (An Emergency Service)
- The IBM damages claim was then at £14m.
- Alternative services from the companies 'Printrak' and 'DEC' were discussed and rejected.
- The effect of forces withdrawing were fully discussed.
- A costing schedule identifying the comparisons between IBM and LMC would be circulated.
- Working conditions for and payments made to fingerprint experts working in Tacoma were discussed. Vice Chairman Mr. Giffard would pay a visit and report.
- Members updated with the damages claim and legal aspects. The Litigation Support team formed by AFR staff.
- IBM were wanting to discuss an out of court settlement.
- Approx. £25,000 had so far been spent on legal advice.
- Pat reported briefly on the 'Back Record Conversion' of Tenprints and the commencement of the Emergency Service which had now been loaded and had produced 44 hits to date.
- Lockheed Martin representatives joined the meeting to make their presentations regarding their proposal to provide their system and what they had anticipated they would do. Their final proposal would be submitted in about a week's time. Many questions and answers ended their presentations.
- Mr. Nick Thornton from PA consultants (accountants) presented his report and advised members on the comparisons between IBM and what LMC had to offer.
- Reports also received by Ted Mason, Hampshire County Council and AFR's legal representative. A decision on LMC would be made by votes on 8th July 1995.

To briefly summarise, all aspects of the consortium's withdrawal from IBM and the implications resulting from the LMC's presentations were recorded in these minutes, which as I said above, were the 'Landmark' decisions made, but I was in the USA when the decisions were made and, although I cannot recall fully the events, the decision not to proceed with LMC must have been made, though I cannot now recall the sequence of events.

I do remember that very soon after our DODs were seized from IBM, we flew out several of our UK fingerprint experts to assist in building and searching a limited Emergency AFR database. This was for an interim period of ten months and was at first, limited to searching scenes of crime marks for the most serious of offences. A few fingerprint experts had volunteered to permanently reside in the US and then teams of other experts were flown out for monthly stints to join them. This emergency AFR system, (EAS) became quickly available to all consortium bureaux and us ex senior police officer contractors were to rotate in turn to become duty officers, supervising the EAS operation and its operation in Tacoma, Washington State. During this period, all the records acquired onto the IBM system, approximately 600,000 were purged from NAMSI's (SMI's) database and re-acquired to facilitate the reconstituted database.

Despite our ongoing litigation with Sagem, we had always held the belief that it was IBM who were the problem. They were always reluctant to call in Sagem's software engineers and we had noticed that on the occasions when they did, problems were quickly resolved. So, it was following the breakdown of negotiations with LMC that we decided to open up negotiations with Sagem in the hope that we could organise our own system by negotiating all the contracts required for us to commence an 'Emergency AFR system' (EAS) for our Bureaux.

It was finally, in April 1996, following a 'step by step' approach, when we signed up with Sagem to provide our continued full service. This was only fifty-six days after we had terminated our IBM contract. But having experienced all aspects of this litigious period, it eventually dawned on the powers that be, that our service had been provided by the stitching together of the relevant companies involved in it. The reconstituted service was not to be contracted for in the traditional manner, with a single service provider, who would normally be expected to provide, install, maintain and manage the system. We had been down that route and the result was far from the effective and controllable situation desired.

What was needed in terms of hardware, was a company capable of housing and maintaining our databases and the provision of workstations to access them. In addition, desk top computers housed in all bureaux were required for communicating with the central site and each other by email.

A contract with British Telecom would also be required to produce an I.T. highway so that the required networking and interoperability involved in the 'Cross-Atlantic' fingerprint searches could be facilitated. In addition to providing the servers and the data on them, all that IBM had done, was to act as the conductor of the orchestra. What on earth could go wrong, if we were to do the same ourselves? The term, 'If it aint broke, why fix it' comes to mind, but of course, our previous system was indeed broken, so what were the implications of that?

The ideal solution would have been to have had the database housed in the same location as the software engineers. IBM were in England, but Sagem's subsidiary, SMI were in Tacoma, Washington State USA. But how difficult would it be to have UK fingerprint experts at 37 UK locations, searching a database in America?

It was fully recognised that most of our IBM problems emanated because of their resistance to have the software engineers involved in problem shooting, I suspect this was because of the location and cost implications involved. However, that was bound to change if both the data management and the software expertise were in the same location.

With SMI's base being in Tacoma, I would never have realised that I was to spend many months of many years working at these premises with other AFR staff and my SMI contacts, Jean-Claude Richard, their Senior Vice President and his personal assistant, Debra Chastain. Our relationships were to blossom but for the time being, now that we had extracted ourselves from IBM, there was a 'mopping up' exercise to finish in England and Wales and the introduction of an Emergency AFR system (EAS) for our member forces.

This was a time when the AFRC took on more staff and contractors. In addition to suing IBM, there was the legal procedures involved in the civil action to pull together. It is safe to say that those working for us were to in effect, compile a case for the prosecution. With ex-senior detectives at hand, the expertise was present, though of course, that effort was to be guided by our lawyers.

On reflection, that 1995 was a remarkable year. To summarise, we were juggling with the following to : -

- Form a litigation Support Unit (LSU) to assist with the civil action against IBM
- Strip thirty seven fingerprint bureau of equipment (Exit Strategy)
- Pull together an Emergency AFR system for our member forces. (EAS team)
- Negotiate with other AFIS suppliers to provide a replacement AFIS service caused by the suing of IBM.

These were the core issues, but each of them required a plethora of mini-projects in order to achieve final goals.

Chapter 9 – EAS, HUBs and USA, Here We Come

Whilst AFRC contractors were working on individual projects, in reality, we rolled up our sleeves and very often, had parts to play in one or more of these projects. We were up and running and actually obtaining 'Hits' on our EAS on 16th May 1995. For a short time, the database was limited to two forces, but at least we had made a very good start and had proved the concept.

On 20th December 1995, we finally were to enter into an 'Emergency Service Agreement' with Sagem's subsidiary company, SMI. Alas, the formation of what was to be termed, 'The Central Site' at Tacoma, USA was yet another huge project to be embarked upon.

Following our withdrawal from IBM, it would have been easy to have just shrugged our shoulders and said, "Oh well, that's it then!" However, a lot of blood, sweat and tears had been spent and the wheels of litigation naturally kept on turning, so AFRC was not going to roll over and die. There was a huge fight to be fought and in fairness, Pat and the CMG were good to have in our corner. Our Police Forces had tasted the benefits of an electronic digitised system and importantly, many more criminals were locked up as a result. In addition, we couldn't blame bureau staff and their chief constables for believing that it was somehow, all of our doing. Something had to be done and it had to be done quickly. The strength of mind and determination of Sir John and Pat and our team played an important part.

The emergency plan was quickly hatched with NAMSI (SMI) and involved a process of working with our Bureaux to a planned system whereby we would load up an agreed percentage of their total tenprints into what were described as 'Coffins' which were shipped by FedEx to Tacoma for the process of 'Back Record Converting' them onto a new database. We could not, of course, denude Bureaux of all of their records at once because they were needed to search and so we devised a rotation system of taking a small percentage and no more, until those sent, were eventually returned. We were operating a schedule to ensure that we were sending about 1,000 tenprints per day, shared among all forces, to be acquired to the Emergency Service database.

In addition to all of those main objectives, bulleted in the previous chapter, member forces, in particular their representative CMG members, were required to be kept informed and more importantly, their agreement to proceed as desired, would be required at every step. To this end, we held a seminar at Kettering to keep them briefed and to assist in carving out the future which was to include replacing EAS with a full fingerprint identification service.

By February 1996 we had instructed specialist IT lawyers Richard Kemp of Garrett & Co of London to draft a contract between AFRC and NAMSI. Richard Bonner also of Garrett & Co was instructed to draft the contract for the 'Network System' with BT and Protocol IPS Limited to maintain our UK hardware. It was this same Fareham, Hampshire based company under the leadership of their Steve Heagren which had similarly maintained our equipment under the IBM contract.

The reconstruction of the service had also provided opportunity for the hardware equipment to be used at NAMSI to be upgraded. The traditional usage of 'Juke Boxes' which housed our DODs was replaced by the 'Random array of independent disc' (RAID) technology. This replaced the swinging arm with a scanning method and this eventually considerably reduced the incidence of mechanical breakdowns.

Such a system was not new to BT and they facilitated this so called, 'Wide Area Network' (WAN) highway which they called T-1 lines which were operated and monitored by Protocol Solutions through a Belgian Company, 'Telindus' whose representative was a Mr. Wilfred Suffys, another charming gentleman who bragged that Telindus could warn us when the line was to fail, even before it failed. (And it could!)

Sagem would of course, welcome the business but now, everything which used to be at Warwick was in a foreign country some 5,000 miles away on the

Pacific West coast of America. Oh well, in LMC's terms, 'WE DEFINITELY CAN DO IT'.

A system of access by bureaux was devised which, in the very early days prior to individual bureaux operating alone, comprised a 'HUB' system whereby at first, I think it was ten hub bureaux were constituted equally spread around the country. Each of the hubs would accommodate the work of three or four of their neighbouring forces and, the sending of tenprints for acquisition which also involved scanning machines called 'Telscan', in addition to the FedEx transportation to NAMSI via the project office. This 'Hub' system spread until by early May, 1996, after all 'Hub' sites had been constituted. This provided all English and Welsh forces between them, with a full service.

Between May 1996 and subsequently, April 1999, 46,700 fingerprint marks lifted from scenes of crime, were identified against the 3,800,000 tenprints then held on the system. A remarkable achievement by any stretch of imagination.

So, it was to Tacoma we were to go to our work place and not just down the road to Droitwich. We were to be accommodated at the Sheraton hotel, located almost opposite to NAMSI in a very pretty plaza with plenty of trees and greenery surrounds but otherwise, unlike Seattle its twin city a few miles up the road, Tacoma wasn't an exciting city at all. It was generally, pretty 'down trodden' in comparison. Tacoma had been developed purely because it was a 'port' city built on the Puget Sound of the Pacific West. It was one of the deepest ports along the west coast, indeed the world, and could accommodate the largest of vessels able to import merchandise, especially motor vehicles from all parts of the world. I recall fields of Japanese vehicles being stored near to the port. It seemed to me that with the building of large shopping malls on the periphery of Tacoma, many of what would have been 'High Street' type shops, including F.W. Woolworth, had closed down due to their trade being sucked out of the city into these malls. My thoughts were that our own cities back at home, might well be suffering a similar fate in the near future, due to similar large-scale malls and Internet shopping, but we would have to wait and see.

I also thought it a coincidence that our AFRC bases at Hindlip and Droitwich had been located just off the M5 Motorway and now our new base in Tacoma was just off the Interstate 5 (I-5) and took about the same time to travel from Droitwich to Hereford as it did from Tacoma to Seattle, about thirty-four miles away along this fast multi carriage Interstate Highway.

The other 'down side' to working there was that Pacific time was eight hours behind GMT. Jetlag played havoc with my head, especially after the return flight easterly when flying home. It took me a couple of weeks to get over it and by then, I frequently had to return.

The most pleasant aspect of these Seattle flights was flying very adjacent to Mount Ranier which was always snowcapped and in glorious sunshine. Even on the ground, the journey to Tacoma by road, involved seeing this, mountain for the whole short trip. What appeared to be a huge mountain, just a mile or two away, was a really confusing perception because it rose so high above everything else, yet in reality, the closest one could get to the Mount Rainier National Park by road, was 60 miles and then you were only at ground level foothills before the mountain began to rise.

The Mount Ranier National Park

All this travel might appear to be exciting now, but it literally, for me, it became a real headache! Thank goodness, it must have been after a year or even two, that British Airways decided to put on direct flights from Gatwick to Seattle, but even so, that didn't cure my jet lag.

Jumping the gun here all the way to the end of our AFRC service in 2001, the CMG presented all UK based AFR staff involved in these flights, a very nice professionally mounted photograph of the BA flight passing Mount Rainier. It was unexpected but very well received and is hung in my office today. The airport serving both Tacoma and Seattle was located almost midway between the two cities and so, was aptly named 'SEATAC', to include the first three letters of both cities. The photo below in black and white belies its delight in glorious colour.

If memory serves me correctly, we were on the eighth floor of the high-rise tower and SMI were so ideally situated on the fifth floor. What a contrast to that which had existed between the Warwick based IBM and Tacoma! SMI's name was still NAMSI then, but we had been referring to it as SMI (Sagem Morpho Inc.) for some time. However, both terms were in use but jumping the gun again here, it wasn't until 1st January 1998 until the company officially changed its name from NAMSI to SMI.

As explained earlier, security was of the utmost importance to both preserve the tenprint forms being checked in both physical and digitised formats and at the same level for the scenes of crime marks being checked. The index board in the foyer of our new high-rise home, described all businesses inside but no mention was made of the AFRC. Similarly, nothing indicating what was on the other side of our internal door was apparent. 'Unique to one-person' high-level quality electronic tags ensured that wearers were tagged wherever they went. All that plus CCTV recording and an armed guard at our reception, ensured that security was at the highest level. In addition, all our workstations including computing equipment were logically secured. Fingerprint machines and other computers were stretched right across the width of the building with offices or rooms at either end. An important room at one end, was a type of resting centre with free snacks, cold drinks and tea / coffee making facilities. It was a very comfortable area which was completely covered in nice soft carpet. Indeed, I recall our American office secretary, Denise Couch, doing backward flick flacks along the whole length. She was a gymnast but it was such a long length that it took some doing. Our work-stations were positioned along both sides of this carpeted area.

High Rise 1145 Broadway Plaza, Tacoma WA

My wife Jo and I had previously spent holidays in New York and Florida and elsewhere, along USA's East coast prior to my retirement. However, during those 'Operation Shakespeare' days, I obtained a 10-year visa on my passport as it was going to be necessary for me to travel frequently to Tacoma for periods of 'Duty Officer' duties. These were usually for around a month at a time and us ex senior police contractors operated in rotation with one another until maybe we were required to carry out mini-projects or anything else required of us.

My visits were to become more frequent and I recall some of the immigration officers at the border becoming curious as to why they were seeing the same faces repeatedly. This was later to have implications which I shall mention later.

So far as SMI were concerned, they seconded one of their shift leaders, Greg Tillett to work with us as a Service Director on behalf of their company. He was not only very useful but a very nice gentleman who I got on extremely well with. He invited me to his home for dinner one evening where he introduced me to his hobby of collecting old machines such as juke boxes (the musical models) and fruit machines.

I was also to develop a very good relationship with SMI's top man, a Frenchman named Jean-Claude Richard (JCR) and his PA, Debra Chastain. My problem with JCR was that although his English Grammar was fairly good, his very thick French accent caused me much difficulty in understanding what he actually said. However, in later times, I thought that it was possibly my relationship with JCR why Pat asked me to negotiate some business with him, thought to cost in the region of £1m. This occurred in April 1999 and I'll deal with that matter also, a little later but it briefly concerned the upgrading of our database memory size and our system's matchers.

So far as I can remember, the UK contingent of fingerprint experts employed there at first contained the pick of them and we were lucky to have the services of a Dick Johnson, head of the Bedfordshire Bureau as leader of the experts seconded to us. He, among others, were to eventually obtain 'Green Cards' permitting their full employment and residence in the USA.

Service notices were distributed to bureaux stressing that only marks found at serious crime scenes would be searched. SMI supplied us with the equipment but, we needed Fingerprint Experts to operate them. Member forces agreed that we could second their Fingerprint experts to work at Tacoma on a Rota basis for about a month at a time. It was also necessary for us to perform our somewhat different 'Duty Officer' role there. This involved the supervision of the whole process including looking after relatively young fingerprint experts being sent to us. Whilst they were all adults, some were very young and, we didn't want to attract attention locally. I felt that us 'Duty Officers' were playing very much a paternal role for them.

Our duties involved us meeting these experts at SeaTac Airport and settling them into the nearby Sheraton hotel, a short walk from our operation. We often chaperoned them to local hostelries where invariably we were required to prove their ages. I was quite pleased that a great deal of effort was expended by Americans in ensuring that only over 21s were sold alcohol, and admitted into Licensed Premises. I was even more pleased when on some occasions, I was also asked to prove my age!!

This was, of course, an exciting period of time for all concerned, we were suddenly thrust into working in America, something we never envisaged would ever happen. We encouraged a competitive spirit among the experts and every time one of them identified a scenes of crime Mark, they were permitted to ring **'The Bell'**. Statistics were obviously kept and the competitive spirit extended to the various teams that were sent to Tacoma in rotation.

My first of many trips to Tacoma occurred on 20th July 1995 when I went to perform a short twenty-three-day stint of 'Duty Officer duties'. Karen Dorans picked me up from SeaTac Airport and this was the first time, I witnessed Mount Rainier which was plainly visible with its snowcapped summit basked in glorious sunshine. This was such a magnificent site and there was an air of brilliant light and freshness about the place.

This first trip was also remarkable for another reason. I was to expect members of a fresh team of experts to arrive during my stint and for some reason, one of them could not travel. Unbeknown to me, the replacement had been arranged through the Gloucestershire Bureau and it had been arranged that my daughter, Sarah would take this vacant slot. I had no hand in that.

As can be seen by the below photographs, there were normally six or seven fingerprint experts to each team who were seconded to us in one-month rosters. Sarah's presence would not have been an ideal situation had it been planned but the nature of the emergency situation had caused this tremendous coincidence. I had often been accused of easing Sarah into her employment in Fingerprints but, she had been engaged in that work for some time in the Gloucestershire Bureau even before I had retired from West Mercia. She later transferred to the West Mercia Bureau to ease her daily fifty-mile round trip to Cheltenham. I had actually tried to dissuade her from applying for that job because she possessed a bubbly extrovert personality and I could sense that she might become bored with searching fingerprints after the novelty had worn off. However, for the period in question, not only was our similar work a bit of a coincidence, but now we would be working together on the same team and I was to be her boss!! She arrived at SeaTac Airport on 29th July 1995 and was due to return on 26th August.

I suspect that she was a little relieved to see me pick her up and that she had 'Dad' to settle her in, but also, she was probably more than pleased that I was to return well before her and so she was out of her dad's sight in America with her mates for a couple of weeks. I must admit that I was very pleased to see her as she bounded, at a pace, down the ramp leading from the immigration department at Seatac.

Ironically, she eventually did get bored and she now remains working as Operations Manager at the RSC, Stratford, close to where she now resides with her family. It did however, take her 24 years before that boredom set in.

Denise Couch, our American 'flick flacking' gymnast secretary / office manager was about the same age as most of the fingerprint experts. Her desk was adjacent to the Duty Officer's and she, together with Greg Tillett, our SMI secondee, were our links to the local area giving advice about where to explore and where not to explore etc.

Miss Sarah Humphreys

At her workstation.

'Daddy' Duty Officer

With Sarah and the rest of her team.

Monthly teams of fingerprint experts came and went but it must be remembered that this was yet another temporary solution until we could be in a position to offer the full database and return to normal searching at all bureaux. In total, this was to take about ten months. It was because we were now operating a scaled down temporary system that part of a Duty Officer's responsibilities was to ensure that the experts on our watches gave priority to searching marks from the most serious of offences. With shift members getting up from their workstations to ring the bell, loud cheers ensued and this only added to the spirit and camaraderie of the occasion and a competitive spirit ensued.

One can imagine that very serious crimes would invariably result in numerous marks being found at the crime scene. For example, a murder in a house might entail hundreds of marks being found and the job of searching that many would take days. On the other hand, a burglary of a mansion where perhaps property was stolen and taken from the premises via the same place as it was entered, might only involve a few marks being discovered.

I was quite strict on this policy but I learned that my colleague Duty Officers weren't so strict. On a later occasion, I was to hear a whisper that Pat, who was in England, wasn't that happy with the number of 'HITS' my shift of experts had been harvesting. By the same token, the pride of ringing the bell by individual experts was to inevitably, end up with some of them searching through the 'jobs' they received and by means of reading the description of them, were in effect, 'Cherry Picking' the best ones which might provide the best and fastest jobs to result in 'HITS'.

It became obvious to me that if one team continued to spend their month searching through the marks that they had 'cherry picked' then they would be leaving behind, all the 'not so easy' jobs to search for the next team. I realised immediately that these practices were not only wrong, but the suggestion that successful hitting of marks against tenprints were resulting from the expert's skill, was also wrong. Indeed, though it never happened, it would be quite possible for a team of good experts to work through 24 hours with none of them gaining a 'HIT'.

My team at the time was a particularly good one, and contained some good experienced personnel. With others, they included the head of the Northamptonshire Bureau, David Goodwin and his Deputy, Simon Marshall. I called the whole team together for a chat and our relationship was such that they gave me their response – **"leave it to us gaffer"**. What that meant, I didn't ask.

They confirmed my suspicions and without saying more, promised me that their 'Hits' would increase. Pat never mentioned his worry to me directly and so I didn't feel it necessary to say anything further when reporting that our team managed to break the record existing at that time for the monthly number of hits. This was probably achieved through a certain amount of cherry picking even though I did ensure that we searched a fair share of 'no hope' marks.

I have often argued the case for managing with encouragement or preferring the 'carrot rather than the stick'. This was probably a good example of how the 'stick' didn't work but the carrot did.

CHAPTER 10 – AFRC Progression and Life in the US

We were free agents in a foreign land enjoying America's hospitality and claiming the expenses incurred at all the various eating places in the district. Examining my first expenses claim in Tacoma, reminds me of the many restaurants we used – The Wintergreen and the Altezzo Italian at the Sheraton hotel, Katie Downs, The Lobster Shop, The RAM, The Spaghetti Factory, The Mandarin on Broadway Chinese, Harbour Lights, Dock Street Landing, The Ark, Fujiya Japanese, Elliott's Bar, Stewarts, Shenanigans, Grounds, Helen's Parlour, **Engine House number 9** and many more were to come. As eating was my favourite hobby, this was certainly one of the plusses, so I had a struggle with trying to avoid those huge portions.

Jumping the gun again here, Sir John Hoddinott had been knighted in the Queen's Birthday Honours in June 1998, so it must have been on one of my many visits to Tacoma that he and I went to 'The Engine House Number 9' restaurant / mini brewery for our evening meal.

The Engine House wasn't a posh restaurant, indeed, its name indicated that it was a converted fire station and probably the opposite. However, it was quirky and became one of my favourites because the pub food was particularly good and also, the poor weak beer often experienced elsewhere was beginning to improve at such mini breweries.

Sir John and I had been before and we took it in turn to pay at the till before sitting down at a table outside. He happened to pay by card and the young man at the till examined it and asked him, "Sir John? Is the 'Sir' your name or a title?" Sir John was very sheepish about this, in fact, he once told me that I could use his title only once per day and that it wasn't to be used after breakfast. On this occasion, he indicated that it was correct and we sat outside, only to be followed by a middle aged woman. She said, "Is what I heard correct, you really are a Knight of the British Realm?" Oh dear, just like the gentleman he was, he politely told her that it was correct, but that he had been very lucky etc, etc, etc. He was so commanding in his presence, but oh, so humble.

So, returning to those earlier days, staying at the Sheraton hotel was fine. It was probably the best in that area, was so close to the Finance Centre where we worked and the rooms and facilities were large and well appointed. Putting up our staff and visitors must have cost a huge sum. It was later, when the opportunity arose, that AFRC were able to enter into a rental agreement for I think, three or four apartments which were contained within a converted paint warehouse at Cliff Street, more towards the waterfront.

Cliff Street Lofts in the background overlooking the US Postal Service Sorting Office. The Roof Garden below.

The quirkiness about them included the fact that huge oak pillars, used to support other floors, came down through most of them. Although this sounds horrific, most of us duty officers enjoyed them equally, if not more so than

60

the Sheraton hotel. It was just a short walk away and being apartments, it contained all facilities one might expect in furnished accommodation. The roof garden was an added bonus frequently used.

Fate had played its hand again, here I was, working as a contractor for handsome daily fees and expenses on the West Coast of America. I had always been extremely lucky during my working life.

Back at home, we convened a CMG meeting at County Hall. This was an important meeting because we had lost six forces who decided to pull out of their membership following our 'fall out' with IBM. I suppose their doubts about us being able to recover their service was an indicator and on the face of it, who could blame them?

We did not want to lose any more forces and additionally, we needed to keep the tenprints of those exiting forces on our system and to persuade them to allow us to load their new tenprints to it as they were obtained. This was a big ask especially as we would not be receiving their fresh marks to be searched.

On my return home, Terry Smith was working full time on a small litigation support unit (LSU), ploughing through thousands of documents looking for those of evidential use for what would be, a very long legal battle. So, when not in the US I swapped to cover the North of England and Wales and Inspector Geoff Aston from Hampshire was seconded to work with us temporarily to cover my absences and to perform other tasks.

A Further CMG Meeting was held on 18th October 1995 at Netley, Hampshire where it was agreed that forces would contribute equally to a litigation 'fighting fund'. We told members that the emergency service had so far loaded almost 86,000 tenprints and 7,000 marks and had achieved 481 'Hit' identifications. This was the time when shortly after, on 25th November 1995, an 'Autumn Seminar' was held at Kettering. The importance of this meeting was because we had invited all our prospective suppliers. The objective was to 'sell' the new AFR service that we envisaged being run from Tacoma and which was now indeed, in train. This very statement is surely an indication that LMC had been left behind? There were many questions being asked by our members who found it difficult to appreciate that our service could be run just as economically from across the far side of the USA. We formed various workgroups and this proved a good means of educating those who could not, initially, appreciate what was involved.

In addition to John Hoddinott and his new Vice Chairman, David Stevens (Chief of Essex), other speakers included four Sagem Morpho representatives who stood a good chance of supplying their Sagem software, Mr. J. Bamford, the Assistant Data Protection Registrar, Keith Fryer, the Assistant Director of the National Fingerprint Training School with his colleague George Sheppard, the former Head of the Gloucestershire bureau, Ron Forster of PA Consulting, the leading IT Management Consultants. In addition, Ken Luff of the proposed National Fingerprint Identification System (NAFIS) for England and Wales who, with the assistance of the company, 'TRW' mentioned in chapter 2, were due to take over from us on 30th June 2001. Indeed, TRW the preferred company that had since merged with Lockheed Martin, were still likely to be involved in the NAFIS project.

My presentation to this meeting was simply entitled, "Service Issues - Structure and Lines of Communication and Bureaux Support'. This was an explanation of my role as Assistant Operations Manager, (Service) a description of what that entailed and what my responsibilities were in support of the membership and so I led one of the four workshops entitled, 'Non-Member Databases – Serious Crime and Practice'.

This was my opportunity to explain how we would overcome perceived problems of losing the six forces, indeed one of my later jobs involved me visiting all of those 'lost' forces each month to identify and collect their new tenprints. All in all, the Seminar was hailed a success and we at least thought that we had made a good job of converting any 'non believer' members and more importantly, hopefully preventing others from 'jumping ship'.

My next visit to Tacoma for EAS Duty Officer duties was for twenty-two days ending a few days before Christmas 1995, but I was lucky enough to be invited to attend the SMI office Christmas dinner and party on 15th December. Although we were still running the Emergency AFR System, at the same time, negotiations were still taking place with companies which might be contracted to build our full AFR system / service.

Building such a service required cementing together the various expertise in particular fields because one field of expertise might well need to rely on others. Hardware could not run without software and data could not be accessed without lines of communication. The hardware required not only being supplied but it required maintenance. In addition, the communications in terms of the 'Wide Area Network', (WAN) required monitoring and maintaining. It was like putting a jigsaw puzzle together.

So far as our local and cross Atlantic communication links were concerned, as earlier mentioned, we had decided to negotiate with British Telecom. This was to be a lucrative contract and, of course, many US companies such as AT & T would have died for it. The whole cake was to be baked by all of these expertise 'ingredients' being signed up for a common purpose and although they were just concerned with their own businesses, they were, in effect, to work as a team.

I mention BT specifically, because on 18th December, 1995 I was to meet three BT personnel at SeaTac who were visiting us in Tacoma to negotiate a contract. I think it safe to say that we weren't going to sign up with any of their competitors as they were the main British communications suppliers. In hindsight, this was probably a 'jolly' for these three BT executives who, although they needed to sign the contract, also took advantage of coming over to see what we were all about. Who wouldn't?

Anyway, I met them and took them for a quick spin around the highlights of Tacoma which, due to the lack of available highlights, took all of a couple of minutes, before introducing them to The Sheraton hotel. We would be taking them out for the evening.

Meanwhile, Pat and I discussed our plans for that evening and we decided that we would take them to one of the sports bars on the edge of Commencement Bay. We used many similar establishments along this bay but C. I. Shenanigans was very nice particularly on a warm evening because you could dine on their boardwalk around the main building watching, on occasions, sea planes coming in to land. The Bay was in effect, the entrance to Tacoma Harbour.

It was at this establishment where they had numerous sports televisions all over the place. No matter where you sat, you had access to a clear view of at least one television screen. They were hanging from walls and even the ceilings. Pat and I knew that the State of Washington ran quizzes over the television service in hundreds of similar establishments and any team of players could join in the quizzes by paying a few dollars for a special remote control handset. This required the texting in of the name of your team so that your scores could be attributed to it and that after each question, the answers would appear, and so would a League Table which indicated the position of every team for all to see on the TV screens.

The plan was that Pat would join up with the BT men on one table to form a team and I would accompany a gang of fingerprint experts on another table to join the competition as competitors with all others in Washington State who were playing the quiz.

We were all a little late in settling down but we managed to purchase our handsets and our team began to text in the name of our team. For whatever reason, we just could not get our machine to accept our team. There was no time left and we would just have to hand in the remote and get our money back – it was a faulty handset.

Anyhow, the game started and there we saw on the screens, the name of the BT team. It was 'THE BEES FROM BT' or similar. We also saw that one of the other teams from 'Up State' was called 'The Lawmen' or something similar. By coincidence, this team was doing very well and that was when I hatched a dastardly plan. I had the idea that we would 'adopt' this team as ours. Pat and the BT men were about 10 yards away from us and so, when each answer was made known on the screen, our table, as did others who had entered the correct answer yelled –"YES" and jumped up and down or thumped the tables with joy. We were now very much into the game with adopting this 'Lawmen' name as our own team. They must have been a superb team because, as we progressed through the competition, they were top of the league and the BT team were very close behind them. It became 'neck and neck'.

This couldn't have panned out better, even if the scenario had been written out as the script. The BT team and Pat were getting most of the correct answers but The Lawmen hardly faltered at all. Just about every time an answer was declared, our table would punch the air and yell – 'YES!!'.

It must be remembered that these BT Executives were no slouches. They had all, most likely been graduates but whatever, they were in the highest echelons of the massive BT Corporation. There was me, a Secondary Modern school educated grown adult with a bunch of young fingerprint experts with a mixed assortment of education. Pat's table were not pleased and we all took delight in catching their occasional odd looks or sneers in our direction.

Hell, it passed through my mind that my plan could even ruin the chances of BT signing up with us and although us beating them at this stupid quiz obviously wasn't going to determine that outcome, I must admit to feeling a little sheepish about what was transpiring. But we weren't in a position to 'throw the game' anyway. We were totally in the hands of this team who may have been hundreds of miles away from us. Our adopted team, 'The Lawmen' were adjudged the eventual winners and the BT came second or third.

The fingerprint experts had enjoyed every minute and didn't they let Pat and the BT team know it. In my mind there was no way that I could let our fraudulent activity (albeit good fun) continue but I wasn't going to spoil the night. So, next morning I joined Pat in his office and, of course, he said something like, "How the bloody hell did your team win that quiz last night?" I placated him by telling him that there was no way that we could have done it and I told him of our little rouse. He stared at me and said, "Naah your lot bloody won it OK; we could hear you shouting out every time". I explained it again and still he didn't want to believe it. It took ages for him to catch on and then he had great delight in telling the BT men what we did. Game over; but I'm sure that everyone enjoyed the evening.

The BT business had been successfully completed and contracts were signed up by all of the constituent Consortium member forces on 4th April 1996. The AFR Service had been fully restored to the UK through our centralised HUB sites which operated with their neighbour fingerprint bureaux.

I took Messrs Warburton, O'Shea and Bell back to the Airport for their return flight on 20th December and flew back myself the next day. By mid-June 1996, we had successfully commenced initial negotiations for a full UK AFR service through a deal between ourselves, SMI and their Parent Company Sagem SA of Paris. I hadn't at that time reflected on the enormity of the project I had been involved in. And by the way, what had happened to LMC?

I had been a part of the roll out of the first and second computerised fingerprint matching system in the UK. Something I'm proud about. I was an Assistant Project Manager (Service) and the Consortium's statistician. By now, our team had been further inflated by others. I recall among them, that Peter Walsh, Head of Bureau for Thames Valley had also either joined us or had been seconded to us. The system was working well and things were certainly heading in the right direction.

Chapter 11 – Dealing with 'The Met' and 'Non-Members'.

As time went by and although negotiations with our partners to be, remained on a sound footing, it became increasingly obvious that searching a database without the complete set of tenprints from all English and Welsh forces, would end in a massive 'switch off' for all existing members and withdrawals from the consortium would continue.

For a variety of reasons, I must admit that I began wondering whether, in the eyes of member forces, it would be worth hanging on until 2001 when ostensibly, the Home Office were, through their 'Police Information Technology Organisation' (PITO) going to be launching their brand new database. I hasten to add that these were my private thoughts that I dare not, at that time, have shared with anyone else. But on the other hand, I wondered how on earth they were going to introduce their new system without having the thousands of tenprints which we had already acquired to our databases. I could only foresee two options:- 1. A 'Take Over' of our databases or 2. Purge our files and 'Re-acquire' all of the tenprints again. Surely, NAFIS couldn't just commandeer them, or perhaps they were going to compensate the AFRC for that privilege?

The whole thing became a blur in my mind and I think I must have just rolled along with the flow, doing my best for the Consortium. After all, I was just doing what I was told and who was I to interfere? I did actually care and did all I could to keep the status quo. We had by now, dropped Lockheed Martin and were ploughing our own furrow along with Sagem Morpho Inc.

I was almost fully engaged in the collection of new tenprints for a while and this involved making regular trips to all of the bureaux who were then, not members of the consortium. However, it had not been forgotten that in addition to our regular members, the Metropolitan Police were also 'non-active' members and my attention had been drawn to the fact that they were in possession of what was their own 'Burglar Bundle'. As explained previously, these bundles were tenprints containing the fingerprints of people convicted of particular classes of offences. In this case, the Met's bundle was of their convicted burglars. I was encouraged by Pat to try my luck by visiting Scotland

Yard to see if I could get them acquired to our system. I learned that Commander Malcolm Campbell was the officer in charge of fingerprints and he was based at the Yard. I made contact with him and he agreed to a meeting in London in early January 1996 just to discuss the situation. It was then that I learned that we had a mutual interest in playing golf. Well, who was I not to offer a challenge? It would have been extremely rude not to have done so, it was just a shame that my clubs weren't in the boot of my car. So, it was necessary to fix another meeting in early February but most probably, this would be on a golf course somewhere when we might fix the delivery of what I was after.

In the meantime, March had kicked off with me visiting the posh new Police Headquarters of Avon and Somerset at Portishead, near Bristol. This was one of our non-member forces and I was there to negotiate the acquisition of their tenprints to our database. Thankfully I was successful.

We had by now, secured contracts with SMI and BT and it was at the same time that I had produced a report headed 'Twenty Good Hits'. As can be seen from Pat's email below, he was like a dog with two tails. Apologies for the quality of the reproduction.

```
FROM: Pat PITT, 100332 3671
TO:    Angela GALE, 100070 3345
CC:    Karen D. DORANS, 100066 1026
       Brian HUMPHREYS, 100520 1142
DATE:  27/04/96 19:57

Re:    Brian HUMPHREYS Hit report paper

Angela,

Brian HUMPHREYS hit report paper has been read by me and is excellent. The are problems with the type face which need resolving before it can go to CMG.

Please have this rectified and immediately issued copied to me, the Chair, Vice Chair, Ted MASON, Peter ROBERTSON, Ian MASKREY Steve HOWARTH, Mr GIFFARD plus me, Karen, Ronnie WRIGHT, UK team members and Pascal COLIN (MORPHO) and Jean Claude RICHARD, Pam STEINER, Bill RIPPI all at NAMSI.

This URGENT.

Copy also to Karen for the User Group presentation.

Regards,

Pat
```

I was obviously very pleased and was like a dog with 'three' tails. But as pleased as I was, it was, after all, some simple computer work which sadly, in the end, caused me to suffer through the jealousy of my colleagues – at least, one in particular.

The timing of this report would suggest that it was the upgraded software which I had negotiated for, with Jean-Claude Richard which had probably caused the upsurge in more hits. We would now be benefitting from the upgraded matchers – 'Arizona 3.1 software'.

Returning to the question of the Metropolitan Police's 'Burglar Bundle', Commander Campbell and I fought it out not many weeks later, at his golf club somewhere on his own turf in Greater London. Malcolm suggested that if I were to beat him, he would allow the transference of the records. I didn't believe that he would refuse even if he had won, so I agreed the deal. Nevertheless, I managed to beat him and the acquisition of 25,000 tenprints of all London's burglars were collected at the end of June 1996 for acquiring to our database.

In Tacoma, the development of a new Help Desk based at Newbury was at the planning stage as was the recruitment of permanent staff to move to Tacoma on a permanent basis, was in train. This was when I was to play what Pat might have thought was a mischievous prank on him but what the rest of us thought was a really good one. True or not, it was pretty well believed that Pat and Karen were in some sort of relationship but in fairness, if that was correct then they never flaunted that. Both were married, yet it was thought that there were problems in both camps. It was no issue for us to be concerned with.

Pat sent us a Memo saying that he was looking to recruit a member of staff to be his permanent assistant in Tacoma. Whilst we all knew that this was a job set up for Karen, he asked that if any of us were interested, we should write an application and put it in a sealed envelope and handed to Angela Gale, the office manager.

I couldn't let my devilish instinct miss this golden opportunity and as I was about to give Pat a detailed statistical report, I put it in such an envelope and gave it to Angela knowing that she would assume that I had applied for the job. I was careful to let her know beforehand that "I might well be interested in that job".

Angela later informed me what had occurred when Pat had rung her to ask if there had been any interest in the job. She nonchalantly replied, "Oh, I've just got the two envelopes from Karen and Brian". He apparently almost fell off his chair – "Brian! What's he got to say about it?" She replied, "I don't know, it's in a sealed envelope as you directed". He immediately told her to open the envelope and read it to him but when she did, she realised that it was just my report. Isn't it great when a plan comes to fruition?

Of course, Karen was the only applicant and the rest of us knew that it would have been futile to have applied for the post. Off she went to permanently work in Tacoma. Both eventually got their 'Green Cards' permitting them to reside and work in the USA. They continue to reside there ever since. During our secondments to Tacoma Karen very often generously invited us to a Sunday Roast. Pat was obviously 'At Home' there with Karen and Paige, Karen's young daughter but I believe both had separate dwellings. The electronically sent Christmas cards I receive each year, are always signed off, from 'Pat and Karen'. Good luck to them.

Anyway, we had by now, set up the emergency HUBS and the Central Site in Tacoma was complete and the Network installed and running. Pat was beginning to recruit some old contacts from the days when he was in charge of the Hampshire I.T. Department. One of these, John Sims had joined us as our 'Implementation Manager'. We often worked together and I thought he was a good chap.

September 1996 saw us complete all members' 'Selected Force' searching parameters. The searching of fingerprints could now be extended to other force collections in addition to their own. It meant that each member force could select which forces, other than their own, could be include in their searches. I recall that most forces would include Merseyside because of their travelling criminals who were then plaguing the country committing crime in almost all other counties. (I recall such a job when I dealt with an armed Liverpool gang who raided our Worcester Post Office Sorting Office)

It was also on 17th September 1996 that our chairman, John Hoddinott completed signatures for all our partner companies, so that we could begin to see the end of what was our 'splintered' service. Glasses were no doubt raised but there was a long way to go before we knew how the eventual outcome of our service would end.

Chapter 12 – Second Generation AFIS but PITO's on the prowl

By now, we had just about fully reconstituted an AFIS service to most of the British Police Forces. With NAFIS possibly going to take over in five years' time, it was important, whether or not they did, that we were fully 'up and running' as soon as possible. The organisation behind NAFIS was the Home Office's quango, 'PITO'. Their view was that Police Forces were so parochial that they didn't particularly like sharing information, and as such, the development of IT involved an unhealthy competitive spirit with one force trying to outdo another. Quite frankly, the situation did require some sort of organisation and orchestration and PITO became the organisation charged with doing just that.

PITO had grown into a massive organisation with a total of 7 Directories – 1. Communications Services, 2. Technical Advice and Standards, 3. Local Police Systems 4. Procurement and Contracts, 5. Identification and Verification Services, 6. Corporate Resources and 7. Police National Computer.

These Directories were under the leadership of the Chairman, Sir Trefor Morris. Sir Trefor was a real Police 'heavyweight' in his time. In brief he had been the Chief Constable of Hertfordshire and HM Chief Inspector of Constabulary. It was probably a coincidence that his old force, Hertfordshire was one of the few forces that decided not to join the Consortium.

NAFIS fell under the Identification and Verification Services Directorate and although the 'roll out' of it wasn't to commence until 2001, some pilot schemes would commence earlier in 1997. This stone was most definitely rolling but had gathered quite a lot of moss. I must confess to being a little surprised that we were putting all this effort into our reconstitution. Indeed, a 'handover' document had already been agreed and signed in Sagem's HQ in Paris, by our Chairman, John Hoddinott and representatives of Sagem SA. The Chairman of Sagem, Daniel Dupy was another signatory.

Despite this 'stone' rolling on, there appeared to be an underlying belief held by our leaders that this 'NAFIS' thing would never materialise. There was an unspoken desire that our 'baby' would survive. It was a precious baby and no doubt we were all very proud to be a party to the provision of the very first automated fingerprint identification service in England and Wales.

This was never freely spoken about but I (and no doubt my colleague contractors) certainly knew that the Home Office would take over after 30th June 2001 as it had promised all those years ago, when John Hoddinott was given the 'go ahead' to establish that mini-consortium to fill the gap. The situation now was such that it was as if the consortium was so successful that it grew to believe that it would, at some time in the future, become that 2nd generation replacement that PITO was to introduce.

I had been producing some charts from Microsoft 'Excel' Spreadsheets and Pat loved them. I must admit that they looked very good in colour but, of course, it was the content that we wanted to bring to notice. I was now able to draw comparisons with the reconstituted system and that previously provided by IBM. Our current successes were running streets ahead of the old IBM system.

My daily rate had increased quite a bit to £141.08 per day. What with my pension, these were the days when I had more disposable income than ever before. My work with statistics was just an 'add on' job but I had already quickly learned that if you are self-employed, you don't go sick or grumble about extra work. What I thought would be a nice cushy situation working from home, turned out to be a complete myth because although I was enjoying myself, I doubt if I had ever worked so hard and for so long. Although I have always risen bright and early, Tacoma was eight hours behind us, so the barrage of communications from there, didn't start until about 3pm and went on until bed time and on many occasions, far beyond that.

In August 1996, I see that even with eight days working at The Project Office and with weekends off, I had travelled almost 2,000 miles and that was just scampering around The West Midlands, Cheshire, North Wales, West Mercia, Suffolk and to Slough for the London train, then Northamptonshire, Lincolnshire, Leicestershire, South Wales, Suffolk again, Grantham, Nottinghamshire, Derbyshire and West Midlands again. This involved just four overnight stays. The Vauxhall Carlton was going well and still not depreciating in value as it was still worth nothing, though earning me plenty in mileage expenses.

A Similar pattern emerged in September with my trips involving seven nights' accommodation and my travelling a total of 2,630 miles. Life on the road was crazy but I did learn much about the geography of England and Wales, especially where the traffic bottle-necks were and thus, when not to organise my trips to coincide with busy Fridays etc.

I paint the picture above to describe what was now a well-oiled mechanism which had culminated in a very efficient re-constituted service which could only be maintained by collecting fresh prisoner tenprints from all forces, members or not, so as to keep our database right up to date at all times.

Keeping the database updated had always been a question in most CMG members minds at that time of uncertainty regarding whether or not we should continue to provide a service to those non-member forces. It was recorded in the Emergency CMG meeting that this critical situation would be looked into. Well, in retrospect, it was achieved by my collections of them from forces who were unable to acquire tenprints directly to the database. To supply them with the equipment to do it, would effectively draw them back into membership and that was what they had opted not to do.

I might add that this was not a job that could be taken on by a van driver simply collected these tenprints in a box. It must be remembered that these were now non-member forces. There was a little administration to take place beforehand and they were not going to sort them out for us or even let us take them away until those previously collected were returned into the slots from where they had been vacated. I devised a marking system whereby I could quickly ascertain their previous location so as to make that transference more of a simple task. In addition, a great deal of diplomacy was required because in some cases, there wasn't a great deal of love lost between Ex-AFRC forces and current AFRC staff, and I was one of the latter. In addition, as a service manager, these collections were very often merged into my trips to other of our member bureaux.

There was so much to do and it was my job to ensure that all of my force Chief Officers and their bureau staff alike, were kept abreast of what was going on. This was so important that I drew up a matrix of visits to be made and contacts to see. These not only included the Heads of Bureau but the Consortium

Management Group Members and the Force's Liaison Officer who normally was the Head of Forensic Services. I also drew up a schedule of items to be discussed. I saw this as very much a selling job. They had, in effect, been let down by the trouble we had encountered with IBM and obviously, similar problems with our new SMI system would not be tolerated.

On my Agenda at this time would be the flow of Tenprints to Tacoma and the turnaround times involved. It was also important to monitor the number of records belonging to the Force that were on the database. This had financial implications. Equally important was to ensure that Forces kept on top of the training issues in connection with the taking of prisoner's fingerprints. Many forces were sadly lacking in that expertise and their officers sometimes, received no training at all.

The Telscan project was also another issue to be discussed as these scanners needed to be rolled out to the forces and their personnel required training in their use. I would also collate details of interesting hits especially those that might have involved 'Cross Border' hits whereby a Scene of Crime Mark had hit on a fingerprint record acquired by a different force. The Data Protection Act was also high on the agenda because some fingerprints for juveniles cautioned, for example, were required to be deleted after five years if the donors hadn't come to notice within that period. Forces were reluctant to 'weed' their systems in accordance with these Home Office directives.

At this time, plans that were already on going to develop a special 'Help Desk' for all our UK users had come to fruition. We had one at the Tacoma Central Site but, when all forces were up and running and acquiring their own records to the database, they would want assistance in the UK. The Newbury Help Desk was built and commissioned in six weeks. It went live on 4th November 1996 to virtually coincided with the return of full implementation of service to all our operating sites.

The success of fingerprint searching is obviously reflected in the success of offenders being arrested and crimes being cleared up. The whole system, however, is not only reliant on good fingerprints being taken but that they are actually taken, when the law permits them to be so taken.

For example, it was a common misconception by arresting officers that if their prisoners had already provided their prints on a previous occasion, then there was no reason to take them again. This is not the case for several 'identification' reasons, the main one being that their tenprints would not automatically be searched and the offender may well have committed further crimes since their fingerprints had been first recorded. Re-taking them would ensure that they would be searched against all fresh marks and tenprints acquired since their prints were first recorded. Much of this was also the result of sheer laziness which would reduce the efficiency of the whole process of clearing up crimes by use of fingerprint identifications.

One of my jobs was therefore to conduct tenprint audits in Custody Centres. These were at the behest of Chief Officers of Police. (With my encouragement) For example, in November 1996, I conducted an Audit of every Custody Centre in Bedfordshire where I discovered a shortfall of 3.49%. This equated to an average of 26 per month which when extrapolated means that over a year, 312 prisoners might escape having their fingerprints taken. The concern here was not totally about the effects on crime detection. These shortfalls could well impact on working schedules by the experts examining them and the numbers might also impact on the contractual situation between themselves, the Consortium and SMI.

Similarly, many of my trips to Hampshire were connected with a new 'Livescan' system which might be useful in reducing the number of false identities being experienced. I submitted a feasibility report to Senior Officers in Hampshire and for the benefit of our own team. I visited all six Custody Centres there and examined every charge sheet for the months of June and November, sixty days in total which gave windows for comparison both in summer and winter seasons.

With the aid of the Force's 'Fingerprint Management System', I produced a matrix of when fingerprints were taken. I also discovered that on many occasions, fingerprints had been properly taken but that the Custody Sheets had not been updated with that information. These instances represented around 5% of the total and they caused a slight imbalance to my findings because it left me with no idea what time of the day they had been taken. Sadly, other instances were found where no fingerprints had been taken when they should have been. These represented 10.58% of the total or an annual shortfall of 1,272 prisoners fingerprints.

Take a minute to Imagine if a loved one of yours had been murdered or raped or even the subject of a high value robbery or burglary. It was very likely that the offender would remain undetected if he or she had previously not been fingerprinted when they should have been.

The shortfalls identified, were given wide publication to other Force CMG Members through my publication of a document which was presented at their meeting. They were encouraged to organise similar reviews in their own forces. I also liaised with Colin Pascal from Sagem as putting right the shortfall would seriously affect contracted throughputs.

As things settled down, I was able to start drawing up comparisons between our old IBM system and the new SMI Arizona 3.1 software which we had been using since 15th April 1996. There was no way that a true 'Like for Like' comparison could be made, but looking at the first weeks as they progressed, it gave a good indication. Even with less forces operating our system now, the charts I produced showed quite clearly that more 'Hits' were being obtained with our new system.

Christmas 1996 was almost upon us. I couldn't believe that this was to be my third Christmas in this self-employed capacity. I was thoroughly enjoying myself, was never more 'well off' and although I was spending much time away from home, Jo was enjoying her extra 'spending power'.

Chapter 13 - 'Livescan' and the Quality of Tenprints

The commencement of 1997 brought with it yet another sub-chapter in the history of the electronic scanning and identification of fingerprints. As explained in earlier chapters, numerous arrested and charged prisoners had hitherto escaped prosecution by managing to get away with providing false details of their identity. The process of discovering these false identities took so long, sometimes many months by which time, the prisoners had long since disappeared or had been dealt with for other matters.

The ideal situation would involve a facility which could scan suspects' fingerprints into the system to be checked and verified, before prisoners left the Police Station on bail. It was only a very short time ago, when that situation would have represented a 'pipe dream' that would be hard to believe would ever come to fruition. Now, here it was, and the name of such a machine was called 'Livescan'.

Whilst fingerprint images could be faxed from one place to another, the problem of searching them revolved around the fact that the fax paper used would obviously be flat and would not contain the hills and valleys (ridges) of a fingerprint. The patterns could easily be seen but would be difficult to be searched. That was the problem!

The inventor of an algorithm which could be used on such machines and which could scan the fingerprints to remote, centralised databases, was Randall Fowler (Randy) who was a very clever PhD student who started experimenting with this problem in his garage. He now owned a company called Identix in Sunnyvale, California. This was in the heart of Silicon Valley and I was to meet him there soon. The Internet extract below, provides more than enough detail to describe what a wizard Randy was.

Dr. Randall C. Fowler

Randy Fowler has a unique combination of Wall Street knowledge, technical expertise, and hands-on experience in financing, marketing, and sales. Currently retired from day-to-day business operations, Randy founded Identix, Incorporated, and served as Chairman and CEO until his retirement in 2001. He created and patented the biometric technology (prior to starting the Company in 1982) that enabled Identix to maintain its leadership in creating the Biometric Industry worldwide. He led the Company through its IPO in 1985 (NASDAQ, and later the American Stock exchange) and subsequent financings including a number of acquisitions and mergers.

During his almost 20 years at Identix, he became the first Chairman of the International Biometrics Association. In addition, he also served as Chairman of ANADAC, Fingerscan, Australia, and Syvan/Identix Joint ventures. The company was awarded Fast 50 and Fast 100 Companies in Silicon Valley in 1999, 1997, 1996 and 1995. Dr. Fowler received the Silicon Valley Entrepreneur of the Year award in 1997, the Kjakan Award of New York in 1998, Professional Awards, as well as Distinguished Alumnus award, Univ. of Louisville, where he currently serves on the Board of Advisors for the University. He presently sits, or has sat, on the Board(s) of Directors for several private/public companies, and mentors young entrepreneurs in development of new ventures.

Prior to founding Identix, he held General Manager, Marketing and Sales, and Technical positions at a number of Fortune 500 companies. He taught for several years as Professor of Engineering at San Jose State University. Randy holds patents in electro-optic techniques for biometric equipment, and for Attitude Control & Dynamic Stability for Spacecraft and Rocket hardware. He earned a Doctorate of Engineering from Stanford in 1969, a master of science in Engineering from Arizona State University in 1964, and a Bachelor of Science from University of Louisville in 1962.

With Sir John Woodcock and Sir John Hoddinott being my first heroes, Randy was in the same league and like the Sir Johns I had worked with, he wasn't just a very clever gentleman, I found him to be just a 'nice bloke' and until I found the above information about him, I wasn't aware that he even held a doctorate. I now feel a little humble in as much as I later made a presentation to him about the British Police Custody System and in particular, the way we processed the taking of fingerprints in our Custody Centres.

So now, without my knowledge then, I was to shortly become not only an Assistant Project Manager, Service Manager and Statistics Officer, I was soon to become a Livescan Manager and Livescan Trainer because we were hell bent on installing this equipment at a 'Pilot Site' at Portsmouth Police Station, Hampshire.

It was in 1997 that we started working on this pilot and I set off for Portsmouth on 13th January to assist in the installation of the first Livescan machine that was to scan a set of fingerprints across the Atlantic to our Tacoma database from a custody centre. I'm claiming another record here, because those fingerprints were MINE!

I booked into The Ibis hotel in Portsmouth which conveniently was just across the road from the Police Station. That was the only convenience it was to offer, but I did stay for the duration of my four nights there where I met up with two 'techno wizards' from Randy's Company, 'Identix'. His people were Phil and Judy and after a few trials and tribulations, they managed to successfully scan my prints to our Tacoma database on what I thought, was a historical, 14th January, 1997. Thank God, no hits were recorded.

I returned to Portsmouth for another two-night stint at the end of that month when Livescan went operationally live from that police station on 30th January 1997. During the first nine days, one male prisoner was found to have two other identities and one female hit on another identity. She was wanted by two other Police Forces. In addition to these remarkable successes, we found that our success rate of 'Scenes of Crime' marks being matched to Tenprints acquired on these new machines was far higher and this was paying dividends; no more ink and rollers and smudged prisoner fingerprints. We had turned another page in Police history and even though my part was miniscule, wasn't I proud to have helped to turn that page.

From then on, I was not only busy assisting in the implementation of Livescan equipment in other police stations, but, of course, the police officers using them, would require training and that was what I was additionally engaged in. The technique was pretty simple, in fact it was a lot easier and cleaner than that old 'ink and roller' method and was very much faster to complete. What's more, this meant that the incidence of failing to record prisoners' fingerprints would reduce considerably because it was less hassle.

Any number of tenprint forms could be printed off in no time at all. Unlike that old system, if one digit was smudged, then that image could be deleted and immediately replaced. Although training took some time across the country, it was only really necessary for me to train other trainers and the practice soon cascaded from one to another.

However, until such time as the process became completely paper-less, it was necessary to ensure that the quality of tenprints printed, was up to the standard of the old forms which had probably been produced by HM Stationery Office many years ago. This was a major step in the use of fingerprints in criminal cases. Prisoners could now have their prints checked when first coming into custody and a result as to their identity relayed back before they were processed and bailed.

We were to calculate that the whole process on average, would take nineteen minutes which meant that prisoners would not be released until results were returned. As already mentioned, the checks previously made at Scotland Yard could take months and then the prisoner giving a false name might never be traced.

Whilst with Randy, I discussed all aspects of the fingerprinting procedures in the UK with him. The 'Custody Centre' set up had been introduced not too long after the 'Police and Criminal Evidence Act 1984 commenced around England and Wales, which wasn't that long ago then. I promised that I would do some research for him to ascertain about how many existed and as luck would have it, I was in possession at home, with a 'Police Almanac' which included this information.

By now, our Livescan machines were being rolled out to other stations. Forty plus separate units were eventually installed in twelve different police forces. My trips during February 1997 included visits to Luton, Dorset and Thames Valley. As contractors and virtually free from close supervision, we were monitored by the use of a system called 'Timesheet Professional'. This was a part of Pat's inability to trust us, maybe it displayed his controlling nature. It annoyed me because, so far as I was concerned, little did he know, that in order to complete my work, I was having to give much of my own time., as I suspect others were. It was an unnecessary imposition and actually gobbled up more time to complete than the worth it provided.

Livescan machines were expensive and so in order to gauge whether they would be cost effective, I needed to conduct audits of 'prisoner' throughputs by examining custody centre charge sheets. The stations visited in this 'sample' month were, Portsmouth, Winchester, Fareham, Dorset, Blackpool and Hutton in Lancashire. I was pleased to be shown the below letter concerning my Blackpool audit.

**POLICE HEADQUARTERS
HUTTON, PRESTON. PR4 5SB**

DRS/SKK

16th June 1997

Dear Mr Stevens

FINGERPRINT TRAFFIC ANALYSIS AT BLACKPOOL

I refer to your letter of the 2nd June 1997, regarding the above.

This is a comprehensive analysis and will be very useful to us in our deliberations during the Pilot. I particularly take note of the potential additional prisoners which would now be fingerprinted as a result of the additional Phoenix categories of recordable offences.

Could you please pass on my grateful thanks to Brian Humphreys for his efforts, our custody office staff in Blackpool were particularly complimentary on the quiet and efficient way he conducted the survey.

We are looking forward to the Pilot and I will be reporting back to you in due course.

Yours sincerely,

David Smith

D. F. Stevens Esq., LL.B.,
Deputy Chief Constable,
Vice Chairman - AFR Consortium,
Bedfordshire Police,
Woburn Road,
Kempston,
Bedford. MK43 9AX

My fingerprint 'throughput audits' not only provided a judgement on the value of Livescan installations at police stations, they also identified the degree of the failures to take prisoners' fingerprints but these multi-tasking days were taking its toll. In addition, I was now required to work on producing some Livescan statistics for the management at Tacoma. AND oh, there was an upcoming CMG conference to feed with a multitude of statistics and "Oh, Brian, could you please explore the quality of the paper fingerprint forms (tenprints) to be used in Livescan fingerprinting."

It was necessary to visit our hardware maintenance company, 'Protocol Solutions' at Fareham with my colleague, Ian Maskery. We spent two days there, to be trained on our bureaux machines but primarily on some software called 'Scopus' which we were to use for logging all fault reporting. During that month I spent many nights away from home in overnight accommodation and I had travelled 1,947 miles.

My next jaunt saw me shooting off to Southend-on-Sea, spending two night there at the Westcliff hotel whilst I conducted a Tenprint Analysis which confirmed that they would be ideally suited to have a Livescan machine in their Custody Centre. I called at the Cambridgeshire Headquarters on the way back to collect more Tenprints for acquisition to our database. Life was beginning to be a non-stop visitor to the various fingerprint bureau, primarily to collect 'non-member' tenprints for processing at the Project Office before onward transmission to Tacoma. It must be remembered that during the time these tenprints were travelling to and from Tacoma, they were not available to be searched by the fingerprint experts.

It is useful to remind readers here, that fingerprint identifications were never made solely by the machines that searched the databases. They would only produce candidates for hits and the number of candidates the software returned, could be adjusted by the operators using the system. In serious cases such as 'murders' operators would be inclined to widen the choice parameters so as to return a greater selection. So, it was always the fingerprint experts that verified the hits through their trained eyes in examining these 'candidate' tenprints to check with the scenes of crime marks found. That is why it was important to reduce to the minimum, the time it took to return the fresh tenprints to the force concerned. To prove a point, hints were very often found some way down the list of candidates returned by the machine. They were invariably not the number one candidate as might be expected.

For now, this might be about the right time to jump to early September 1998. My research for Randy Fowler about the quantity of Livescan machines likely to be used in England and Wales was complete and I knew that he would be anxious to discover what sort of business, his company could expect by supplying them all.

I was due to perform another Duty Officer stint at Tacoma but before doing so, I flew direct to San Francisco via Chicago, where, during the next day, 3rd September 1998, I made a 'PowerPoint' presentation to him at his Sunnyvale located company. Although Randy had already been supplying a trickle of them, he was obviously delighted at what I was able to tell him. It was so obvious that the recording of fingerprints by that old fashioned 'Ink and Roller' method was going to be a thing of the past.

This giant step from recording fingerprints by use of ink rolled onto a brass plate to rolling clean fingers onto a clean glass scanner plate, raised implications concerning the quality of the tenprints when they were eventually produced on paper by the printer. The paper used in the previous process would have been supplied in ready printed form on approved paper. Selecting the correct type of paper for the old method must have been explored many years ago but this new 'Livescan' method required a complete re-think. After all, the end result was to be printed out on a printer, just like any other document; but we were unsure as to whether the quality of the paper used in our Livescan printers would make any difference to the experts' examinations, at the point in time when they were actually being looked at by the human eye. The quality also must be such that the fingerprints would not slowly fade away as does other printed material on cheap paper.

We had now moved into a completely different method and once again, I was very much a part of this historical shift. I was given the project to research the best quality of paper to be used for both the electronic and the old ink and roller method because both would be in use until England and Wales were completely covered by Livescan machines. It would probably take at least two years for the complete transition to be made. This meant that I needed to conduct 'Market Research' with fingerprint experts and then find and work with paper specialists to find the best paper to use for both methods.

I had identified a company in Leatherhead, Surrey by the name of PIRA International. They are described on their website as follows:-

Established in 1930, the initials PIRA originally stood for the Printing Industry Research Association. The aim of the organisation was to be "a technical research bureau for the pooling of technical information and to conduct scientific investigation of technical problems" for the printing industry. In 1936, PIRA became a grant-aided research association supported by the equivalent of the Department of Trade and Industry - the DSIR. PIRA was also renamed PATRA - Printing and Allied Trades Research Association. A new packaging division was formed in 1943 following work to look into the problem of service equipment arriving badly damaged in the Middle and Far East combat areas.

In 1967 PATRA merged with BPBIRA (British Paper and Board Industry Research Association) and was renamed PIRA with three main divisions - Paper and Board, Printing and Packaging. The range of business services has expanded over time to cover market research, strategic and technical consulting.

April therefore saw me preparing for this work and I wrote PIRA a long letter from home on 15th. I believe this was the start of that project.

In June 1997, following a couple of days working at The Project Office, I went on a three day trip which took in my first visit to the PIRA paper experts in Leatherhead. I met those who were to conduct our experiments with us. I had already formed a small team of the best fingerprint experts recommended, for it was these who were going to be using the forms and were thus qualified to review the qualities and properties required of them. We discussed how we would conduct the experiments through the use of the various papers. This was a lengthy, on-going project and involved many trips to PIRA and which finally culminated in late 1997 with a choice arrived at through the combined opinions of the industry and fingerprint experts.

Whilst this project was in progress, I continued my visits to the Portsmouth pilot site and the Hampshire Police Headquarters at Winchester which again caused me to 'stop over' for two nights in Hampshire.

It was during this period that some excellent Livescan results were being reported from the sites then using them. The forces without Livescan were now longing – no, begging to have them installed. Their reputation had now spread right across the country. I visited the Merseyside Force to conduct an audit analysis at Sefton and Wavertree Police Stations incurring a two night stop over. That was immediately followed by a similar audit at Guildford, Surrey where another two days at Guildford Police Station with an overnight stop. It was becoming clear that because of the introduction of custody centres which served more than just one police station, that they would all exceed the criteria for Livescan equipment, which indeed, made my life a little easier.

Throughout this period, our pilot site at Portsmouth demanded a lot of time with visitor demonstrations and the training of additional trainers. The beauty of Livescan was that in addition to the custody centres being able to confirm identities before prisoners were bailed from the Police Station, their fingerprints were automatically saved directly into the tenprint database in Tacoma for immediate searching. There would be no need for later 'scanning in' through 'Telscan' or indeed, sending them by air to Tacoma, USA. But for now, a hardcopy was required should further back record conversions be required. The future was looking very bright.

Chapter 14 – Visitors from America

On 5th August 1997, Pat had arranged for Jean-Claude Richard, (JCR) the Chief Executive Officer of SMI in Tacoma who I had met many times before in his impressive offices, to visit the UK and it was my pleasure to host him around the various locations in which he would have had an interest. As I have said before, his very thick French accent made it difficult for me to understand everything he said, so quite frankly, I was more than relieved to wave him goodbye. Little did I know, however, that Jean-Clause was to be my employer some years later.

I took JCR to our operations centre and help desk at Newbury and to one of our busier bureaux at Thames Valley Police Headquarters. We also visited some Livescan locations but I shall always remember the splendid lunch we had, whilst sat outside the Trout Inn on the banks of the River Thames in Oxford. I could have trusted the Head of the Thames Valley Bureau Peter Walsh to have taken us to probably the most picturesque pub in England.

The Trout Inn Oxford

I sensed that JCR was very pleased with what he saw even though at that time, there were only five Livescan machines fully operational in four forces. I was however, assured that he would be taking back the knowledge of how successful they were and that many more were in the pipeline.

My memory that Pat had been in Tacoma is supported by the fact that my diary indicates that on 26th August 1997, three weeks after JCR had landed, I met Pat at the East Midlands Airport and that we had lunch at an M42 Service Station en route to the Project Office. The below Memo indicates that that was the reason for me meeting him there.

Memorandum

To: Brian Humphreys

CC:

From: Superintendent Pat Pitt, AFR Consortium

Date: 08 September 1997

Subject: Statistics

Dear Brian

I would like to express to you my appreciation for the statistics that you prepared for our meeting at East Midlands on 26th August.

I was most impressed with the detail that you put together and the output of our discussion was most useful to the Consortium.

Kind regards

Pat

Superintendent P A PITT
(Operations Manager)

It would have been unusual for us to use that airport and from the looks of the date, it is very possible that I had delivered JCR to it for his flight home and at the same time as I had met Pat from another flight.

In September 1997, I set off 'up north' on a four day trip calling at various bureaux on my way. My objective was to conduct Livescan 'Tenprint' audits at the Northumbrian force's custody centres at South Shields, Seaburn, Southwick and Sunderland Police Stations. This also included a visit to their Ponteland fingerprint bureau. I stayed at the Park Avenue hotel, Seaburn.

A system very similar to our Livescan was now in operation in the USA and in particular, at the Maricopa County Jail in Arizona where it was used in connection with the proving of prisoners identities. So, in that context, Pat asked me to chaperon a lady I was to meet off an American flight at Heathrow on 14th September. She was a Bert Stegan (I assumed Roberta) who was in charge of the fingerprint system employed at the county Jail. I was to learn that this jail had been given somewhat of a reputation in the national media, both at home and in the USA, due to the methods employed by Maricopa's Sherriff, Joe Arpaio. Indeed, I recalled having watched a TV program about it. In addition to normal Sherriff's duties, Joe was also in charge of the prison. It's worth taking a slight de-tour here to describe this very unusual prison and its Sherriff.

The prisoner population in Maricopa County Arizona, was the 4th largest in the world. It was bursting at the seams and as a result, prisoners were routinely being released from custody prior to completing their sentences. Sherriff Arpaio reasoned that if military tents were good enough for the US military, then they would be good enough for his prisoners and at the same time, would save the state $70m which was the estimated cost of building a new, larger facility.

He therefore commanded a 'Tent Jail' constructed through utilising 'inmate' labour. It consisted of Korean War era tents donated by the US armed forces. A 50ft. observation tower was also constructed on the site. Joe directed that a large sign which simply said, 'VACANCY' be mounted high up on it.

The final cost of the project was approximately $100,000 and it is capable of housing over 2,400 inmates.

88

The inmates in this 'tented jail' were 'volunteers' who were required to agree to work an assigned job and comply with the Sheriff's grooming standards. Inmates declining to work or refuse to groom themselves and defecate in communal areas were relocated inside the facility in a more 'hardened' environment, along with the rest of the jail's population.

Bert had been used to operating scanning systems for fingerprint recording and matching and so she had been invited over here to have a look at our Livescan system and to offer any advice. She was married to a supervisor warden at the prison.

One of Sheriff Arpaio's most visible public-relations actions was the introduction of pink underwear, which the Maricopa County Sheriff's website cites as being, 'world-famous'. Arpaio subsequently started to sell customised pink boxers and pyjamas with the Maricopa County Sheriff's logo and 'Go Joe' embossed thereon. His success in gaining press coverage with the pink underwear resulted in his extending the use of the colour. He introduced pink handcuffs, using the event to promote his book, *Sheriff Joe Arpaio, America's Toughest Sheriff*.

Bert was accommodated at The Pear Tree Inn, Smite, near Droitwich and on her first awakening there, she had managed to blow up the hotel's electrical system and her hairdryer at the same time! She had used the wrong voltage. I met her with wet hair and quickly returned home to collect one of my wife's hairdryers for her to borrow. She later discovered that the hotel provided hairdryers and there was one in a drawer in her room??

We visited our Livescan pilot site at Portsmouth and on a later date, we set off on a four day trip around Sunderland, South Shields, Ponteland and Newcastle. We returned to the Project Office on 25th September and I returned her to Heathrow shortly afterwards. Jo wasn't all that enamoured with my new pink pyjamas and they suddenly disappeared!

Chapter 15 – Livescan's Progress

The Central Site at Tacoma was now firmly established as a 24hr, 7day per week, facility. A 'Mark Operations' unit had been established there through staffing by experienced fingerprint experts willing to uproot their families and move to Tacoma. The increasing numbers of Livescan units meant that prisoners arrested in the UK required their prints to be checked against other Tenprints to establish their identity and checked against Scenes of Crime Marks to see if their fingerprints hit on any of them. All this was to be done prior to the prisoner leaving the Police Station and therefore when 'Hits' were achieved, they needed to be verified by the human eyes of these skilled experts.

The Mark Operations Unit, in fact started their work in September 1997 when the number of Livescan Units stood at three. During the ensuing two years, that number had grown to twenty eight with even more to come. The full time staff at Tacoma had increased from an initial two experts to seven by the turn of the millennium.

So far as our database was concerned, the number of Tenprints we held had grown from 2.6 million in April 1996 when we started the 'Emergency Service' operation, to 3.25 million by the end of 1997. It was to continue growing and by December 1999 it had grown to 3.824 million, a 32% increase in just 45 months. Based on an extrapolation exercise, our database was expected to include 4.25 million by the end of our contract in June 2001.

During the same period, our 'Scenes of Crime' marks had grown from 3,771 cases to 171,993 cases to December 1999. I should explain that each case, was often referred to as a 'job', and on most occasions, each job would include many different 'marks'. Our little project had really managed to turn that chapter of fingerprinting history. It is only on reflection now, that I, and indeed all of us concerned in the project, are very proud at what had been achieved.

By 31st December 1998, the five Livescan machines in operation in 1997, had grown to twenty two sites and at 31st December 1999 we reached 45 sites. We were achieving some phenomenal results with over 26% of all Tenprint to

Tenprint 'hits' being of the 'Cross Border' variety. These were hits which Forces would have missed had they not been able to search other forces fingerprints. Results were still being returned to Livescan Custody Centres at an average speed of 19 minutes from when they were initially scanned.

Livescan Sites were eventually taken on by Hampshire, Bedfordshire, Dyfed Powys, Durham, Northumbria, Lancashire, Gwent, South Wales, Merseyside, North Wales, Cumbria, Surrey, West Yorkshire, Greater Manchester, Thames Valley, Essex and West Midlands.

As Hampshire was the Force that pioneered AFIS in the UK, they could be expected to pioneer the Livescan concept. In fact, as we rolled out machines to their Custody Centres, including one at Newport on the Isle of Wight, they were eventually capable of acquiring all of their Tenprints by the Livescan method. They had a machine installed in each of their 10 Custody Centres.

In addition to this massive Livescan 'Roll Out' project, fresh Tenprints continued to be required to be collecting from the 'non-member' Forces and my trips to Huntingdon, Cambridgeshire, Staffordshire and the West Midlands continued. It had been a sad day for all the Custody Office personnel at Steelhouse Lane, Birmingham when later in September 1998, I attended with Engineers to remove their Livescan Machine because their force managers had decided not to continue their membership when we reconstituted the service. The Sergeants, Constables and Custody Office back up staff thought that their senior managers were barmy and they were correct.

I was to shortly take on (had been lumbered with) the secretaryship of our quarterly CMG meetings, the next one being at Worcester and not too far away. In addition to the organisation of it, the final months of 1997 saw me with continued attendance at the non-member bureau to collect tenprints. I also visited numerous Livescan sites and was in regular attendance at PIRA in Leatherhead for yet a further meeting concerning the 'Tenprint Paper Project'. If there was any spare time, and there wasn't, I continually worked, mostly in my own time, on my both Livescan throughput analysis and the other statistical information requested of me.

Compared with IBM, our relationship and successes with our Tacoma partners, SMI bore no comparison. We were far more efficient, providing a better service, which was far quicker even with those 5,000 or so miles which separated our UK fingerprint bureaux from our databases in Tacoma.

1998 started with a desire by Sagem to change the name of their North American wing in Tacoma from NAMSI – (North American Systems Incorporated) to SMI – (Sagem Morpho Incorporated). I suppose the previous name was a little longer and what's more, it didn't include the name of the Parent Company, Sagem. The new name was, in any event, already in common use.

At this juncture, my working life with AFR was almost totally 'Livescan'. So very unwittingly, here I was creating history again because although I had no involvement in creating the machines, or expertise in fingerprint identifications, I became very much a pioneering 'Salesman' in effect, because I was persuading police forces to take on the concept and thereafter managed the implementation of the machines and the training of those who would be using them. I knew only too well that it was working well. Not only were my fingerprints to be the first ever complete set to be sent to the database in America, I was compiling the statistics which showed remarkable improvements in the success rates of every piece of measurable data involved in the fingerprinting business, ranging from their quality to 'Cross Border' hits and most important of all, the success rates in matching prisoners tenprints with fingerprints left at scenes of crimes.

Our success rate had increased, not only due to better quality fingerprints being taken, but they were being recorded on better quality paper. Another factor which also could be attributed to our system's success, was that there would have been less shirking of officers' responsibilities to record their prisoner's fingerprints in the first place. No longer was that messy procedure a problem to them and the tenprints could be printed off in a much faster time.

The first quarter of 1998 saw me working at twelve further custody centres to ensure that they were fully functional. In addition, I spent a great deal of time continuing to collect Tenprints from the Non-Member Forces and administering them for shipment at the Project Office in Droitwich. It was just not the fingerprints that were unique, each tenprint had to be given a unique bar-code label and very often, I would assist the admin staff to do this.

Chapter 16 – Promotion and Jo Pays a Visit

April fool's day 1998 kicked off quite well as far as I was concerned, because my daily AFR rate was increased from £145 to £150.07. Believe me, £5 was a lot in those days. It also ended the first quarter of the year and in those three months, we had successfully implemented thirteen Livescan Systems around England and Wales. Many others were commissioned in and around Hampshire and aside from my 'Duty Officer' duties, I was once again, to fly off to Tacoma for my next stint commencing there on 12th April 1998.

In addition to many other things, Pat had asked me to calculate the amount of compensation we were owed by SMI for the system outages but in addition, I was to be engaged in a great deal of planning for the upcoming CMG meeting. I spent the first few nights at the Sheraton hotel, nicely located a minute or two's walk from our offices at The Finance Centre, Broadway Plaza.

My actual work in Tacoma was to last until 30th April 1998 but I had planned to take some leave whilst there so Jo could join me. However, due to our Cliff Street apartments being occupied, I transferred from the Sheraton to one of the other two slightly upmarket apartments we rented on the other side of Commencement Bay. This was the first time I occupied one of these apartments and on the plus side, due to the distance from the office, I was provided with a hire car at the Consortium's expense.

These apartments were situated right by the side of the North Shore Golf Club. Indeed, the Apartment I occupied; number 515 had a balcony which actually looked down onto one of the fairways of the course. So, there was I, having caught the 'golfing bug' many years ago and without the time, let alone the golf clubs, staring down on a fairway and unable to take advantage of it. Things were tumbling into place for me and at the end of my stint there, instead of being paid for my flight home, I remained there to take a holiday with Jo, who flew out to join me. It was only Jo's return flight to pay for and I managed to get that at a discounted rate through our own booking system. The apartment wasn't required for others and so we stayed there but the car was, of course, then paid for by myself. The plan was that Jo would arrive on

1st May 1998 when I would start a period of holiday and we would both return to the UK together after our ten-day holiday.

Before her arrival, I had much work to do, in addition to my 'Duty Officer' duties. I had no idea what the calculation of SMI's systems 'down time'

The photograph I took from the balcony at Apartment 515, Fairways Apartments, Fairwood Boulevard, North East Tacoma.

entailed and I needed to start planning for the next CMG meeting. I had planned our holiday during the week previous to Jo's arrival and had driven to Snoqualmie Falls which was inland and about an hour's drive. This was such a beautiful place that I had made up my mind to take Jo there as part of our holiday.

I also paid a visit to see some Tacoma Rotary pals I had befriended whilst visiting that Club which met at the Sheraton hotel. Bob and Stacia Cammarano were nice people of Italian ancestors and were engaged in a drink transportation company. This was just a short visit because I wanted to ensure that I knew the way to their house because it had been arranged for me to take Jo there for a meal.

Meanwhile, back at home, Jo had been planning for another holiday, but this time, it would be in very hot Turkey. It was during my stint working at Tacoma on this occasion that my colleague Terry Smith and a Hampshire Constabulary video cameraman by the name of Alan Hilary came out to make a film of the Tacoma part of the operation. A very good DVD was made later and which I used on many occasions to promote what we were doing.

Anyway, 1st May arrived and I was pleased to pick Jo up at Seatac Airport and take her out to my 'Fairways Apartments' on the North side of Commencement Bay.

Jo arrives at Seatac – Your car awaits you Madame.

The use of a driver and stretch limousine to continually collect and deliver us and the many seconded fingerprint experts arriving and leaving, was actually cheaper than hiring taxis on an individual basis. So as can be seen, I used the same service to collect her. (At my expense). I was hoping that this would start her holiday off with a touch of luxury and generally, a good impression, even though I knew she would feel a little self-conscious.

In addition to our apartment being right on the edge of the fairways of North Shore Golf Club, it was also rather quirky inside because the sleeping area was up a flight of stairs to a mezzanine floor with a balcony overlooking the living area. In other words, the huge double bed wasn't in a bedroom, it was just on a raised level. It sounds awful but, as the grandkids used to say, 'it was so cool'.

I knew that Jo would be whacked because being eight hours behind GMT and although she arrived at around 6.00 pm, her body clock would be at about 2.00 am in the morning. So, having unpacked and in the knowledge that we would be in Seattle in the morning shopping for jeans for everyone at home, it wasn't too long before we got to bed. (Good Lord, in those days it was roughly two dollars to the pound)

Our first 'non-shopping' trip was to the Olympic Mountain Range South of Tacoma. It's a beautiful ride and the views are out of this world. I had planned that our main trip would be to Canada. The border, just South of Vancouver was only about 180 Miles north of us up the Interstate five and we hadn't been to Canada before.

So bright and early on Monday 4th May we set off for Canada but first, taking a slight detour for Snoqualmie Falls, fifty miles north east of Tacoma in beautiful mountainous country. We decided to have breakfast there and as we entered the small village of Snoqualmie, we found what looked like the only establishment likely to serve it. I did hesitate a little when I saw the notice by the entrance, 'HELP WANTED'. We ordered exactly the same from the breakfast menu except that my eggs were 'Sunny side up' and Jo's were 'easy over' or vice versa.

The magnificent falls at Snoqualmie

We left Snoqualmie and headed north east towards the I-5 again towards Anacortes. This was about 80 miles further north of Seattle and is where ferries are based for the San Juan Islands. It is because the Ferries are State owned and operated, that the fares were heavily subsidised and travelling around the Islands wasn't an expensive item. I think on this occasion we went as foot passengers but whilst working in Tacoma in the past, I had ventured out to them on different ferries and on occasions I had taken my car. On one such occasion I went over to Allen Island and was stopped driving it because I was unwittingly heading for the residence of the Island's owner, Paul Allen. He was the co-founder of Microsoft with Bill Gates, another San Juan Island resident. The San Juan Islands will always be one of my favourite places. Being alone in Tacoma on the odd occasion I had a day off, wasn't exciting and these were the islands I therefore often visited.

On this occasion, we just sampled a return trip to one of them. Although I have never seen any Orca Whales, if you are lucky, glimpses of them can often be caught but I wasn't ever that lucky. As can be seen on the map below, one of the Islands is named after them.

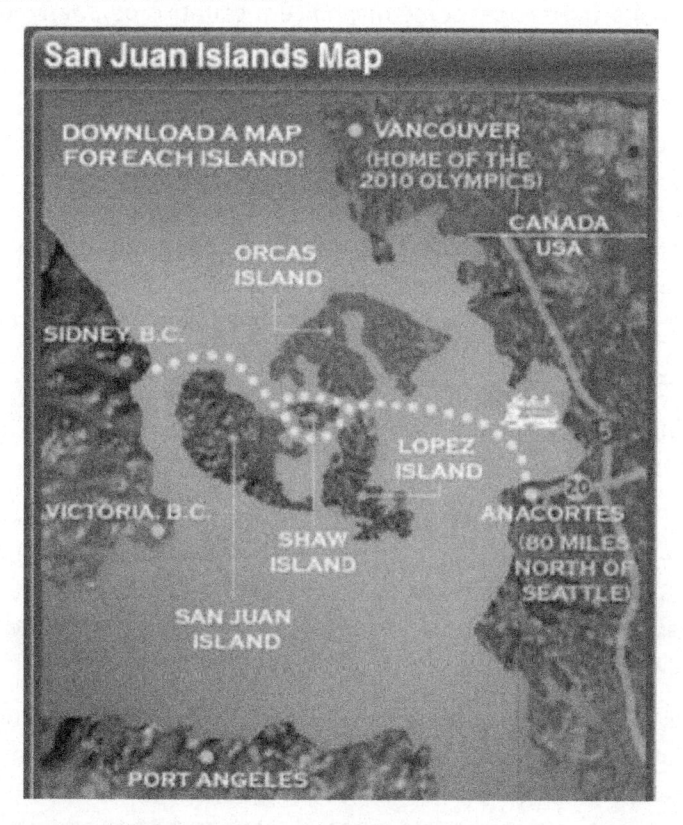

It was whilst we continued our journey towards Vancouver that my stomach began to rumble. It was one of those occasions when you know that you will soon be visiting the loo, or if not, you will be in deep trouble! The memory I have, concerns the time after we had crossed the Canadian border and found ourselves in downtown Vancouver.

I was absolutely exploding inside and was driving around frantically trying to find a place to park. In the end I parked in a 'No Waiting' area leaving Jo in the car to fend off any parking ticket. As I was racing around on foot, I realised that in order to visit the loo, I hadn't any Canadian coins with me, so on seeing a hotel, I dashed into it, pretending I was a guest - just in time.

We continued along the Trans-Canadian Highway; 'Highway 1' as it is called. This is the coast-to-coast route running not too far north of the American border. The route takes in crossing the 'gold rush' area of the Rocky Mountains and transverses some magnificent countryside. Many tourists do this trip by train with the carriages hugging the sides of mountains and often running alongside the road on which we were driving.

On the one hand, this was a magnificent scenic trip but on the other, I knew that I had contracted food poisoning. I was forever looking out for public conveniences. The need for them never seemed to stop and the stomach pain was something else. Quite frankly, I have never had food poisoning before and I felt as though I wanted to die. I will cut this short by just sharing a few memories such as going to bed with a bath towel wrapped around my lower half just in case I coughed. Also being sat in very nice restaurants watching Jo and others eating glorious looking steaks whilst I sat with a tumbler of water. Also visiting many Pharmacies along our route trying to get an even stronger medicine to stop the flow!

We stayed in some very nice motels along the route and especially when we got to Lake Louise. This was that great hotel on the edge of Lake Louise where daughter Sarah and Mason had stayed some time ago. We weren't as affluent as them, so we stayed in the Lake Louise Deer Lodge hotel just a few hundred yards away. It looked very cosy and it was. (And cheaper)

The smell of the food as we entered during the early evening was great, except that I daren't have any. Jo wasn't insured to drive the car and I recall only too well, suffering the drive along the whole of this journey. Prior to this night, we had stayed in two other motels, one was the Sandman hotel at Langley and after reaching Banff where a kind Pharmacist sold me some extra strong medicine which I had a feeling he wasn't supposed to do, without a prescription, we stayed at a place called Kamloops. We were away for four nights in total but there are two further memories which come to mind: -

1.   We had been following a very long line of Heavy Lorries for mile after mile across the Rocky Mountains. We were the lead car of another very long line of cars. Thank goodness we came to an uphill stretch where they had especially widened the road purely to provide a facility for cars to overtake the many slower lorries, such as those we were now following. We were still going uphill so it was necessary for me to accelerate to complete the overtaking and leave room for those following, to do likewise.

As this was happening, I was suddenly aware that at the top of the hill were positioned police officers with a radar gun. They had the cheek to book overtaking cars at exactly the spot where it was necessary to increase speed to overtake. What made me even more furious, was that the officers admitted that they knew everyone would be speeding there and they needed to get a few 'in the book' to keep up their monthly tally!

I happened to subtly drop out something which gave the hint that I had been in that business and he asked me what I would do in England if I stopped a Canadian citizen speeding who was about to return home. (As I told him we were) I responded that I would merely say, "Have a nice day".

He replied, "Well, have a nice day and here's a souvenir". He ripped off the ticket and gave it to me. I was so annoyed that that road had been especially widened to allow overtaking, I vowed there and then, that I wouldn't pay the fine. Those officers would have been disciplined for doing that at home and I didn't pay the fine. After returning home I received a letter from a 'fine' chasing company. I wrote a humorous letter back which didn't work because I eventually received another one. I didn't bother to respond to it which is why I probably shouldn't go back to Canada again as I may still be on their 'WANTED' list!

2.   The other memory of this trip, was when we met the American Immigration Officers at the border on our return to the US. I lowered my window for the officer to speak to us. He said, "And what are we bringing back to America today Sir"? I responded, "Diarrhea and a Speeding Ticket"! Without hesitation he waved his arm in a 'go forth' motion and said, "NO CHARGE" – Off we went!

Although part of my 'Life Story' this final chapter in it, is supposed to be about fingerprints, but I thought that this holiday sojourn would be a nice break from them. However, time now to revert back to work even though Jo and I had visited other very nice touristy areas of the West Coast and had dinner with my Rotary friends, Bob and Stacia. We both returned to England on 10th May 1998.

My work then in Tacoma had involved Pat's request to calculate the periods of time when our SMI system was unavailable due to the occurrence of 'outage' times during the last quarter. I can't recall exactly what brought this on but our contract with SMI provided for penalties and service charge credits for every minute they failed to have the system available or nominated staff in place. The last thing that we wanted was to have the system down but should that occur, our contract provided for the receipt of cash refunds as compensation payments. I add that more often than not, the system needed to be taken down for routine maintenance and this was the most frequent outage.

My research culminated in a report that SMI would be required to pay us $326,746.81 or almost a third of a million dollars. Whilst that seemed a lot of cash just for one quarter, it was a small fraction of the amount they received in payments. This was after all, a service system turning over millions and millions of dollars and the compensation they owed would have represented a drop in the ocean. Pat was so excited that he couldn't wait to get me back in Tacoma to work with a Regina Scarrett, a consultant with the World-renowned Accountants, Arthur Anderson. (To check my figures, no doubt!) However, I'm not sure as to whether that visit was ever made, at least for that purpose.

Because I had been on holiday with Jo and had flown back home with her immediately afterwards, I hadn't been aware that Pat had sent me a memo dated 2nd May 1998. It was very short, and headed – Excellent Work. So, because it was short and documents do not copy well, I'll just repeat what it said in full. Forgive me for showing off but it simply said: -

Brian An excellent piece of work in the USA. Congratulations are in order. You have helped me considerably. Signed Pat.

Thinking back, it would have been soon after this that he asked me to take over the management of the CMG Meetings. Although I hadn't realised this at the time, in retrospect, what with living so close to the Project Office and even though I was one of the latest recruits to the project, I enjoyed working with the computer, far more than my colleagues who were living in Liverpool, Nottingham, Greater Manchester and Hull. Because of those logistics, I might well have been of greater benefit to Pat than the others.

To recount, Pat had been described to me as possessing something of an Ogre image, but it was difficult now, to place him in that bracket when I constantly seemed to have been in his good books. I emphasise again, that I did not like his style of management and many suffered as a result of it, but with that description in mind, one would never imagine him taking time out to write such memos. This was good management and a lesson that I had already been taught by Sir John Woodcock when I worked as his staff officer at HM Inspectorate of Constabulary.

I also emphasise that whilst things possibly could have been achieved more easily by use of a different style, no-one worked harder than Pat to get to grips with all the technical issues that computerisation threw at us. Like me, he had been suddenly taken out of his comfort zone of operational policing, to head up this AFR Project. His achievements could only have been arrived at by 'working his proverbial socks off' and there is no doubt that he threw his whole self into it – maybe also, at the expense of his marriage.

I must have realised then, that as the 'baby' of the team, the others, or some of them, would have been a little jealous of the extra jobs I was being given and, the fee rises that went along with them. Anyway, whilst I knew that Pat's moods could fluctuate at a whim, I would be lying if I said that I wasn't proud of what I had achieved. Doesn't praise, trigger inspiration?

His directions to me now indicated that I would need about three weeks in Tacoma and to book my passage when I would be alone over there with him. Whilst I had looked at this subject of 'service charge credits' before, I would be digging far deeper on this trip. I was to be flown to the USA for about three weeks, being paid quite handsomely, accommodated and fed so the amount owed would need at least to cover all that. In addition, Pat wanted to give me support by employing probably the best Accountants in the World, Arthur Anderson. I wrote to Pat indicating that the job I had already done wasn't that difficult and although having the name of a contact at Arthur Anderson would be advantageous, I wasn't that keen so long as I could access the work sheets that we had previously used. I was now getting a little worried especially, when I received an e-mail from a Lela Davidson of that company. She had been informed by Pat of my impending visit and this is what she wrote: -

Mr. Humphreys

"I am a consultant in the Seattle Office of Arthur Anderson and worked with Gina Starrett to create the database model used to calculate service credits owed to AFR from NAMSI. I understand you will be travelling to Tacoma after the New Year to work with service credits. My schedule is currently quite open and I would be happy to meet with you at your convenience. Additionally, if there is any information I can provide you about the model, let me know. I am also available to make any additions to the model you may find desirable (i.e. additional reports). I have some suggestions for improving the data entry and archiving processes that I would like to discuss with you.

The last time I sent Gina an updated version was May 12 1998. I believe the date of the file is April 30th 1998".

Oh dear! Here was a top consultant from one of the best accountancy firms in the world, talking a foreign language to Brian Humphreys who was now feeling so inadequate and scared I didn't know how to reply. At that time, although I had earlier credited Gina Starrett with the advice, I had been given by her, her advice was largely verbal and my calculations were arrived at just through a simple Excel spreadsheet without using any 'service model' designed to calculate them. I cannot remember now, having met this person but I must have done.

My simple mind told me that in order to calculate the amount owed to us for service outages, all I had to do was to multiply the contracted amount per minute outage payable, with the number of minutes of outage service time. Designing a 'Service Model' to calculate this told me that either there was quite a lot of 'Bullshit' flying around or that we were being deliberately confused so that they could charge their huge consultancy fees.

At that time, we were using some software called 'Scopus'. It was designed to produce tickets detailing the problems suffered for each fault on the system. I suppose they could be called 'Fault Reporting Tickets'. It was obvious, at least to my simple mind, that my first job was to create a catalogue of such tickets and I worked to have all the Scopus tickets printed out for my arrival which was to be sometime in early 1999.

Apart from the Christmas period, the year ended for me by visiting Livescan sites in the West Midlands and Hampshire including the Isle of Wight. At Christmas 1998, we had 22 Livescan machines and two Telscan units up and running. It had been a hectic but successful period to say the least.

Chapter 17 – The CMG Secretaryship

The next Livescan machines were to be installed at Preston and Leeds. Other Livescan visits which occurred prior to our daughter Lisa's wedding were at Luton, Bedford and Basingstoke.

As hinted in the last chapter, my Livescan work had now become routine but still the increase in their installations had not yet come to an end. And so, turning the clock back a little, my work at the AFR Consortium by now, had included taking over the secretaryship of CMG meetings which had previously been handled by the office manager, Angela Gale. I cannot now recall why this change had been made because she lived closer to the office than I did.

This first meeting which I arranged took place at the Worcester County Hall Council Chamber on 21st May 1998, just eleven days following our return from Tacoma. For the period leading up to it, I was mostly engaged at the Project Office preparing the various papers for the delegates. The period afterwards, involved tidying up the issues raised and preparing the minutes.

Being as this was closely followed by our eldest daughter, Lisa's wedding, to say that this was another hectic period would be an understatement. It seems futile now, to describe the setting up of a large meeting to be difficult. I can assure readers that although not particularly difficult, it was on a scale far bigger than any meeting I had been involved in, and far more important.

The mountain of different papers under the red covers previously explained, provides a snapshot but one must consider that Chief Officers from just about every police force in England and Wales would be in attendance and Sir John Hoddinott would chair the meeting. Every agenda item required packs of papers in their own right. It was also the simple things, such as meeting the delegates at Railway stations and some at Birmingham airport on the day preceding and all the domestic arrangements that went with that which in its totalisation, did not make this a simple meeting at all to arrange.

The planning of the meeting was a Project Office affair and included all Project Office staff. They must have been sick to death with the continual use of the photocopier which produced a mountain of paper. In that context, it was nice of Sir John to send us the below note, though now, barely legible. A similar memo was sent by Pat but it is so faint and was to replicate briefly that said by Sir John. For that reason, I have omitted it from here.

> Dear Colleague
>
> At the Annual General Meeting of the Consortium on 21st May 1998, CMG were congratulatory of the performance of the Consortium's System and its team.
>
> I too, as Chairman, would like to record my deep appreciation of the effort and enterprise that goes in to delivering to our Members a first class AFR and Livescan service, 7 days a week, 24 hours a day.
>
> The performance of the Consortium reflects creditably on you all.
>
> Yours sincerely,
>
> *[signature]*

And so, the setting up of new Livescans and all that went with that and the continued collection of tenprints from non-member forces continued up until 27th June 1998 when once again, Jo and I holidayed in Turkey. Thankfully, the secondment of Inspector Geoff Aston from the Hampshire Constabulary had eased my general service commitments in order that I could continue with Livescan work. So far as my 'Assistant Operations Manager (Service) duties were concerned, Geoff was extremely helpful with overseeing the management of the flow of tenprints from forces so that the Emergency Service database could be continually updated.

Meanwhile, our specialist I.T. lawyer, Richard Kemp (Kemp & Co. London) was busy drafting a memorandum of understanding for the provision of Livescan to member forces. Richard was, and remains, a widely recognised IT lawyer and since 1997, was recognised as being among the world's top IT lawyers. In 2014, he set up his firm, Kemp IT Law.

By the end of the 2nd quarter of 1998, we were operating fifteen Livescan machines. I recall spending quite a lot of time over a period of about a week or more at Steelhouse Lane, Birmingham. This, no doubt, was as a result of the West Midlands Police being so large with many trainers to be trained. Their Livescan operators at Steelhouse Lane were very excited at what it could do and in particular, the short turnaround times achieved when receiving the search results. But their excitement was to be short lived.

Further Livescan business was to be conducted in Durham, Dyfed Powys, Surrey, Berkshire, Lancashire, Yorkshire and Hampshire. That was to conclude my Livescan work for July, but the CMG was to convene an 'Extraordinary CMG Meeting' on 25th July 1998. I was in Tacoma and so Geoff Aston and Angela Gale did the arrangements. I learned that its purpose was to update members on the negotiations concerning the LMC proposal and its cost.

The other main issue of the meeting concerned the four forces that had withdrawn from the project and the method and cost implications of retrieving their new prisoners' tenprints. This was going to be my job but that wasn't known at that stage. By that time, the West Midlands excitement was deadened because they were one of the four forces who withdrew from the project. The others were Staffordshire, Cambridge and the City of London forces.

Discussions continued and it was accepted that forces would continue to be charged on a 'percentage of records held' basis. Also, methods of dealing with the fluctuation of the value of the dollar to the pound needed to be discussed. All members were now finally unanimous in their support of the LMC proposal, and Inspector Aston was tasked with preparing a press release.

Not being present at the meeting, I can only surmise that the acceptance of LMCs proposal had not been finalised and that this extraordinary meeting was called merely to update the progress regarding caveated votes. Obviously, something must have happened for that situation to have changed because as history will dictate, we continued with our EAS, HUB system and final full service with Sagem Morpho. However, among many budgetary issues raised, members had agreed that negotiations should now proceed to draw up the contract with LMC. The next meeting would be held on 6th December 1995 but one was called to take place at Hampshire on 18th October. In addition to those budgetary issues, the main issue concerned updates on the litigation process against IBM. Mr. Robertson, the Hampshire member promised to circulate a bulletin concerning the contract and litigation positions to all members for the information of their Police Authorities.

Chapter 18 – The Red Team Review

This 1998 period looking onwards was an important pivotal period in what must be remembered was, after all, a 'temporary solution' to fill that decade of Home-Office procrastination to supply the Police Service in England and Wales, with a digitised fingerprint system. What had been Sir John's baby, was now the baby of the entire team. But whilst we worked as a team, for what turned out to be many years, we ought to have known every wrinkle involved and every twist and turn on a daily basis as to the Home Office's progress to achieve their long-term objective of coming up with the replacement goods. But was no news to be good news? No-body seemed to know.

In retrospect now, we had probably been so successful in what we had achieved, that there was every desire that maybe our AFRC system might well be the system which the Home Office would be introducing. On the other hand, there existed a strong possibility that we might be sunk despite our own success. My experience with the Home Office would make me back the latter.

But as an outsider looking in, to what undoubtedly Sir John had been aware of to a greater extent, though as it appears now, that he may not have been fully aware of what was going on, PITO (Police Information Technology Organisation) was a huge, some might say, 'white elephant' quango of the Home Office and would not be simply barged out of the way. They would have spent millions of pounds in designing what, in their eyes, had to be, a huge improvement on what we had produced. (As good as it was)

Another problem we had suffered, identified again in retrospect, was the fact that our Consortium Management Group consisted of an ever-fluctuating band of Assistant Chief Constables, most of whom would be seeking progression with Deputy and Chief Constable appointments in mind. They had far too much on their individual plates to be over concerned with what was going on with their fingerprint bureau systems. Most were content with letting their heads of 'Forensic and Fingerprint Bureaux' personnel get on with it but on the other hand, some were keenly interested.

In addition, we had four police forces withdraw from the project and this would have caused their ears to have 'pricked up'.

With all that, there was now a secondary issue which concerned those Livescan machines which undoubtedly, their forensic teams, especially their fingerprint bureau and custody centre personnel would have been singing its praises. Livescan could not go unnoticed and at that time, our IT lawyers were drawing up Memorandums of Understandings (MOUs) to continue existing Livescan Operations beyond our exit date of 30th June 2001.

But, playing the devil's advocate, how were their prisoners fingerprints going to be searched on a database which wasn't in control of the Livescan service provider? One can imagine that all of these questions required clear cut answers for at least, their Chief Constables to be in a position to report back to their respective Police Authorities. (Police Authorities were replaced by Police and Crime Commissioners in 2012).

The fact that this would take them beyond the life of AFRC appeared to be of little concern to most forces. They wanted Livescan so much and seemed to be oblivious to the fact that their contracts would be overlapping the consortium's end date of 30th June 2001. Should any resistance be felt, then surely it would have been a fairly simple matter to have replaced all businesses that were then in place, with similar companies. Any form of resistance by them or our consortium, would surely breach the deal set by Sir John and the Home Office that resulted in the signing of the Consortium Management Agreement (CMA) which, so far as I knew, had been set in stone. Unless any future major developments would change that, our exit on 30th June 2001 seemed very final.

One can imagine that CMG meetings were suddenly very important and more questions were being fired from the floor than hitherto. It seemed inconceivable that the successes the system and Livescan were achieving, would end up being 'snuffed out' without any review of the current situation. Much water and AFIS experience had flown under the bridge since those early days and the NAFIS issues were to be discussed at the CMG Meeting scheduled for 11th November 1998. It was for that reason that in early October 1998, I flew to The Marriott Airport hotel, Orlando to meet up with

Karen Dorans to organise what was to be called, 'The Red Team Review' in preparation for that 11th November CMG meeting.

This meeting was to be very much a 'softener' to ensure that all CMG members were going to be 'on side'. Delegates were stopping at the Raven hotel, Droitwich and so Pat asked me to stop there on the night prior to the meeting so that I could tell everyone what a good job was being done. This meeting was a critical one and part of our strategy was to invite representatives of all our suppliers to speak to the meeting and tell the CMG members what a good job they were doing. It was a real 'back patting' session.

Jean Claude Richard our French CEO at SMI came up with a bright idea of presenting gold, silver and bronze discs (DODs) to representatives of the various forces that had achieved certain numbers of 'HITS' on their systems. Although not many people could wade through his thick French accent, this pictorial gesture told the story. SMI would have benefitted if forces took up the 'New Deal' Livescan contracts and continued to maintain our databases.

In order to plug our case well and truly home, I remember collecting all of the acetates used by the presenters so that I could copy them and distribute them by post to all CMG members. (Just in case they didn't 'get the messages' on the day.) It was also at that meeting when a decision was made to describe all the issues, including our successes and fears which would be fully described in a review document for the perusal of CMG members. This would obviously help to make up their minds as to whether we were to jump or be pushed or even welcomed to stay put. It was in effect, a proposal to CMG members that we continue with our Livescan contracts including those extending beyond 30th June 2001.

The project had grown to such an extent that it would have been utter nonsense for it to be scrapped for the sake of a new generation taking its place. The worst that could happen was that at least NAFIS could somehow 'take over' the system and staff that was now in place. Pat in particular, had striven so hard, as indeed, had all of us. I obviously believed in that concept and that we should continue with what we were doing, but It was obviously necessary to carry our CMG members and their police authorities with us.

They were the people paying the bills and they had to be encouraged, but also, the Home Office too, would need convincing that that, would be the way forward.

I was naturally pleased to receive a memorandum from Pat dated 12th November 1998. Due to its poor reproduction, it read –

"Dear Brian, I would like to thank you for all your efforts to ensure the smooth running of yesterday's CMG Meeting. I am aware of the amount of time and effort that goes into organising such an event."

Pat and I had attended an all-day meeting with our Lawyers, Kemp and Co. in the city where we slogged out a skeleton strategy regarding our position with NAFIS. It was an exhausting affair and I was pleased to walk up the road after the meeting and dive down into a City Bar called 'Davy's City Pipe'. This place was heaving with young 'Hooray Henrys' and I wondered why the full room of occupants hadn't dashed off home as it was the start of their weekend off. I soon realised that it was absolutely useless trying to get out of London at that time of the evening, especially on a Friday.

The entrance to Davy's Wine Bar in Fosters Lane, Cheapside, London

Our huge CMG 'push' was to take place at the following CMG meeting which was especially called for as an 'Emergency CMG meeting' which would be held on 1st April 1999. (We were hoping that April fool's date wasn't going to

110

be appropriate). The sensible conclusion resulted from a promise that a review into the whole affair would be published for the information of all CMG members, their Chief Constables and their Police Authorities. My vision was perhaps a 20-30page document explaining all the why's and why not's. I emphasise that that was my vision but of course, we ended up in Orlando, Florida on two, ten-day visits in October and the following February. This was to include personnel from both Droitwich and Tacoma, putting together a huge two-volume document each of about three inches thick and obviously costing many thousands of pounds. We had already made our first ten-day meeting in October and the final meeting took place between 18th and 28th February 1999.

The two meetings must have cost thousands to ship the documents that we required. I recall that we took over two huge conference rooms in the Marriot Airport hotel where we were to be based and that when the document coffins arrived, they covered a huge area of floor space in one of them. Their contents were numbered and each described by me, with a label.

We had already submitted various 'Red Team' documents to our briefing barristers. Indeed, in mid-February, 1999, Pat and I had travelled by train to see Mr John Swift QC at Greys Inn, London. Together with others, he was briefed on what we had achieved with the NAFIS 'Red Team Review' situation. We afterwards visited our solicitors; Kemp & Co and no doubt visited the nearby Davy's basement wine bar afterwards.

With no prior knowledge of what was to come, I received a memo from Pat dated 11th February 1999 informing me: -

"Please refer to my Staffing memorandum that has just been issued. I would be grateful if you could please ignore the 60% Staffer Duties / 40% Livescan split in relation to your role." I am planning that you move to full time "Staffer" duties and will negotiate the rate with you. Your main responsibilities will be NAFIS counter attack and system upgrade." Many thanks - Pat Pitt.

The 'Staffer' role (Staff Officer) was to be for Sir John, his Vice Chairman, David Stevens and presumably, Pat himself. He was very much aware that I had been a Staff Officer for Sir John Woodcock, HM Inspector of Constabulary. (Later HM Chief Inspector of Constabulary) I was obviously pleased that the powers that be, appreciated what I was doing.

For the sake of continuity, our second visit to Orlando was in effect, to review the review and it took ten days for the large assembled team to put it to bed, or at least in another draft format. Whilst I would certainly support what we were doing in producing a review, I personally thought that we had overkilled what was required and had turned it into a huge waste of money. That was a view which many of the CMG members I spoke to believed, although I did not promulgate that view.

In addition to this review, Dean Stelfox, a Solicitor with Kemp and Co., our City Lawyers, was busy writing our 'Exit and Continuation Strategy'. The two documents combined would be our double barrelled weapon in what I was eventually to believe, was a futile attempt to survive the giant wheels of the Home Office and their plans to bury us on 30th June 2001.

From the time I had returned from Orlando, I worked flat out to get the 'Review Report' delivered. By now we had rented the next door premises at Droitwich so we had doubled our area. Those added premises were intended to be used as a 'Training School' though it wasn't used very often. So, the Project Office staff and I were able to utilise the upper floor of our new unit, to operate something of a conveyor belt system in putting it all together.

As the CMG secretary, I was to spend more time than usual, at the Project Office, planning these meetings. The Review documents had been dispatched to all member Chief Officers and CMG members in sufficient time for them to read it but my guess was that not many would have digested it due to its sheer length and their lack of knowledge of what was happening. It most probably had the effect of drowning them in paper!

Despite some inner thoughts as already described, I nevertheless put everything I could into trying to achieve AFR goals. At least, the memo was a pleasant surprise. I can honestly say that during this period, I, like all other contractors were performing roles as team members and just rolling up our sleeves and getting on with it. I had acted in complete oblivion to the earlier memo which placed me in the 'Staff Officer' role. We were all working in any way considered best to get the job done.

I was extremely pleased that Sir John had taken time out to write me a personal memo which I wasn't going to share with my fellow Colleagues: -

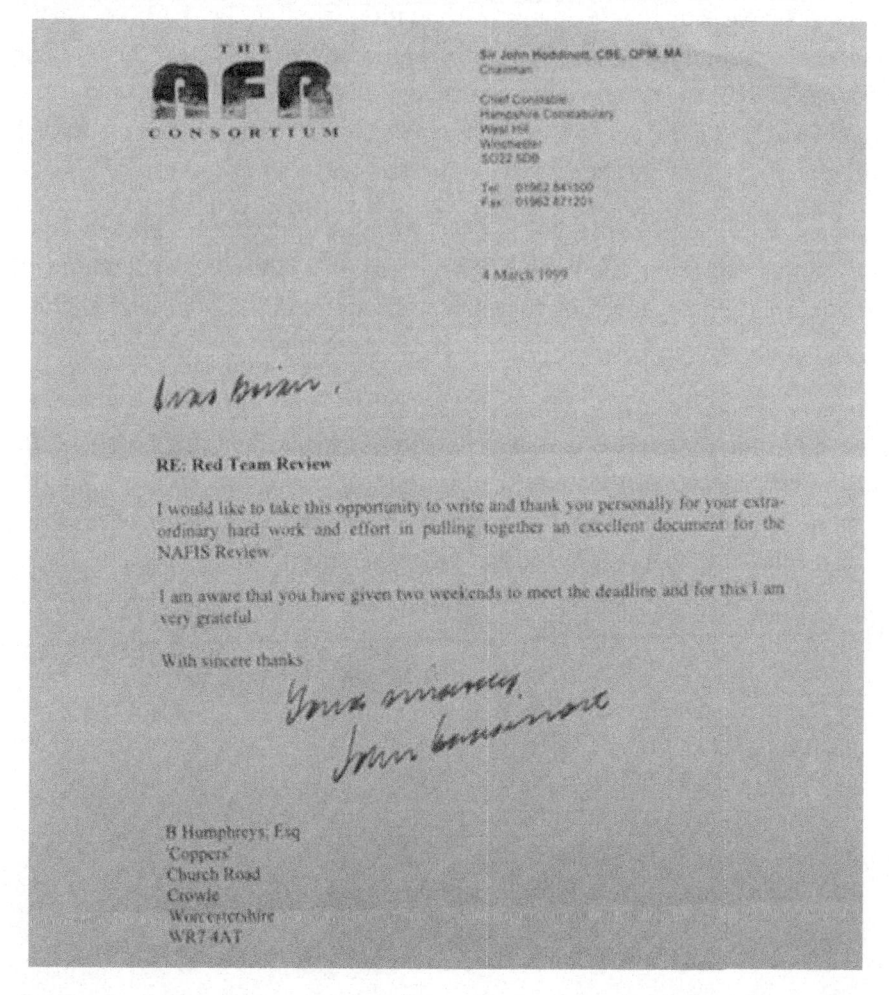

> **THE AFR CONSORTIUM**
>
> Sir John Hoddinott, CBE, QPM, MA
> Chairman
>
> Chief Constable
> Hampshire Constabulary
> West Hill
> Winchester
> SO22 5DB
>
> Tel: 01962 841500
> Fax: 01962 871201
>
> 4 March 1999
>
> Dear Brian,
>
> **RE: Red Team Review**
>
> I would like to take this opportunity to write and thank you personally for your extraordinary hard work and effort in pulling together an excellent document for the NAFIS Review.
>
> I am aware that you have given two weekends to meet the deadline and for this I am very grateful.
>
> With sincere thanks
>
> Yours sincerely,
> John Hoddinott
>
> B Humphreys, Esq
> 'Coppers'
> Church Road
> Crowle
> Worcestershire
> WR7 4AT

Life went on in the Livescan world as normal until the end of 1998 however, some relaxation was had on Saturday 28th November when a dear friend of mine, now departed visited Twickenham but only to see England beaten by the old Australian enemy. Gerry Pearse was the regional director of Lloyds Bank and it was his (and my) bank who sponsored the England team at that

113

time. We had the best seats and were hosted to lunch and afternoon teas afterwards in the 'Red Rose Room'.

The whole object as stated above, was confirmed quite openly by now and indeed to repeat, Dean Stelfox from Richard Kemp's company, had completed some good work on that 'Exit and Continuation Strategy'. By this time, we had already convened a meeting at Identix regarding the 'New Deal for Livescan' strategy with Mike Pearson and Dan Dellagardo of Identix. Present were Kemp & Co, Pat, BT, JCR of Sagem Morpho Inc. and Steve Heagren of Protocol. Della Quimby of the accountants, Arthur Anderson was also present.

As a result, Sir John wrote to all CMG members and their Clerks to Police Authorities explaining the new deal arrangements which we had made with Identix. This had already been fully explained at the 11th November 1998 CMG meeting, but it didn't hurt to press the message home.

We were obviously now, full steam ahead with trying to maintain our services post 30th June 2001. This would stifle the questions being asked about the reason why forces were being asked to sign MOUs for the various 2,3,4 or 5 year extended terms, which in some cases, would take them beyond the Consortium Management Agreement (CMA) period.

Chapter 19 – Interpol Calling?

I have no recollection of how our involvement with Interpol commenced. But the first I had heard of it was when Pat discussed it with me because it was as a result of our conversation, that I then started to visit the library at our Police Staff College at Bramshill, Hampshire, to commence researching all aspects of West Indian Policing and its police forces.

Apparently, Interpol were anxious to network the many Caribbean Islands' fingerprint operations in similar fashion to how that was achieved with our 37 police forces in England and Wales. I was to learn that nothing much differed in the way that could be achieved but one of the major downsides concerned the imbalance as to equipment and the skills possessed by these islands in comparison with that found in England and Wales. The equipment could be supplied but the skills were a different matter. From the little I learned, I believe that Interpol had made the first move in their courtship of us and we would not be slow in showing off our successes. On reflection, it was no wonder that they 'came a calling'.

It was during this long courtship, that Pat asked me to visit Jean-Claude Richard, SMI's CEO to negotiate a £1m extension and upgrade of our databases and matchers. From my point of view, there had been an air of mystery surrounding this directive because although Pat was a workaholic living and breathing nothing but the task, I believed that he found it difficult to be personable in a business type fashion. I may have assumed, rightly or wrongly that he didn't enjoy face to face negotiations but would rather 'send an e-mail'. I say this because he was already at Tacoma and he could have so easily conducted this important deal with Jean-Claude himself, yet he preferred to use resources to fly me all the way to Tacoma to complete it. Surely this was beyond 'Staff Officer' duties?

I recall this event well because on one of my earlier flights I purchased a mini hand-held computer not much bigger than a mobile phone. It was during my flight to Chicago on 7th April, that I actually completed a spread sheet of all the costs involved and what was, in effect, to be my pitch. I had purposely set out to do this in order to pass the many hours which these flights involved. It seemed more productive than the crosswords I used to do. The result of completing this just before we landed, was the successful negotiation with

JCR much earlier than expected. Our two hour negotiations resulted in securing what I thought was a good deal and I knew Pat would be happy because we had landed the deal way within the parameters, which he thought were reasonable.

My return was scheduled which provided me with some extra time but it cost me as I visited Seattle and, on an impulse, foolishly bought Jo quite an expensive dress from Bon Marche. Believe me, spending £209 on an item of ladies clothing was not only foolish in my mind but I had never ever bought a dress for Jo before without her being present. I can remember that because I didn't know her size, the Russian sales lady at Bonne Marche offered me the telephone to call Jo. I did and in addition to her agreeing the purchase just from my description, she appeared to be excited about it. I bought it and I cannot ever remember seeing her wearing it! That says a lot for my fashion sense!

Returning now to Pat's rationale in sending me into the front line of the negotiations with JCR, I was later to comprehend what might have been a clue to this. I had been making numerous telephone calls, trying to fix business meetings with Caribbean Commissioners of Police and their government ministers. I suppose I developed the 'gift of the gab' when persuading secretaries that I really must speak to their top person. My strategy was at the appropriate times, to 'make verbal love' to those more often than not, ladies who represented the barrier of my access to their bosses.

I had been working in a room next to Pat's office and we could easily listen to each other's telephone conversations. On one occasion, he came into me and said, "I've been listening to you bullshitting Humphreys, how about I give you a contract to make appointments for me?" I started to laugh but soon realised that he was actually serious. I passed it off by saying something around the fact that he needn't bother to do that. On reflection, however, rightly or wrongly, he saw value in me as his staff officer and whenever there was a letter or a report or proposal to write, it generally fell to me with him saying something like, "Humph, write it up and use your old HMI Staffer speak." He had obviously placed me on a pedestal due to that HMI Staff Officer job experience. (If only he knew)! It did, however, make me realise that overall, I had probably had an easier ride with Pat than perhaps, others on the project, I also felt that that might eventually come back to bite me.

So, Pat had been in negotiations with a certain Peter Nevitt of Interpol who had completed his 30 years' service as a Metropolitan Police Officer and who had entered into employment with 'Oracle' as a frustrated ex-copper. His frustrations concerned the duplication of criminal intelligence being stored in various world-wide pods, and the resultant errors ensuing, often as a direct result of that duplication. To cut a long story short, by the turn of the Millennium, he had become Interpol's Director of Information Systems.

It was considered between them, that some sort of alliance between our two organisations might have the effect of reducing the costs involved in our exit from the CMA by approximately 80%. As I've already suggested, the Caribbean Islands were an excellent portrayal of a Hotch-Potch conglomeration of varying degrees of skills in many different areas and 'Policing' with all that word implies, was just one example. Communications, intelligence gathering and specifically, all aspects of fingerprint searching, the categorisation and storage of fingerprints and most importantly, the identification of them, was sadly lacking to various degrees from Island to Island.

Having discussed the origins of what transpired many times with curious friends and associates, I have found it simpler to explain that Interpol had learned what had been achieved by our team and suggested that the networking of our many different forces, and the searching of fingerprints across the Atlantic, would represent little or no difference with the many Caribbean countries in the West Indies. Though a very simplified explanation, it was indeed, very true but my later research had indicated that it wasn't going to be quite as simple as that. In terms of fingerprint skills and systems, the difference between the best and the worst, and indeed, those in between, were far wider than would have been expected or even hoped for.

The Bahamian Islands, for example, were to the fore and the Bahama police force with the Bermuda force, were the only ones to possess their own 'stand-alone' systems. Together with the Cayman Islands, they were tax havens and financial hubs of the world. They were also very westernised with the Bahamian Islands close to Miami and both closest to the US Eastern coast. As a consequence, allegiances had been struck with US Government agencies and funds acquired to stop the drug trafficking operations in the US who, because of that, were only too willing to assist in the funding and training of their officers to stem the drugs flow.

On the other end of the scale, some of the police services in very small Islands were hardly in possession of any fingerprint skills and on one Island, I found that fingerprints discovered were looked at by human eyes to see if any patterns were similar to those recorded on tenprint forms which had not even been classified into their various classifications. It must be remembered that some of these Islands were still emerging from an almost 'Third World' status. Their 'Gross Domestic Product' could always be found languishing near the bottom of the table and in almost all Islands, a heavy reliance was dependant on its agriculture. I wasn't expecting much different to be honest, and the occasional open sewage drains along the sides of what might be described as pavements was often a stark reminder as to where I was.

In addition, some of the Islands were governed by French and Dutch motherlands and this made the working in unison between all islands a very difficult prospect. Also, there were hardly any signs of associations between the Islands and the patriotism of them as individual communities was probably the reason why. There were only two main ones but one of them, CARICOM (Caribbean Community) mainly concerned the promotion of integration and equitability and an overall improvement of standards of living and work in their islands. It was formed in 1973 by the fifteen member states of Antigua and Barbuda, Bahamas, Barbados, Belize, Dominica, Haiti, Jamaica, Grenada, Guyana, Montserrat, St. Lucia, Suriname, St. Kitts and Nevis, St. Vincent and the Grenadines, and Trinidad and Tobago.

I did make reference to their various aims and objectives, but apart from being of general interest, I found very little concerning specific references to the policing of their Islands.

So, my main port of call was the 'Association of Caribbean Commissioners of Police (ACCP). The purpose of this association is exactly what it says in its title, yet although their conferences were regularly held and there were signs of improving unified commitments, patriotism was to stifle the amount of co-operation that was possible. The Association had probably been based on our own ACPO; indeed, I was to find an ex-Metropolitan Police Officer in charge of their administrative headquarters in Barbados. Both associations comprising commissioners in the Caribbean and chief constables in England and Wales. They would meet on set occasions but in both cases, whether they would share 'best practice' is another issue.

Maybe this was an example of the origins of the frustrations harboured by Peter Nevitt as mentioned above. My initial research was going to be office based and was going to take some time. Goodness knows what I would have done if it were not for the Internet.

For the time being, however, there was other domestic work to be attended to. We had purchased some extra land adjacent to our garden at Crowle and my battles with the planning department were to absorb much of my time. However, despite my so called 'staffer duties' visits to Livescan sites continued.

Our 'Mark Operations' at Tacoma had now been active for almost two years providing a 24/7 service for Livescan. We now had twenty eight machines in operation and had moved from an initial average of forty eight tenprint to mark searches per day to a then, average of 300 per day. These were being led by a manager and six British fingerprint expert staff who were now in permanent residence in the US. This Livescan work had already produced 2,300 hits. What an impact that would have made in not only crime detection, but the prevention of prisoners getting away with giving false identities and hence, their criminal activities.

However, the atmosphere within the AFR circles was now beginning to become tense. Our member forces had something of a dilemma on their hands. They knew that for all intents and purposes, the service they were receiving from us was to cease on 30th June 2001. PITO, the Home Office's quango would take over with whoever they would contract to be their service provider. We were doing all we could to identify the problems they would have, and so, the battle against their 'NAFIS' was well under way. We were providing an excellent Livescan service in 'Custody Centres' and thanks to the 'Exit and Continuation' strategy, we were in a position to be able to continue to do so after 30th June 2001.

Within this period, two forces, Surrey and the West Midlands, declared that they would not be continuing with our AFR Livescan Service. I would not be sharing my thoughts but I too, had become concerned about how we were going to be able to continually feed the tenprint database if we were not in control of it. However, the huge problem that NAFIS faced, concerned the fact that they would not be providing a 24 hour service. What? That was the main benefit of Livescan and hundreds of prisoners would once again be using false identities and getting away with it. A 24/7 operation was critical and probably the best of all its advantages. This stupid decision was to drive me into producing a paper – 'LIFE POST NAFIS'. I gave this wide circulation to all forces as it highlighted all of the perceived problems with what was planned by our successors.

I spent my time then, racing around the two forces in question, Surrey and West Midlands. Their 'Custody Staff' were outraged at their forces decisions because they, not their bosses were well versed with all the success which Livescan had brought. We formed another 'Red Team Review' at the Raven hotel in Droitwich where we put together costing plans for them and other forces as a proposal for the possible continuation of our service to them.

The West Midland's Livescan machine was decommissioned under my supervision at Steelhouse Lane Police Station in early July 1999 when numerous staff approached me asking what on earth had their bosses done? I had been assured by them that the decision to abandon Livescan was made by their leaders with little or no reference to the user staff. Maybe someone had just been looking at the cost; if so, that was such a short sighted view. Until then, we had 33 Livescan machines in operation.

The situation was to become dire and at about that time, an 'Exit and Continuation' strategy meeting was held in San Diego, USA which, although my attendance is recorded, unfortunately, I could not attend. However, all of the important players, including our service providers, were in attendance. They were from our solicitors, Kemp & Co., Protocol Solutions, British Telecom, SMI, and Telindus. Meanwhile, on 8th July 1999, Pat paid a visit to Lyon, to meet up again with Peter Nevitt to continue mulling over the Interpol 'Proof of Concept' which by now was gathering a certain amount of momentum. In addition, because I was to become more involved with this, towards the end of July, I thankfully handed over the secretaryship of our CMG meetings to Sally James. She had been one of the additional staff taken on at the Project Office. Sadly, the Guildford machine was decommissioned on 11th August and I was also there to supervise that sad occasion.

Unbeknown to us at that time, 1999 was also to be something of a 'Landmark' year within the Consortium's 'Management Team'. As is indicated in his below memorandum to us, Sir John was to retire from his beloved Hampshire

Constabulary. David Stevens, Chief Constable of Essex and Vice Chairman was to take the chair.

It was earlier in that year that I received quite a substantial fee rise to £163 per day to perform staffing duties for Sir John and Pat. This was mentioned in the memorandum I had received concerning my changed role.

10th September 1999

Dear Colleague,

On the 1st September I handed over Chairmanship of the Consortium to David Stevens, Chief Constable of Essex. I therefore now have no formal position within the Consortium although, as you might guess, I shall continue to watch your fortunes in great detail.

I should like to take this opportunity of thanking all of the Consortium staff in the United States and in England and Wales who have made such a huge contribution to ensure not just that the concept of computerised fingerprint matching works but, more particularly, by their individual and joint efforts they made sure that a lot of criminals have been locked up when they otherwise would be roaming freely to commit more crime. I am confident that all your work has helped in the general reduction of crime figures.

I know for certain the Consortium would not have been as successful unless everybody working for it had put in such enormous effort and personal commitment, especially when the going got tough. There have been difficulties, sometimes even crises, but I have always been able to act in the sound knowledge that none of you would ever be found wanting in commitment, effort and ideas. There is not long left now for the Consortium to operate and another system will take over. You know I think it is a great shame that the British police service will not have available to it the best possible AFR solution. But as that time approaches, you may be confident that you have done your bit and a lot more besides. For that I, my colleagues, and lots of working coppers around the country need to be very grateful to you for all that you have done.

With best wishes for the future.

Yours sincerely,
John Bonsurgeon

To All Consortium employees

Sir John's retirement represented a bombshell to me personally but alas, it wasn't going to be the end of his involvement with us.

Chapter 20 – Onwards and Upwards towards Interpol

I was still running around the country encouraging forces to keep going with Livescan and indeed, despite our losses, our Livescan number increased to forty five by the end of the year. Peter Nevitt had visited Tacoma and Identix and sent an e-mail to Pat about how much he was impressed. By the end of the third quarter of 1999, thirty four Livescan machines were in operation.

Despite my status now as 'Staff Officer', I had never fully removed my 'service manager' hat, plus the fact that in most cases, it would be futile of me visiting a force's custody centre where Livescans were located, without visiting the bureaux which in every case, were not in the same locations. In any event, as was mentioned in the memorandum describing my 'Staff Officer' duties, I regarded my efforts in Livescan responsibilities as being in 'counter attacking NAFIS'. It was also more cost efficient for me to combine the collection of the new tenprint forms from the non-member forces during these travels.

By the end of October 1999, Pat and Peter Nevitt were regularly communicating with each another in particular, Peter Nevitt indicated that Interpol's member countries had been commenting on how the AFR concept was being welcomed with enthusiasm. The cream on the cake was the fact that Interpol's General Assembly had agreed to donate £10,000 per Caribbean site and that the Cayman Isles force had agreed to host such a pilot project. At that time, I had produced my 'LIFE POST NAFIS' document and that, combined with this Interpol news, would represent further strings to our bow by giving an added emphasis to the importance of our project. We just need one foot in the door and the Royal Caman Islands Police Service was going to be that 'foot'.

By mid-November 1999 MOUs concerning the proposed extended Livescan service were signed up by all our suppliers and SMI had produced their proposal to fully participate with them. All this excitement had been incorporated into a seminar held in London on 23rd February, 2000 to promote in particular, the extended Livescan Service.

The fact that we had somehow stretched our tentacles into an International service was emphasised later in November, 1999, when I accompanied four senior Mexican police officers to Livescan sites in Hampshire. This was the time also, when we were to learn that PITO had struck a deal with TRW, an American fingerprint system company which had also been making advances to Interpol. However, at a strategy meeting convened on 21st December, they assured us that their intentions were to stick with us post June 2001. However, this prompted Pat and Richard Kemp to confer with Interpol's lawyers (Sandrine Capsales) to design a 'confidentiality agreement' between Interpol and AFRC so as to stop leaks to PITO. The good news was that such progressive steps were not in any way, a hindrance on our UK operation. To the contrary, the new Millennium had turned and we were now operating with forty-five Livescan machines.

It was only when, seven days into the new Millennium that Pat sent me a memo asking me to prepare some management information on 'performance' for the Interpol Proposal. Sir John Hoddinott was to sign the actual proposal but he wanted to include some impressive data in it. I knew that Pat wanted me to go 'overboard' in producing something special because he actually wanted me to produce it under my company's name, (Brian Humphreys Operations) so that my time did not impinge on Consortium contracted days. This meant that my AFR contract was extended and my invoice was paid by AFR Associates Ltd.

So that was the green light for me to produce what turned out to be a separate appendix titled 'The AFR Consortium – A statistical Insight'. This was a forty six page A4 document filled with not only statistics shown in various explanatory graphs and charts but which were accompanied by stories describing the various steps involved in the progression of the AFRC story. I'm proud to say that the management of our AFRC were delighted with it. I was amazed to see the complete document as 'Appendix A' to the Interpol Proposal.

In addition, the accountants, Arthur Anderson were commissioned to produce a financial evaluation of the Consortium and this also turned out to be another large document produced by a Bruce Budge of that firm. So, between Bruce and myself, we had produced a double barrelled salvo of documents which were bound to impress those at Interpol who were contemplating a marriage with us. Whereas Arthur Anderson's invoice was probably in the thousands of pounds, mine amounted to just £383.05.

As might be expected, this important stage in our history, was thought to be going to be an integral step to be taken towards any decision concerning our future. So much so, that an 'Interpol Project Proposal' writing team was convened at our Droitwich base in the same training room as was used in writing the 'Red Team Review'. SMI flew over their Phil Thompson who was almost immediately replaced by Greg Tillett in double quick time. We had worked with Greg before and he, unlike his predecessor, was a terrific help.

On 31st January 2000 I collected three Interpol representatives from Birmingham airport and only four days later, the very first Interpol 'Proof of Concept' project commenced in the Cayman Islands following the loading of their fingerprint data on our system. I was not involved in that at all other than during that pilot project, I was engaged in researching the policing arrangements of most other Caribbean countries. It was at about that time that we learned that PITO were snooping around our organisation and were being mischievous in trying to break up the proposed marriage between us. Indeed, important administrators in the PITO camp had actually visited Interpol's headquarters at Lyon but they were 'sent packing'.

Meanwhile, my research into the policing of Caribbean countries continued. This involved many aspects including not only the policing of them but their financial strengths and weaknesses and their demography in general. In order to do this, I had been separately contracted by that AFRC Associates Ltd Company who had paid my invoice for producing that statistical appendix to the Interpol proposal. I merely assumed, rightly or wrongly, that Pat and possibly Ron Wright had got together and were backing their horses both ways just in case the Consortium was to fold and that should that be the case, they could somehow, use their AFRC knowledge in other directions. It also, would not impinge on our AFR members business, so maybe that was a prudent step or maybe I was barking up the wrong tree. But why else would I be separately contracted to do that job and why else would they want to operate under a different company?

I commenced this research in early February 2000 and it involved the preparation of a paper on each and every one of the many individual Police Forces in the Caribbean. Most of my material was creamed off the Internet and I prefaced each paper by dealing with the history, geography and demographics of each Island before delving into how they were policed. One thing was for sure, and that was, no matter how closely related to each other in terms of distance, geography and culture, they had not heard of the words amalgamation, merger, alliance or network. Indeed, I have often said that you could commit murders in each of the Islands under different assumed identities and your deeds would never be uncovered or at least, would not be linked together by a fingerprint match. All this, in despite of the existance of the ACCP. (Association of Caribbean Commissioners of Police)

The Interpol Proposal was a huge document split into a main sections with an additional folder of Appendices. As a whole, it was compiled by full consultation with all parties concerned – Sagem HQ Paris, SMI Tacoma, BT, Identix, and all other of our AFR contracted businesses. (Protocol, Telindus etc)

The actual document was titled – SAGEM - INTERPOL – International Biometric Identification Bureau February 2000. My document at Appendix 'A' ('The AFR Consortium – A Statistical Insight') was dated 29th January 2000. Other non-statistical appendices concerned future aspirations and details of the other proposed companies forming the alliance was included. It was also accompanied by a separate report compiled by our Security Officer, Ron Wright under the name of AFR Associates Ltd. 19 Houghton Avenue, Cullercoats, Tyne & Wear. This is the personal address of Ron Wright, our AFR Security Manager. It was titled, 'The West Indies – An Operational and Business Case for the Provision of an AFR Service. The separate Appendix Folder to it contained details of all 23 Countries which Ron and myself had been working on previously. As touched upon earlier, I became curious as to whether Pat and maybe Ron and even Sir John, may have been preparing to ride the wave themselves should it become high enough to decimate the status quo. Otherwise, why was this separate Limited Company formed? I may well be wrong but my suspicions were aroused.

The whole proposal required delivering to Interpol's Headquarter at Lyon but only following a final tweeking by SMI executives in Paris. That responsibility fell to me and on 23rd February, 2000, when I took off from Birmingham

Airport arriving in Paris where I took a Taxi to the Sagem Headquarters to meet the President of the Company, Francois Perrachon.

I had met Francois before but I hadn't realised just how important he was. I arrived at his very impressive offices where just a few adjustments to the document were made. I had already booked my seat on the High Speed TGV Train to Lyon and I could see that I had little time in which to get to the Paris Gare de Lyon Railway Station. I indicated my plight to them and they had a taxi wait outside the front entrance for me. I eventually jumped into the Taxi and my French hosts indicated to the driver where I needed to go – Gare de Lyon.

That Taxi ride was probably the most hair raising trip I had undertaken in a car. The driver must have been told of the urgency involved in my catching the train. In reality, although I had booked a seat, it mattered not because it was not intended that I deliver the proposal to Interpol until the following morning. Anyway, the driver darted off the main roads and shot along parallell service roads before re-joining the main roads. He squeeezed his cab through the narrowest of gaps and paid no heed at all, to speed restrictions. To say that I was apprehensive would have been the understatement of the year. I was actually terrified!

There was a time during the journey, when I genuinely wondered if he was under the impression that I had to be at Lyon by that time and not at the Gare de Lyon in Paris. I tried to make him understand that I did not want him to take me to Lyon, just to catch the train to get there. I knew that he could not understand what I was trying to say and in any event, we finally arrived at the station where I breathed a huge sigh of relief, especially when I found the seat on the train that I had booked. My ticket included the booked seat number and it was then that I realised that all TGV train travellers were given a specific seat and that the train consisted of two levels. How refreshing it was to travel on this TGV compared with our trains. It was comfortable, fast and easy and I seemed to arrive in Lyon in no time at all.

Interpol had booked me into an apartment suite not too far from their Headquarters. They used this establishment for their guests who required overnight stays. It didn't seem like a hotel, in fact I didn't think it was, but a search of the Internet now tells me differently. I thought it was a block of very posh apartments as the rooms I occupied could easily have been lived in by a family. I wondered then, if these apartments were owned by Interpol as there were no glitzy signs advertising it on the outside. They were called, Le Residence La Reine Astrid.

After booking in and securing my valuable documents, I walked for a while to explore the nearby park and river and to 'sus out' exactly where the Interpol Headquarters was located. I found it and it looked as though it was something out of 'Star Ship Enterprise'. I could see diagonal looking glass tubes inside the building which were elevators or mobile walkways. It was so sci-fi looking, I had visions of people being sucked along these tubes. My experience in entering the place during the following morning was to confirm my suspicions about such a futuristic building it was. It may well have been my first glimpse inside the building that now reproduces those images in my mind of the glass tube conveyor system I saw. The image below is a view of the front of the building.

Interpol Headquarters Lyon, France

The distance between the hotel and the Interpol HQ was 1.3km and it took just a pleasant 15 minutes walk around the park. The park was a huge affair and the whole area was right on the banks of the Rhone and not far away from the convergance of it with the Saone. A really beautiful area. I had dinner out and returned to bed for the big event in the morning.

My first visit to Interpol Headquarters took a lot of getting into and I was to protect and carry the quite heavy documents, so I took a taxi. It seemed that their security started off with the idea that they would not permit access to anyone. It was up to me to supply, God only knows what proof of identity and good reason to enter. Following numerous checks and phone calls made in my presence, in French, of course, I gradually eased my way into the building, signing this and signing that and being issued with this and that and after having my fingerprints taken. Suffice to say, that I delivered my very important cargo and made a call back to the office that the mission had been completed. I returned to Birmingham Airport that same day.

Chapter 21 – 2001 Draws Nearer and Bermuda here I come.

During my visits to force bureaux or Livescan sites, I obviously became very acquainted with many of the officers serving in the forces concerned. Hampshire was the lead force and although I had retired before him, one of the Assistant Chief Constables there, was a Peter Linden Jones who, no doubt was recruited to the AFRC by his Chief Constable, Sir John Hoddinott.

Peter and I were to occasionally work together and we became good friends. I was quite busy with our Interpol Caribbean Project and Peter became involved with promoting the 'New Deal' Livescan initiative. We were now in March 2000 and as briefly mentioned before, this was when my research into the Police Forces and the policing of the West Indies took me to the magnificent Library at the Bramshill Police Staff College, Hartley Wintney, Hampshire. I had persuaded the powers that be there, to issue me with a 'Lending Library' ticket and I was able to photocopy data from many of the available reference books.

The UK Livescan Initiative 'Project Scope' was now widely circulated and this, together with the Interpol Proposal gave confidence in policing circles, that SMI would continue the service requirements post 30th June 2001. In the meantime however, Peter was to accompany me to various Livescan sites as he would be required to possess an indepth knowledge of the whole process. I also recall us working together in one of the Caribbean countries, I believe it was Jamaica.

March 2000, was a particularly busy period and Pat was getting a little concerned that our Interpol initiative was beginning to slow things down by 'changing goal posts etc.' He visited Jean Claude and Sagem's President Francois Perrcharon on 19th March and records that Peter Nevitt's comment that the West Indian's reaction to AFRC was 'phenominal'.

I was to pay another visit to Interpol's headquarters but a week prior to that, I paid a quick visit to our City of London based solicitors, Kemp & Co., I think for something in preparation for that meeting. It turned out to be an absolute massive affair with about half of all fourteen delegates being from Interpol and the other half representing us AFRC personnel or associates.

We went 'mob handed' with Pat, Hampshire County Council's solicitor, Ted Mason, Ray Elvy, Surrey's head of fingerprint bureau, a Kemp & Co.Solicitor and Jean-Claude Richard and Thierry Provoust from Sagem. We were to discuss operational and fingerprint issues with an Interpol team consisting of Peter Nevitt, Murray Hill, Jimmy Wang, Dominic Suc, Mark Blanchflower, Interpols Head of Fingerprint Bureau, Sandrine Capsalas and Chris Eaton. The meeting very much concerned the practical issues in our merger but other minor issues such as becoming a 'Charitable Corporation' and our exchange of contracts etc. were discussed at the same time.

April arrived and this brought an increase to my daily rate. I now jumped from £163 to £168.54 per day. Not a very big deal, but a fiver went quite a long way in those days. It was this April Fools day that I also arrived in Seattle again to perform another stint as 'Duty Officer' at our Central Site in Tacoma. My tour was to have been a short one ending on 11th but Pat wanted me to produce some charts and documents in connection with our UK Livescan Initiative for the upcoming ACCP's (Assn. of Caribbean Commissioners of Police) Annual Conference on Grand Cayman. Part of what I did involved describing in greater detail, the scope for the detection of false identities which was very relevant to Caribbean countries. He therefore extended my contracted 210 days by three days and I eventually returned to the UK on 15th April 2000.

By this time, it was 'all hands on deck' and I continued with various service and Livescan visits. Even with modern day communications, I wasn't sure how I was to spend all my time on Staff Officer duties if my principals were in other countries. I had spent a few days in the Gwent force at Pontypool, Cwmbran and Newport in addition to their force headquarters. Sadly, it was whilst in Newport that I received a pager message to visit my mother's home at Hereford. She had been found by her visiting home help and carer, collapsed in the kitchen where she had lain all night because she couldn't get up from the floor. That was to be the start of many medical visits to hospitals etc. and which eventually culminated in her having to be cared for in Stratford House

Care Home and later at Hampton House Care Home, Hereford for many years until she died there aged ninety four in 2007.

Back at work, the Annual Meeting of the Association of Caribbean Commissioners of Police (ACCP) was being held on Grand Caymen during the week 14th to 20th May. I did not attend it but having worked on it in Tacoma a few weeks earlier, I knew what it was all about and I continued to work on the results of the Conference once it had concluded. We were obviously hell bent on encouraging the Caribbean Islands police forces to take a huge step up from their very old fashioned ideas and working practices which the use of our technology would provide.

One could imagine that any police force's conversion to the digitisation of fingerprint recording and storage from that old 'Ink and Roller' method, might attract publicity from local media including members of parliament when preaching how valuable they were in 'Law and Order' issues. It was with that in mind, that I spent a couple of weeks researching such outlets so that I could create a database from which I could make contact with people and organisations who might, in some way, promote and advertise the value of our Livescan machines in the custody centres located within their constituencies or otherwise at their areas of jurisdiction.

I touched down at Seatac Airport again at the end of July 2000 for another period of work at the 'Central Site' in Tacoma. This trip, however, would involve an onward trip to Bermuda. We had by then, agreed with Interpol that we would continue with the successful 'Pilot' scheme we had started in the Cayman Islands, and which we would now offer to all other Caribbean Countries who were interested.

By now, the concept had been sold at the Annual Meeting of the Caribbean Commissioners of Police in Cayman which shouldn't have been too difficult especially as we were offering to load 10,000 Tenprint forms donated by their worst or notorious prisoners for free. These were to be searched by launching their scenes of crime fingerprint marks against all tenprints on our system, including the 10,000 of their own. Although I wasn't privy to the financial arrangements, this free service would have been made possible through the £10k per site bounty we were being paid by Interpol.

We had also been very lucky in Cayman because it was only the second 'Mark' launched on our system, that solved a long outstanding murder of a taxi driver who was stabbed in the back by his fare, in order to steal his takings. This murder had been undetected for a good few years and in no time at all, the pilot project had detected it for them. As might be imagined, this 'HIT' was to feature in a DVD video we made for marketing purposes and indeed it cropped up many times, including in the many presentations I was to later make in the Caribbean. On one occasion in Turks and Caicos, David Thursfield a close ex-colleague of mine and once Deputy Chief in the West Mercia Police, was now the Commissioner of the Royal Cayman Constabulary. He was thankfully able to relate this story at first hand, with far greater detail than I could have done. It was as if we were a double act, extolling the virtues of our system and that occurred on more than one Caribbean meeting I was to attend in the future.

I was very pleased that I had been selected to do the ground work in Bermuda by myself, and so, before leaving for Tacoma I made contact by telephone with, what I thought to be, the best hotel in its capital, Hamilton. The Hamilton Princess hotel would be my base for the several visits I was to make there. The plan was, that in addition to getting myself acquainted with the police and all other interested organisations and politicians, I was to organise a grand dinner at the hotel, inviting all those I would be touching base with in our quest to build a 'Multi-Agency' system. The main players being the Police, Customs and Excise, Prisons, Immigration departments and Airport security departments or owners.

The plan involved me visiting all these important people during the week prior to them attending the grand dinner at the hotel which I was to arrange. The meeting would be chaired by our chairman, Sir John Hoddinott who would arrive on the day prior to the meeting. My objective in setting up the delegates and the dinner was obviously not difficult but it was made a great deal easier through my earlier, pre-visit contact by telephone with the British born head of the Bermuda fingerprint bureau, Howard Cutts. I made him my best friend and we got along very well. He kindly made contact with the right people to explain who I was and what I was doing. In effect, he was my 'foot in their door' and his presence there, helped to negate that old problem I was always to suffer from, which was to shake off the belief held by these people, that I was just there to sell something. That was in fact, around about correct, but it was my ex-police experience that also helped. Being there at the behest of Interpol and with the ACCP's knowledge, also opened these doors. Our ambitions honestly coincided with our desire to detect more crimes and lock up the people committing them.

I also chanced my arm in asking Howard that if the opportunity presented itself, would he, on my behalf, invite them to the dinner and fix up some of the meetings with these people in advance for me. Indeed, that would have made the opening of the door, easier for him.

I was to learn that there's not a great deal to do on Bermuda and after all, who could turn down a free dinner at the best hotel on Bermuda? The dinner / meeting was to be held during the evening of 16th August and Sir John would leave during the next day, several hours before me. We obviously hoped that his status would play heavily in our favour as his job was to chair the meeting.

Sir John's important presence reminds me about what had happened as a result of my telephoning the Hamilton hotel to book our rooms prior to my leaving England for Tacoma and which I (eventually) thought was quite funny.

I gave Sir John Hoddinott's details for his room. There was a pregnant pause and the chap on the other end of the line said, "You mean 'Sir'... as in..... 'Knight of the Realm'?" I said "Of course". He then suggested that we could perhaps have some upgraded rooms and no mention of inflated cost was made. Without wishing to pull any favours, I obviously thought it rude to refuse this offer. Well, you would, wouldn't you?

Being a wealthy Island, and with mostly british born and trained fingerprint operatives, Bermuda was the obvious Island from which to start spreading our 'proof of concept' project. I was lucky to have tucked Howard Cutts under my wing and all those I invited to the 'Dinner / Security' meeting agreed to attend. Of course, there wasn't much to think about as it was free. I hadn't met Howard before and I was so pleased with the arrangements he had made, that I took him out to dinner one evening and memory makes me believe that he also attended the dinner with his commissioner, Jean-Jacques Le May.

Thank God I was on expenses; I've never been in such an expensive country before. Howard did warn me that whatever I was doing, would cost a 'bomb'. I just don't know how ordinary workers on Bermuda can afford to survive. Its remoteness from the nearest mainland, 640 miles from North Carolina, obviously adds to the cost, though tax incentives act as a balance for the local inhabitants.

I was told not to hold back on the expenses so obviously I didn't want to upset anyone by being 'cheap'. In addition to the heads of the 'security' agencies on the Island, I invited several Government Ministers because it would be them who would give the ultimate sanction for the purchases we were hoping they would later make.

The Princess hotel, Hamilton. Not my upgraded room but typically laid out the same

I couldn't believe what a fabulous environment I was working in. The weather was good, the sea warm and the Pina Coladas were cool and tasted great. I was staying in a suite which overlooked the sea. I had never before seen such a hotel suite with all its added little rooms and facilities.

There was a huge settee in the middle of a giant lounge with a separate dining room, come study. A huge dresser with drawers and cupboards etc. It could have housed a family. I had this constant fear that my bill would include an enhanced rate for the rooms but it didn't. I was indeed quite pleased with myself because although Sir John never swanked about his status, I knew that he would enjoy his room when he arrived.

It was thanks to Howard that prior to the dinner, I was able to scoot through many of my earlier meetings with individual ministers and heads of the security agencies. My job was not only to get them to the dinner / meeting, but to sell them the worth of what we were trying to do, before they attended it. To be frank, this didn't take anywhere near the six days that I had been given and to be honest, I was provided with some free time.

My cousin's wife, Mary from Glastonbury, gave me details of her cousin who lived on the island. She was another Mary who was divorced from her husband Tony. They were a wealthy couple who had lived on the small Hinson's Island which was visible from the main island. Mary was now living on the mainland. I made contact with her and she took me for dinner at her tennis club, the Coral Beach Club. The dinner had a 'Sea Food' theme and I had never ever seen such a magnificent display of every type of seafood you could imagine. Lobster, Crab, Oysters, Prawns as big as my fist – it was tremendous. Sadly Mary was suffering from cancer and she lost her battle, not long after my visits there.

I had also made a good friend of the Canadian Commissioner of Police, Jean-Jaques LeMay. Although Bermuda is a 'British Dependant' country and in the North Atlantic and not strictly within the 'Caribbean', it had, and continues to have, a firm association with it, and for all intents and purposes, including social, political, trade and business purposes, it may just as well be in it. Jean-Jaques was a member of the Association of Caribbean Commissioners of Police (ACCP). With Cayman and the Bahamas, it was a country far more advanced than those other Caribbean countries I was later to visit. The government's trait had been to employ experienced personnel from other countries to lead the way in their various businesses, education and training. That was why Jean-Jaques LeMay had been seconded from the Royal Canadian Mounted Police, to Bermuda. Similarly, many members of its police force, including fingerprint officers, had been employed from Britain, Canada and the USA. Much of the training of its officers occurred in those countries.

I emphasise that the same policy of 'transferring in' applied to many other important professions on the Island.

My time in Bermuda however, was when the tide was beginning to turn. The mostly 'black' government ministers were of the belief that these secondments had probably 'done their job' and that their country had been promoted to a higher status as a result, but it could now stand on its own two feet. Things were beginning to bubble and rumour had it that at the conclusion of Jean-Jaques LeMay's secondment, he would be replaced by an indigenous commissioner. His deputy at that time, was a 'black' man called Jackson who, although a very pleasant chap, in no way matched the skills and professionalism of Jean-Jaques. For the country's sake, I hoped that such a transition would not occur.

Jean-Jaques would obviously be attending the dinner meeting but nonetheless, I fixed up a more informal chat with Sir John and I during the morning of it. It went well and we obviously explained in greater detail, the benefits of such a system on the island. Unlike most other countries, Bermuda was comparatively wealthy and there was no doubt that they would be 'on side' and very much in favour of our system. Following our chat, Sir John and I walk around Hamilton town and ended up in the restaurant at the famous Trimmingham's Store. He asked me if I had telephoned Pat to put him in the picture about the dinner; who would be attending etc. I think he was pleased about the arrangements so far made. With Howard's help, we had managed to persuade all of the 'big guns' to attend. I explained that I had sent Pat the odd e-mail but Sir John suggested that we ring him.

We approached the hotel on foot and decided that we would make the call from Sir John's room. As we entered it, my mouth dropped. His room was just one of the ordinary standard rooms and not a suite like mine. I couldn't believe it; they could have fitted three of his rooms into my suite. I also couldn't believe the obvious mistake that had been made. How on earth could they put me in a suite and a 'Knight of the realm' in a bog standard room? I didn't show my exasperation and played it down a little just mentioning that I thought his room wasn't as good as mine, without mentioning the vast differences. He seemed quite happy with his room, so what should I say or do? What would you do in my position?

I said nothing more which gave me time to make a more considered decision. We made the phone call and later on, had a very successful dinner / meeting with I'm guessing about 20-25 people in attendance. I had already deployed some security measures for the meeting and so, with the instruction not to hold back on the expense echoing in my ears, I instructed the waiters to leave the room when we started the business and to leave plenty of wine available so that we never ran dry. There was no doubting that Bermuda was well up for their giant leap into modern day networked searching. They were even excited about it. However, even with all that food and drink inside of me, instead of sleeping with contentment over an excellent meeting, I had a most restless and disturbed night, tossing and turning about the mix up of the rooms. What should I do?

I rose early and immediately visited reception where they admitted their mistake and profusely apologised. I had by then, made very good friends with all of the desk receptionists which ensured a constant supply of copy paper should I need it for my computer's printer etc. They conceded that we should have both been upgraded but for some reason, my room was the only one. I said nothing over breakfast and bearing in mind Sir John hadn't been on the island for very long, we enjoyed another 'touristic' type of stroll in the town. He was due to fly out in the early afternoon, and I think my flight was during the next day. It was during our stroll that I said something like, "I have a confession to make". – "Oh?" "When we went to your room last night, you recall I made comment that mine was a better room than yours. Well, we were supposed to have the same type of rooms". His interjection was, "Well, there's nothing wrong with my room honestly, it's got plenty of room and I'm very content with it".

Phew!! In my sort of apologetic tone, I had now advised him twice and needn't go into any further detail. Saying anything more would be unnecessary and, in any event, would bound to make the hole I was digging for myself, much bigger.

We sat down over a coffee where we both concurred that the previous evening had gone exceedingly well. But it was then that 'Sod's law' kicked in. He casually asked me if he could store his suitcases in my room because his flight was to cause him to check out much earlier than me. Without much thought I said, "Of course you can, have a shower if you wish". As soon as he agreed to that and thanked me, I realised that he would be seeing my room. What an idiot, I should have offered to collect his luggage for him……Oh but what about the shower? – Duuuuh. I couldn't have guessed his reaction when I later opened the door to him.

Sir John was a marvelous, placid gentleman. I loved him dearly, in that manly sort of way. He was honest, well mannered, never swore as far as I knew and, of course, he didn't reach his dizzy heights by being soft.

He stepped in, dropped his suitcases and exclaimed Fuck*** Hell! What have you got here, a ballroom?" Oh God! He went on and on but he did have that chink of a smile on his face which was just peeping out from beneath his exclaimed facade. I didn't think of it at the time but it reminded me of a line in the song, 'From a Jack to a King' by Ricky Van Shelton – *"And Just in time, I saw that twinkle in your eye".*

He was, after all, only on the Island for a few days and I knew he didn't mind really, but he kept up the pretence that I had planned it all. I was on the ropes and said, " I've already raised it with them John. When we go downstairs, they'll tell you about the mix up."

Anyway, when the time came, I realised that as well as earning me a few favours, my friendship with the receptionists was such that on this occasion, they were able to 'blag' me. Sir John was by my side and I begged the male receptionist to check my call and booking requirements and to apologise to Sir John etc. "Tell him it was your mistake," I pleaded. The receptionist looked me straight in the eye and said, "I remember you Mr Humphreys, specifically asking that you be put in the best room"!! His stare lasted for more than a few seconds and he didn't flinch. He had taken my breath away and it seemed ages before I started to chuckle, "Come on, you know about the mix up, you've already apologised to me". The smile then came to his face and he sincerely apologised to Sir John.

That very true story also serves to explain what sort of man Sir John was. I always used to call him 'Sir John' even after him telling me not to. It just didn't seem right and when I sometimes slipped it out he would bark, "I told you, Brian, once before breakfast and then its John". My excuse used to be, "Well I haven't had breakfast yet"! What a great man he was.

Plans for the other Caribbean Islands had not even been discussed at this time but realising that this Bermuda trip was the fore-runner of much work to be done in the Islands, and what with being contracted to do some ground work for SMI, I took the oportunity before leaving Tacoma for Bermuda, to open an American Bank Account with the 'US Bank' which was located on the ground floor of the very building in which we were based on Broadway Plaza, Tacoma. My SMI cheques would be paid directly into that Bank and over time, I arranged many wired amounts from it to be paid into my UK bank. I did have a consultation with a tax acountant in Tacoma to see if it was worth paying Inland Revenue to the States but I quickly concluded that it was more hastle than it was worth and so I have always declared my earnings in the UK wherever my income originated.

Having returned home from Bermuda suffering with the usual jetlag, I had to get my head around the 'mixed up rooms fiasco'. I was, however, also to learn how the 'mix up' of the rooms occurred. I had to settle the very large bills at the hotel with the AFRC Credit Card. I cannot remember the total now, but I know it came to many thousands of pounds. I showed off to Jo and showed her the account. She said, "Congratulations". I said, "What for?" She said, "well you've been Knighted!" I looked at the account and there at the top of it it had my name – Sir Brian Humphreys! Although both rooms were to be upgraded, whoever decided to upgrade the 'Knight of the realm' only, put me down as he. I wondered whether Sir John's account had Mr. John Hoddinott at the head of it!! Oh Dear, do you think I would have mentioned that to him? You've guessed it - Certainly not!

I had landed back at Heathrow onmy birthday, 18th August but my exploration in foreign waters was to teach me that after such a long trip, my car park charge had amounted to £238.50 for 24 days. I immediately suggested to Pat that with many more long visits to come, it would be more sensible for us to have a driver pick us up for conveyance to and from wherever we were required to fly on long haul flights. It was, in any event, a dangerous drive home from the airport because not sleeping too well on these overnight flights, tiredness became an issue for driving home. From then on, we were always conveyed as suggested and it made a great difference not only to costs but to our comfort.

Chapter 22 – Flirting with SMI

So far as SMI's facilities were concerned, another one of the positive spin-offs from Livescan, was the production of their product called 'Morpho Touch'. This was a mobile scanner, at about the same size as one of the larger mobile phones when they were first produced. It was portable and obviously hand held and could be taken on any operation in order to scan suspects fingers to the tenprint and mark databases.

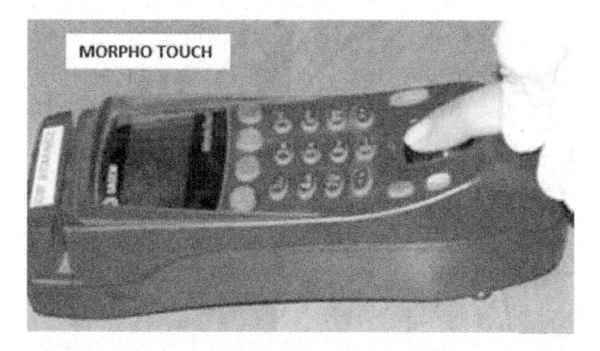

In later years, these were very helpful to Immigration Departments in various countries when they raided for example, workplaces where suspected illegal immigrants were being employed. The police uses of them are so obvious that they require no further explanation here. Their system could also produce cards containing the holder's photographs and fingerprints. This was a fantastic concept with so many perceived uses which was one of the reasons we suggested that our databases would suit a 'Multi Agency' situation. It therefore made sense that if I or anyone else in our team were to tout business for SMI machines, then we had better get to know how they operated and how to use them.

We were, after all, contractors employed for our senior police officer experience of catching criminals but however, for all intents and purposes, we were selling more for SMI, than ourselves as contractors for AFRC. I realise that this was an 'I'll scratch your back if you scratch mine," relationship which actually started me on a closer employment relationship with SMI.

I became aware that although Pat was having me paid by the consortium, he started to re-claim my costs by billing SMI. This was typical Pat and it wasn't as if there were insufficient funds in our own pot. It didn't concern me except that there were periods when I was really unaware as to who I was working for. It was always Pat who appeared to be pulling my strings, no matter who was paying me. However, this situation was later to raise its ugly head after I had signed a contract with SMI.

And so, it was arranged for me to be accompanied by Ray Elvy, a senior fingerprint expert at Surrey's fingerprint bureau and a very nice chap he was. We both needed the training to better understand their equipment, especially Morpho Touch. This was useful to me because although I could present myself as a 'retired' senior police officer, as a civilian, I was once again, in danger of being regarded as just a travelling salesman. Ray was a serving Police Officer as well as a Fingerprint Expert and was able to give me some credibility.

As a self-employed consultant, my feet were now firmly in two camps. It was a 'win win' situation for all concerned. SMI saw that the more we spread the concept around the Caribbean, the more of their kit they would sell. Also, we would be happy in building up our database to include the Caribbean, perhaps in the forlorn hope that 30th June 2001 would never see our demise after all.

The object of Ray and I being with Sagem was that their staff could train us in its use. I think Jean-Claude had 'twigged' his problem of us (me in particular) not being able to understand his thick French accent and so it wasn't long before we were working with Joel Hugg, one of their employees who knew what he was talking about. The whole idea was that having been trained, Ray and I would set off for Bermuda because by then, Interpol were happy that we press on with the 'Proof of Concept' pilot there.

The 'Morpho Touch' kit could also be adapted to perform the function of a security 'door opening' system. The bank of fingerprints would be located in a server so that by placing a finger on the pad, it would recognise it and open the door. It would also record each and every transaction so that supervisors could have a hard copy report about all employees passing into and out of different doors and buildings etc.

So far as Ray and I were concerned, in order to demonstrate the equipment, in addition to the actual mobile hand held touch pad, we needed a small computer to act as a server and a printer to print out the various reports. We would be travelling all over the place and so Sagem had designed what was, in effect, a suitcase made of crush proof material, in which the equipment could be carried. It was just like a large modern day Samsonite suitcase with a retractable handle and on two wheels for mobility.

Our training took place on 5th and 6th September and on 7th, we set off for the first, of what turned out to be, many trips with this mobile demonstration kit, to Bermuda. This was to be the first of many Caribbean countries we would visit, for which I had already paved our way. We were also joined by John Sims who had worked with us before. John was an old support colleague of Pats who used him as a consultant in the Hampshire Police when, I presumed that Pat was head of their IT department. We all got on well and spent until 22nd September demonstrating the kit to as many Police, Customs and Immigration executives and Government officials, that we could. We also demonstrated it at the prison. There literally wasn't an agency that wouldn't have wanted to be involved with this remarkable piece of kit.

With every agency we worked with, we additionally prepared 'Process Models and Operational Requirements' for them. The objective being to make them even more aware of the tailor made benefits pertaining to each individual agency.

The age old problem was always going to be the expense of it all. From memory, we didn't tramp around with prices in those early days; the idea was to whet their appetites. I was always to ensure that we would demonstrate to whoever was pulling the purse strings. In Bermuda's case, this was the Government's Director of Finance (Olga Scott).

In addition to showing off the equipment, I also worked at the three Police Stations on the Island to conduct tenprint flows for a process model and Operational Requirement.' I can assure any reader, that during these trips I worked very hard indeed but I cannot hide the fact that returning to work in Bermuda was a delightful experience which I wanted Jo to share.

We were based again in that wonderful Hamilton Princess hotel and so as a special treat, instead of returning to the UK on 23rd September, I arranged to take some leave so that Jo would join me for a holiday.

We had a lovely holiday and as expensive as Bermuda was, we always had to pass a Jewellers called Solomons at 17 Front Street. Jo always admired a heavy looking gold neckless with a very nice photograph pendant attached. I was to learn that the little pendant cost just over double that of the neckless. Her wishes were enough to coerce me into making the purchase and I suppose it was a mark of how much disposable income we possessed during those heady days. Her present cost me £1,403. Not a normal purchase at my state of affairs!

My Second trip to Bermuda at the Hamilton Princess. Top left, the hotel taken from the little ship 'Patience' which ferried guests between the two 'Princess' hotels.
Top right, relaxing in the 'Ordinary' room – No Suite on this occasion!

We had planned to return home together but I was asked by SMI if I would travel on to Antigua to do a similar job there. I had never visited Antigua before, nor was there any Ex-Pat British Officer there, to arrange introductions. The other major problem I was faced with, was that Jo had got herself to Gatwick on public transport in the knowledge that when I returned after our holiday, we would be collected by my already organised driver. I put the problem to SMI and they agreed to stand the cost of the driver and car to pick Jo up at Gatwick and take her home whilst I went to Antigua. My fees had risen to £200 per day and this diversion had cost SMI an additional £100.

Chapter 23 – Antigua, Here I Am!

Not long after Jo's flight had left Bermuda, I took off for Antigua or to give the country its full title, Antigua and Barbuda. SMI had booked me into the Royal Antiguan Resort for six nights and it was late on Saturday 30th September when a taxi drove me to the hotel without my luggage and demonstration kit which had not arrived on the aeroplane with me.

There were no street lights visible and all I could see was in the headlights of the taxi. What a difference to Bermuda. I was not impressed. The roads were rotten and 'pot holed' and I could see wooden 'shack type' dwellings on the sides of the roads. I soon realised that Bermuda had been very untypical of the rest of the Caribbean, well so far as Antigua was concerned anyway.

Royal Antiguan Resort

The 'Royal Antiguan Resort' was such an impressive name that I had hoped for a lot better than it turned out to be. Compared with buildings I could see in the headlights of the taxi, the hotel looked presentable from the outside. It was on a pleasant beach and there were very nice gardens surrounding it with a gigantic pool. But it was dark and late when I arrived, so I decided to get some sleep and explore in the morning, which was a Sunday. The only word I can think of which adequately described the hotel is 'dowdy'.

However, I can remember the pleasant restaurant where breakfast was taken in competition with the many sparrows and other birds that flew in, to rob the guests of morsels of food. It was, of course, covered but due to the wonderful climate, there was no need for outer walls or windows. It was also very remote from the capital city, St. Johns.

Basic Room, cheap furniture and surprisingly, a TV but I can't remember if it worked.

It was a Sunday and all I had was my hand luggage. As usual, I made the receptionist my best friend and made frequent telephone calls to the airport about my lost luggage.

I had not been to Antigua before and being unexpectantly diverted there, I had no time to research who it was I would want to speak to. It was like being dropped behind enemy lines. This was going to be a blank piece of paper and

I was obviously going to have to use my mouth to find out all about the island and who it would be best to link up with.

It was very hot during that Sunday morning and there was nothing I could do about my luggage, so I decided to get a taxi into St. Johns just to have a look around and find out where the police headquarters was located. To give this force its proper title, it was 'The Royal Police Force of Antigua and Barbuda'. I was to discover that there wasn't much of an association with it being 'Royal' in any respect.

I was far from impressed with the town but very impressed with the 'happy clappy' sounds and song bursting out of church doors which had been flung wide open on the main street. It was, after all; a Sunday and I was in a foreign environment. I had thought that Bermuda had been my first Caribbean Island, but no, Bermuda was going to be a 'cut above' the others and in any event, it was in the North Atlantic. I had not yet seen other 'proper' Caribbean countries, yet I was sure that this Antigua had an air of it being rather typical of the Caribbean. I was all by myself and to be honest, I had wondered how safe it was for me to walk around the town which was pretty well deserted apart from the sounds coming from that church which somehow, gave me an air of security among the few others who, with me being the only white person on the streets, must have been wondering who the hell I was.

I didn't wander too far but before I came across the police headquarters, I found the main Police Station in Newgate Street. This would have been named after Newgate Prison, London, the site of which now stands the Central Criminal Court (The Old Bailey). Wondering whether I could learn something, I wandered into the enquiry office where I was amazed to see that all the prisoners were on view in one large cell behind a wall of bars which was situated just behind the reception area. It was very much like those scenes in old Western movies and it was very overcrowded with the prisoners taking delight at shouting at me through the cell bars.

No way would that be allowed in any country or so I thought. I introduced myself and had a chat with a couple of officers and I learned that an Inspector Henry Christian was the head of the fingerprint bureau but because it was a Sunday, that headquarters where he was based, would be closed until the morning. I guessed as much and without my luggage anyway, I had virtually wasted two days due to the weekend. I only had three days left from a blind standing start, so, this left only two full days plus the day of my departure to get to grips with who I ought to meet.

I had spent nights one and two at the hotel (Saturday and Sunday) and my luggage and the demonstration kit arrived on day 3 (Monday). Therefore, if I was at least to make contact with all of the main 'players', I needed to discover who they were and reverse my normal process to arrange a meeting first, before any individual meetings with them. So, all of the arranging needed to be done on the Monday, to fix the meeting for the Tuesday. I needed to make a friend at police headquarters and treat him to lunch. Thankfully that was to be Henry Christian, whose name had been dropped to me when I paid that unannounced visit to the Police Station.

I was to find that Henry was an obliging gentleman and I drained him of all the information I needed. Whilst I knew that it would be the individual meetings I had hoped to arrange, would be the main selling arena, I knew that time constraints precluded that and that a second visit would inevitably be necessary. I hadn't yet even checked with the hotel that it could accommodate my joint meeting but if I was lucky, I might squeeze in enough time to see some individuals, before I flew back home on the evening of 5th October.

The one saving grace was that I was always in touch with the rest of my 'Business World' through the little lap top computer I carried with me. When I think back now, I can't believe the problems I encountered in order to get an e-mail sent or received. Broadband and Wi Fi was not that popular in those days and my first job whenever I checked into a hotel was to link up my computer to the telephone in the room so that I could link to a 'dial-up' facility. This was more difficult in some hotels, than in others. The better hotels had a spare docking female slot actually in the telephone itself. At others I had to get plugged into the wall after unplugging the telephone or using a doubler plug which I carried with me.

The next job was to find the nearest 'Dial Up' location and this involved me tuning into my 'Internet Provider' and conducting a search. I recall that in some countries I visited, the nearest 'dial up' point was actually in a different country (Very often Caracas Venezuela). So having got connected to the internet, I would then log on and receive my numerous e-mail messages then quickly disconnect to save on the phone bill. A similar process was required to send emails. All AFRC operatives worked completely around emails, and I often dreaded opening them up. It was nothing for me to sometimes wake up to over 100 e-mails. In those times, one couldn't just pick on individual emails to open at leisure. They all had to be downloaded simultaneously to an 'In Box'. Having then saved them all, I could then pick and choose which ones to open. Similarly, all responses or new emails sent by me, were saved into an 'Out Box' and only when I was ready and obtained a dial-up connection, would I send them all simultaneously. What a difference now. In retrospect, my whole 'after police' experience had unwittingly placed me streets ahead of most other people in the UK and perhaps the world, in the use of Internet technology and computing in general. It was a new concept and much maligned by those who swore they didn't need it. Most have it now, which perhaps, speaks volumes.

By now, with a wasted weekend and with having to catch a flight home in a couple of days, I had much to do. To overrun the story a little here, I later managed to see three people at the St Johns Police Headquarters and one very important person in the Antiguan Government, no less than the Attorney General, all were 'ON BOARD'.

Inspector Henry Christian and his wife.

It was very necessary to know their names and position before hand and this sometimes involved having to chat up switchboard operators who were always busy and, in some cases, just anxious to connect you anywhere. I was going to again, have to make some verbal love to someone!

So, I had a good start with Henry Christian. He would hopefully be my ticket to see the Commissioner. I spoke to him in his fingerprint bureau, if that is what it was. It was a cramped office with and with limited space, tenprints were scattered all over the place.

Henry was a good man and more importantly, he looked after me on my many visits to Antigua. I had much to thank him for and In later years, I was to learn that he had been promoted up the ranks and was the Deputy Commissioner from at least 2012 until I think 2015.

Such was the situation in Antigua as with any other place, but I cannot remember Commissioner Truehart Smith's secretary's name but my chatting her up paid dividends. It needs to be remembered, that I had not made contact with anyone in Antigua, before I arrived. I was a stranger in a strange country and no-one had heard of Brian Humphreys nor SMI or the AFR Consortium.

Commissioner Truehart Smith

For now, I'll include just the photograph above which I took of Henry and his wife during a weekend at Nelson Heights.

The Attorney General for Antigua was also another very important government official who came into my sights on that trip. Right throughout the Caribbean Islands, politicians have a far greater sway in policing than is experienced in the UK. The Honourable Dr. Errol Cort was the Attorney General and Minister of Justice and Legal Affairs. His Chambers in Radcliffe Street, were not very salubrious and I paid many visits there to discuss things with him. Later in 2004, he put himself up as a candidate to run against the Prime Minister, Lester Bird. Both were defeated. More on Dr Cort and allegations made against him later but for now, my dealings with him consisted of a brief chat in his offices and at his presence at my presentation.

It was during one of those future visits to him that he confided that he wanted to replace the then Commissioner, Truehart Smith. More on Dr Cort and Commissioner Trueheart Smith later because my dealings with him, covered many meetings and different scenarios over three trips to Antigua. Suffice to say here, that so far as I was concerned, Truehart was another very nice gentleman. We got on extremely well and I learned on my next visit to Antigua that he wanted to invite me to his wedding, but more on that later also.

Right. It was back to the hotel in much haste. I needed to get on the phone and start inviting people fast. The hotel hadn't a clue what I was doing and I just prayed that they would play ball with me organising a largish meeting in a function room which I also hoped hadn't already been booked by another client / party.

The hotel was fine at a price and it was just the logistics of the presentation now which had to be finalised. I hired the large room and had it kitted out with soft drinks, glasses and light snacks. I also had to ensure that the hotel had the equipment I would require such as a flip chart and tripod with marker pens, an overhead projector etc. This required me buttering up one of the staff who I enrolled to help me set it up, I think he enjoyed it. His reward was having his photograph taken in the presentation room we had set up. He felt very much 'involved'. It was necessary for me to brush up on what I was going to say and how to say it whilst operating the demonstration kit I had used it in Bermuda with Ray Elvy but, now I was alone.

St Johns isn't the best place. The infrastructure is very poor; as I've said before, it mustn't be forgotten that many of these Islands were emerging from almost 'Third World' status. All this, plus me having to persuade important people that they could adjust their diaries to attend my presentation, didn't help me have a good sleep on that Monday. In addition, I hadn't done a similar presentation before and so I needed to burn up that midnight oil.

The Prime Minister was Lester Bird, a British and US educated barrister who had taken over the premiership from his father Vere Bird Snr. Lester had an elder brother who may have succeeded his father but for him being found out for criminal activities – gun running etc. I don't suppose they could overlook that!! They were of the Antigua Labour Party (ALP) who were later defeated by the United Progressive Party (UPP). There have not been many years go by without some form of corruption allegation aimed at Antigua's politicians. I was also to witness how they could play an influential hand in the Policing of the country. I have no evidence whatsoever but my experience was such that I wouldn't personally be trusting any of them.

The Room is all set up for my Presentation and Demonstration of Morpho Touch at The Royal Antiguan hotel on 3rd October 2000.

So far as the Police Headquarters was concerned, my ever lasting memory is of seeing chickens strutting about the place and police mechanics repairing a police car at the back of the building. There were no hydraulic hoists or inspection pits. I saw that in order to work on the underside of a car, they had it tipped up and supported on just two wheels on one side by using two wooden props, almost like long pit props. I was later to experience how poor the force was in relation to available finance and the dearth of equipment they had to endure. Surely the finances of this force weren't up to providing the necessary equipment required but one never knows what grants are available from the Government or other agencies in these circumstances.

I had discovered that a small room was available for when Interpol members ever visited the Island. The sign, 'Interpol Office' was on the door. The office was therefore locked up but on a subsequent visit when I was required to work there, they gave me the use of it being as I was working on an Interpol funded project. I remember opening up the room and seeing that apart from a small wooden table and one chair, there was nothing in it except a telephone perched on the table which was equipped with a fax facility. I based myself there and it was ideal to store my lap top, printer and demonstration kit. I could also use the telephone and fax but on this particular occasion, I was without paper for the printer, which negated my use of the fax machine. I popped along the corridor to Truehart's secretary and begged for some paper. I will always recall her words when she said, "Brian de cupboard is bare!" I instinctively knew that she was serious even though for a nano second, a chuckle almost popped out of my mouth; she was deadly serious. There are many, many other instances I could quote as examples of their poverty but as well as having memory problems, it would be unfair on the Royal Antigua and Barbuda Force for the reasons I have already stated – they were an emerging nation and I was there to help, not to be an encumbrance. I smiled and I suppose I would have begged some paper from the hotel which was my normal trick. God, if this place was so poor, how were they going to fund an AFIS?

Luckily, my presentation was well attended and on the whole, I was pleased with the way it went. I always thought that we were on something of a false air of expectation because their keenness was bound to have something to do with our offer of searching 10,000 of their Tenprints against their 'Serious Crime Marks' for free. They were hardly going to turn that opportunity down but, judgement day was always bound to arrive. I knew it!

Attorney General, Dr. Errol Cort arrived with Commissioner Truehart Smith and I think Truehart's deputy, Elton Martin. Whilst I cannot now picture the other attendees in my mind, I can recall quite easily my thoughts about Dr Errol Cort. I learned that he was the current Minister of Justice and the Attorney General and had been the leader of the opposition and was also Minister for Finance. He was the 'King Pin', a very powerful man who, just by his sullen and offhand attitude, I had tagged was 'trouble'. He made few observations and gave me the impression that he almost begrudged my attendance 'ON HIS ISLAND'. This was just my imagination working here but he was definitely then, not going to be susceptible to my sweet talking. A very cold and suspicious character. He warmed up a little later on, during my subsequent visits but for now, in my view, he was not an ally.

My net for catching invitees to my presentation had spread across the whole sphere of Security on the Island and according to my 'contacts' database, the following organisations and persons representing them would have been in

Dr Errol Cort

*Honourable Steadroy 'Cutie' Benjamin
Minister of Labour, Co-operatives and
Public Safety*

attendance in addition to those I have already mentioned.

The Minister of Labour, Mr. 'Cutie' Benjamin. As can be seen, his real name is Steadroy Benjamin and I can only assume that his 'Cutie' title had been given to him as a result of his high pitched feminine voice. I never asked the obvious question but a 'flyer' carrying his CV in the run up to an election makes no mention of his family domestic situation. He has acted as a 'Defence Barrister' in high profile criminal cases including the ex-Prime Minister's brother, Ivor Bird who had been arrested for attempting to smuggle three kilos of cocaine into the country.

At the time, Cutie was the Minister of Labour and I invited him so that he could see the advantages that a 'Multi Agency Fingerprint Database' would bring, especially when it came to checking on the identities of persons to ascertain whether or not they had been issued with work permits. He is another who was called to 'The Bar' in London and with a legal background. He also, had not been without accusations of wrongdoing and the first web page returned when I made a Google search for him, revealed that he had signed a photograph of a person he knew to be dead for an application for a passport.

There had been uproar in Antigua when the DPP, through the Antigua High Court directed that he should not be tried "Because he knew the family in question"?? Again, it seems that not many of these top politicians have escaped some sort of scandal or other and they usually are based on the exercise of their power and political influence. Mr Benjamin also brought his Permanent Secretary, Mr Eden Weston. In addition, the Labour Commissioner, Mr Austen Josiah and his Deputy, Mr. Hesketh Williams also attended. I recall that a good way out of town, almost in the middle of nowhere, was the Office of National Drug and Money Laundering Control Policy. (ONDCP) Whilst I wasn't to visit it until a future trip to Antigua, I had initial difficulty in understanding who had organised it, and what exactly, it did. It was always a pleasant visit because it was a brand new building with AIR CONDITIONING! Something that most other buildings didn't have in St Johns.

The gentleman in charge was a man called Wrenford Ferrance. An unusual or untypical Antiguan, if indeed he was Antiguan.

Senator Wrenford Ferrance
Director of National Drugs and Money Laundering
-Control Policy

He was, however, a friend of the Prime Minister and among the offices held, I saw him described as 'The Prime Minister's Special Advisor on Drugs and Money Laundering'. (I had hoped that this wasn't an indication of how he was to advise the Prime Minister how it should be done!!) What I couldn't understand was, whether this was an operational unit or just an information and intelligence gathering machine. The building was huge and from memory, I cannot recall anyone other than Wrenford, being there. We got on very well though I realised that he would have an interest in being 'pally' because he would have reported directly to the Prime Minister about why and all the wherefores of my presence on the Island. That was a benefit to me but he wasn't that keen to explain these things and so I was forced to try and 'sell' the 'Multi Agency' initiative in the knowledge that whatever this organisation was about, it was definitely in the game of fighting the war against drugs and money laundering. I had a good hunch that the Prime Minister would soon become acquainted with what I was doing.

My subsequent search of the Internet has probably made things a lot clearer because I discovered the below article in an Antiguan Newspaper which concerns the celebration of the ONDCP's eighth year in being. The article was written in January 2012 and so this indicates that its inauguration would have been in 2004, four years after I began to visit Antigua. As suspected, it was obviously in the early planning stages when I first visited it but my 'digging' made me wonder if another Caribbean 'fiddle' had been discovered. Here is the article : -

Friday, 20th January 2012 - By Carib Arena News:-

Lt Col Edward Croft and Prime Minister Spencer

Prime Minister Baldwin Spencer on the right

Antigua St John's - The Office of National Drug and Money Laundering Control Policy (ONDCP) has celebrated its eighth year as one of Antigua & Barbuda's lead specialized law enforcement agencies.

Throughout its existence, the ONDCP has successfully partnered with the Royal Police Force of Antigua & Barbuda, the Antigua & Barbuda Defence Force, the Customs and Excise Department and the Immigration Department.

On January 13, the ONDCP paid tribute to the dedicated men and women of the organisation during a staff appreciation luncheon held at Splash Antigua Ltd. In attendance was Governor General Dame Louise Lake Tack, Prime Minister Baldwin Spencer, and other dignitaries. In his speech to the employees, the prime minister urged the members of the ONDCP to "remain steadfast to your objectives not only when things seem easy, but also when the going gets really tough. Your guiding values are directed by

integrity, objectivity, accountability, professionalism, and loyalty with the underpinnings of a clearly defined vision (to become a lead Caribbean lead law enforcement agency combating illegal narcotics, money laundering, and terrorism financing) and mission (to eliminate transnational drug trafficking, money laundering and the financing of terrorism). These are not simply words and statements but words and statements that must be demonstrative of the character of the women and men who comprise the ONDCP." During the period from January 2007, when the director was appointed to present, the ONDCP has had several successes, resulting in over 12,000 lbs of cannabis and 1,167 kilos of cocaine seized, with an estimated street value of over $193,000,000 or about US$71 M. It was also observed that during the aforementioned period, 101 persons were arrested, and 83 were charged with various offences. Most of the 38 persons convicted have served prison sentences, while the remainder are awaiting trial. Notably, in 2011, cash seizures amounted to over $390,000, while 1,854 lbs of cannabis and 169 kilos of cocaine were seized. The Director, Lt Col Edward Croft, in his presentation attributed the success of his organisation "to the dedicated men and women of our organisation, who as a team of professional law enforcement personnel have diligently aimed to fulfil their mandated duties. He further stated that it is his intention to make Antigua & Barbuda a very unattractive destination for drug trafficking, money laundering or terrorist financing". -IT WENT on...

As a little aside from this recent Newspaper Clipping, the Director of this establishment, as seen next to the Prime Minister in the photograph is Lt Col Edward Croft. When I worked on the Island, Edward was then working as the 'Staff Officer' to the Officer Commanding of the Antigua Defence Force and we got on very well. He was in attendance at my presentation with his Commanding Officer, Colonel Trevor Thomas.

Anyway, back to Wrenford Ferrance and what appeared to me to be in 2000, a one man operation, the ONDCP. Further current research indicates that he was more attuned to financial matters and had been the Director of the International Business Corporation. He had been appointed the first Director of it in 1996 to tackle the lax banking regulations on the Island which encouraged the laundering of money. His building was relatively new and that would fit into that picture. No doubt he had spent a year or two, setting the whole thing up but this above press cutting now explains that the ONDCP is very much an Operational Unit with a strong establishment of officers combating Drugs and Money Laundering offences.

I have mentioned Colonel Trevor Thomas and his Staff officer, Edward Croft above representing the Royal Antigua and Barbuda Defence Force. (RABDF) Well I knew that the Island had a Police Force, an Immigration Department and a Customs Department but what, was such a tiny country doing with an Army? Again, my involvement with them will be explained more fully later but for the time being, just to introduce the main 'players' I had dealt with, suffice to say now, that the Royal Antigua and Barbuda Defence Force, (RABDF) is indeed, the armed force of the Island. It has responsibility for Internal Security, Prevention of Drugs Smuggling, (Bit of an overlap here with the ONDCP) The protection and support of fishing rights, prevention of marine pollution, search and rescue, ceremonial duties, assistance to government programmes, provision of relief during national disasters, assistance in the maintenance of essential services and the support of the police in maintaining law and order. In other words, whatever comes along. I suspect it was the world's smallest military consisting then of 245 people.

Their Commander Trevor Thomas was such a nice man yet he was a giant with such a commanding appearance. When we shook hands, my large hand was smothered by his. There was not an ounce of fat on him and he must have been around 6' 8" tall. In 1982 fourteen men of the Royal Antigua and Barbuda Defence Force were deployed to Grenada during the 'Operation Urgent Fury". In 1990 twelve soldiers were sent to Trinidad after a failed coup attempt by radical Black Muslims against the constitutionally elected government headed by Prime Minister A.N.R. Robinson, and in 1995 members of the force were deployed in Haiti as a Part of 'Operation Uphold Democracy'.

The Immigration Departments of these Islands were always high on my priority list, as the influx of illegal immigrants was a huge problem to these islands. Mind you, I was later to learn that most of their problems were of their own doing. I discovered that whilst all visitors had their passports stamped on arrival and were given a slip of paper concerning their entitlements on the Islands, including their due date for leaving, no records were kept and no follow up enquiries were made. In other words, whilst tourists were allowed a three months stay, they could stay as long as they liked so long as they didn't come to notice. Nobody would be checking!

Mr Edric K. Potter was the Chief Immigration Officer. Whilst they had bases at the Airport, their main Headquarters was at Old Parham Road, St. John's. As described above, they were in a real mess when it came to illegal immigrants. In addition to the airport, the many little docking stations around the island would have made it very easy for lighter vessels to dock. I recall being on a boardwalk on one occasion, when a small yacht tied up and on listening to the conversations as they were filling up with fresh water, I gathered that they had sailed in from Australia. I was there and watched them come in but no official was there waiting to examine passports etc.

Mr. Potter and his Deputy, Clyde Walker were very interested but, again, during my subsequent visits to them, I was always under the impression that their hands were financially tied and, in any event, they were very much controlled by those in power and responsible for security matters at the highest Government level. I also made friends with the Superintendent in charge of Airport Security, Errol George and the Port Authorities Manager, Raphael Benjamin and once again, whilst their thirsts were whetted, the procurement of this equipment was a matter way above their heads. It was, however, nevertheless necessary for me to impress them with the equipment because the benefits would obviously be passed on to their masters.

My rapid visits around the Island also included the Customs and Prison Departments but some of these visits will have occurred on later visits due to my tight timescale. However, the day after the presentation, I went to the Legal Affairs and Customs Department, The Defence Force at Camp Blizzard and to visit the Head Airport Security officer at the Airport.

Following other visits on 5th October, I took Henry Christian out to Dinner. He had been so helpful to me in guiding me around the Island. It was he who also took me to the airport for my return flight to London. I found all who I met on Antigua very personable and overall, my impressions of it were favourable though I couldn't rid myself of the smell of corruption. My first official visit to the Caribbean countries was over and I enjoyed it though it was a hard slog. I was soon to return.

Chapter 24 – Meeting Interpol, and off to Jamaica and Barbados.

With just one complete day back at home, I was off again to Heathrow Airport to meet Pat Pitt and Dave Moffatt at the Hilton hotel for an update meeting. Dave was an Ex Greater Manchester Police officer who had since joined us. Pat was obviously anxious to learn how I had progressed on Antigua. It was on the next day, 10th October that I flew to Lyon ahead of the others to set up a meeting with Interpol during the next day.

It was also on that same date, that my AFRC contract was changed to remove restrictions on the contracted days. But, in addition to financially benefitting me, it would also benefit the Consortium. Nevertheless, it allow me to work extra days taking into account the work for SMI that I had been doing. Clearly, that was an indication that my AFRC work was not going to shrink and my AFRC contract had been extended to 30th June 2001 which, according to the Consortium Management Agreement, (CMA) was the last day on which the AFR Consortium would operate. Whatever, I would be working to the bitter end.

Having set myself up at the Lyon Hilton hotel, I later returned to the Airport to pick up the other AFRC presenters. I also received a note to the effect that an additional eight Livescan sites had agreed to extend their contracts beyond the 'Exit' date. (Overrun Forces). That brought the total so far to 31.

Our joint presentation was given to Interpol officials and members during the next day. I have already written how impressed I was with this 'state of the art' building and its security measures. The room where we made the presentation was similarly 'state of the art'. Once again, my job was to drum up excitement about the project and deliver the operational prospective.

We had had some tremendous successes with Livescan so mentioning some individual cases helped to offset the inevitable boredom that reiterating statistics brings. These were the occasions which taught me that if you need to sell something, then being excited about the product breeds excitement into others. Our presentations went down very well. In addition to myself presenting the 'operational' perspective, Pat and Richard Kemp our City Lawyer of Kemp & Co spoke of how they too, saw things unfolding. JCR was now in his homeland France, so I expect there were more in the audience who would have understood his SMI perspective. Finally, from our side, Ray Elvy gave the Fingerprint Expert's point of view.

This was a 'two way' joint presentation not only from AFR to Interpol but from Interpol to us. In that respect, Peter Nevitt, Interpol's Systems Director opened the batting for them followed by many of the Interpol executives all of whom, showed every sign of their desire to join us. By this time, the film that we had been making was now in full publication and it featured Peter Nevitt from Interpol introducing it and persuading countries to join the Project - it was called "The AFR Service Bureau' - Making the World a Safer Place - The Biometric Partnership. Showing it saved me a lot of explaining. I have a copy in my office.

Three days later, on 15th October 2000, I arrived in Jamaica for my first visit there. Its police force had a peculiar name – 'The Jamaica Constabulary Force'. I thought that perhaps they couldn't make up their minds so they plumped for using both 'Constabulary and Force'!

In addition to JCR's French accent, of all the problems I had in the Caribbean, it was here in Jamaica that I had the most difficulty in understanding the local dialect. It was spat out like a machine gun and so difficult to understand. On many occasions I needed to feign deafness and ask people to repeat a little slower. It was embarrassing, but I think I got away with it.

I was to stay at the Crown Plaza hotel and then fly directly to Barbados on 24th October and return home on 1st November. This was a total of sixteen days in Jamaica and Barbados and in both countries my aim was to similarly meet with top Police Chiefs and Government ministers to hopefully persuade them to sign up to this joint agency Interpol fingerprint initiative.

The Crown Plaza hotel was far better than my hotel in Antigua though my reception at their fingerprint bureau opened up a nightmare of fear and suspicion. They did not want to release their fingerprints into our possession to be loaded and searched, and in addition, unlike most other countries, no weeding of their records had ever occurred. I was to discover tenprints belonging to criminals who by then, would have been well over 100 years of age. My vision snapped to one of these 'ton up' boys climbing up a drainpipe to commit a burglary. No way could I persuade them that their tenprints ought to be destroyed. The 'you never know' syndrome had clicked in and to go through each of the thousands of tenprint cards conducting a weeding exercise, would have lasted for ever. Oh, what a mess.

However, excepting Deputy Superintendent Harrison, the head of bureau who was all 'doom and gloom', I grew to be very close to the staff in the Jamaica Bureau. I learned that their predecessors working there had been trained many years ago by a team of Metropolitan Police Officers. Their training and methods, including methods of classifying fingerprints, had not been updated since those early days. They were working on 'hand me down' methods which were hopelessly out of date.

The problem we had, was that all other Caribbean countries firmly believed that much of their crime was being committed by travelling Jamaican criminals visiting their islands. This was a situation much like in England where most forces believed that travelling criminals originated from Merseyside. There was no way that other Caribbean countries would sign up for a paid, networked fingerprint service if Jamaica were not going to be included. We therefore had to help them as much as possible and I was very much aware that because Jamaica held many more out of date fingerprint forms than other countries that we would eventually agree to increasing their free load by doubling the agreed 10,000.

Crime in Jamaica was dealt with by the CIB. (Criminal Investigation Bureau) The Fingerprint Bureau was an integral part of it. The fingerprint bureau for Kingston was located at East Queen Street and apart from visits to the Force's Headquarters at Old Hope Road, that was where I spent most of my time. In the early days, I just had to persuade those working in the Bureau that an Automatic Fingerprint Identification System (AFIS) was just what they wanted. Seeing Government officials and those Chief Officers at Headquarters would be a waste of time if I couldn't persuade the bureau staff and most of all, Deputy Superintendent, Harrison, that that was going to help them. He was to prove exceedingly difficult and I needed every persuasive tactic to make him believe that I wasn't there on any other agenda.

It wasn't as if they didn't need help. It's difficult for me to describe what a lawless country I found Jamaica to be. There was constant talk of gang warfare, drugs dealing and murders occurring every day. The National

Newspaper was 'The Gleaner' and on its front page it gave a running total each day of the numbers of murders occurring during the past 24 hours.

I later searched the Internet for such stories and the following found during 2010 might go some way to paint the picture, in addition to being an interesting read:-

From 'The Gleaner' Feb 3rd 2010

As the Jamaica Constabulary Force (JCF) implements strategies to tackle the country's crime problem, it has embarked on a process to improve investigative capability within the ranks of the Criminal Investigation Bureau (CIB).

*"We are putting a lot of focus on building the capacity of the CIB. We are looking for people with the right aptitude, energy and discipline to build that capacity," said Senior Superintendent Carlton Wilson, the officer in charge of investigation and training there. (NOTE: Carlton was one of my contacts there. A good man but was a Detective Superintendent in the **'Personnel'** Dept. of CIB)*

Wilson said, subsequent to evaluations, a number of CIB personnel could be reassigned to areas where their skills are better suited. CIB personnel are largely responsible for investigating major crimes such as homicides, robberies and shootings.

The senior superintendent said his team would be intensifying its probe of the existing 180 gangs operating island-wide. More than 870 persons were slain in gang-related incidents last year. The JCF Major Crime Statistics revealed that 1,680 people were murdered last year, 1,293 of that number victim to the gun.

Only 481 of those murders were detected. However, cleared-up conclusions include the fatal shooting of suspects, without necessarily harnessing sufficient physical or circumstantial evidence linking suspects to offences.

The crime statistics also indicated that CIB personnel effected fewer arrests compared with the previous year.

Gleaner again Published: Tuesday | May 25, 2010

The armed forces yesterday strongly repelled the relentless firepower of gunmen, allegedly from Fletcher's Land, **who launched an assault on the Central Police Station in Jamaica's capital, Kingston.**

*A **Gleaner** news team was pinned down for more than 40 minutes at the intersection of East and East Queen streets in downtown Kingston as militants loyal to reputed gangster Christopher 'Dudus' Coke' traded bullets with the police.*

The gunmen, apparently emboldened by the attacks on six police stations a day earlier, turned their venom on the Central Police Station. But alert crime fighters hit back with a vengeance, resulting in a fierce gun battle around the headquarters of Kingston CIB.

A day earlier, the Hannah Town Police Station was attacked, pillaged and burnt. So too were the Fletcher's Land, Darling Street and Denham Town stations in western Kingston. The Spanish Town and Cross Roads stations were also fired on.

As the guns blazed, terrified civilians going about their business in the downtown commercial centre - less busy not only because of the spiralling violence but on account of a national holiday - scampered for cover in just about every direction. This story continued to be described – **BUT THIS EAST QUEEN STREET POLICE STATION WAS WHERE THE BUREAU WAS LOCATED AND WHERE I HAD BEEN WORKING.**

Jamaica News: 46 Jamaican murdered in the past 12 days or 96 for the second month of 2010

The crime doesn't stop and it seems we have no slowing down in sight, about 46 murders in the past 12 days or 96 for the month of February 2010. If we should count the 145 from last month, we would have 241 murders for the first two month of 2010. The crime in Jamaica is so bad that if the local media should report each and every murder incident each day their website and gleaner will be filled with murder incident and they won't have space for other important social news and events. Ask what to do? Where to start? And it seems no one knows how, or care to put a stop to this, it's just not on the front burner it's not a priority.

There we have the picture, but at least East Queen Street was never attacked by gunfire whilst I worked there. However, I was to learn of a situation which took some believing. It was because of this relentless gun warfare that the CIB decided to patrol in unmarked cars with plain clothed officers armed with machine guns. When called upon, they would dash to such incidents and blast away with their machine guns. The problem was, that the gangs thought this to be a good idea so they also patrolled the streets in unmarked cars with their occupants carrying machine guns! You see, the public weren't to know the difference between the covert Police and the gangsters. The Police had provided the hoodlums with the perfect cover in which they could go about shooting down members of their enemy gangs. WHAT!

You wouldn't catch me going on holiday to Jamaica man! My report about Jamaica obviously included the fact that I needed help in the Bureau and this was to be forthcoming in future visits. We also needed to see Frankie Forbes, the Commissioner who was proving notoriously difficult to contact and track down. I tell you; you could write a novel!

To carry on to Barbados was something of a relief. I took a taxi to the Grand Barbados hotel which was alright but not top quality. Its location was perfect though, right on the beach with another of those little piers leading out into the ocean and where the hotel's restaurant was located above that clear blue Caribbean sea. The unfortunate memory of my stay, however, concerns an evening when I swam in those beautiful waters, right into a swarm of Jellyfish. I can only describe the sensation as being perhaps similar to falling naked into a load of stinging nettles except that these stingers really hurt.

I went to reception soaking wet and paraded my stings to the staff. The one said, "You need some alcohol". My dreams of a large glass of whiskey were soon dashed when she produced a bottle of neat alcohol and cotton wool to bathe my stings.

My work on Barbados was not without its difficulties as I shall explain later but on the plus side, I was to be adopted by a readymade office of personnel who had been put together to administer the Association of Caribbean Commissioners of Police. (ACCP) Just as the ACPO Secretariat in London administer the ACPO Association of England and Wales, the ACCP office looked after the Caribbean equivalent. Yes, I was to be their friend and what's more, they had bright and cheery air conditioned offices right next door to the 'Virgin' travel offices, plenty of paper and stationery requirements and a photocopier. I was sure that they would help me proffer the 'Proof of Concept' initiative in whatever way they could.

The hotel restaurant at the end of the pier.

The Grand Barbados hotel, just outside Bridgetown town but within walking distance.

The actual address of the office was Ground Floor, Parravicino Office Complex, Hastings, Christ Church, Barbados. To top it all, the office was being run by an ex Metropolitan Police Officer, (I think an ex Inspector) by the name of John Parker. He was coming to the end of his secondment and the plan was, that having set it up, he would be succeeded by his then Deputy, Keith Renaud a Superintendent seconded from the Trinidad and Tobago Force. The support staff comprised of two lovely ladies – Marcia Manning a researcher from Jamaica and Shirley, the secretary and switchboard operator. I couldn't have wished for better support and I was welcomed so much so, that they included me in their weekly Jamaican 'Pattie' lunch. These were homemade meat pastries much like a Cornish pasty which, I think were made by Marcia.

One of the ACCP Office's jobs was to produce a regular magazine for all their Caribbean Commissioners and I knew that their hospitality was going to end in my doing something for them. They asked me if I would write an article for this magazine and I naturally agreed because this was another way in which I could get the message circulated about the Caribbean. I later wrote the article which with Pat's final touches and SMI images, eventually was published under Pat's name. More on that later.

As if this ACCP office wasn't already a great help to me, I was accidentally to enrol the help of a very high official no less than the Attorney General and Deputy Prime Minister, Sir David Simmons. (Name dropping again!) Sir David was one of the nicest and most honourable men I have ever met both at home and abroad. I had been busying myself around the usual offices of Customs, Prisons, Immigration, and Airport Security etc. and out of courtesy, I spoke to his secretary and through her, I arranged a meeting with him to appraise him of the nature of my visit. He wished me well and his assistance came during my second visit to his offices following my having difficulty with the Chief Immigration Officer. More on that later, but for now, here is what I discovered about Sir David on the Internet:-

Sir David Anthony Simmons – Courtesy of Google Images

Sir David Anthony Simmons K.A., B.C.H., Q.C., LL.M. (Lond.). *entered the Faculty of Law at the London School of Economics and Political Science in 1960 and graduated with an LL.B. degree in 1963. After additional reading he was awarded an LL.M. degree in 1965. Sir David lectured in law in London until his return to Barbados in 1970. Between 1970 and 1974, he was a part-time lecturer in law at the Faculty of Law of the University of the West Indies.*

Sir David has had an outstanding career as a lawyer in Barbados and was appointed Queen's Counsel in 1984. He served continuously for 25 years in the Parliament of Barbados from February 1976 to August 2001, on which date he retired from active politics. Twice he served as Attorney-General of Barbados; first, from 1985 to 1986, and, more recently, from September 1994 to August 2001. On many occasions during the latter period, Sir David acted as Prime Minister of Barbados. He assumed office as the 12th Chief Justice of Barbados on 1 January 2002.In 2003, he was made an Honorary Fellow of the U.W.I. and was also awarded the Honorary degree of Doctor of Laws (LL.D.) by the University of London - the first Caribbean person to be accorded that high distinction by that University. In 2006, Sir David was elected as an Honorary Bencher of the Honourable Society of Lincoln's Inn, the Inn of Court at which he qualified as a Barrister-at-Law. As Attorney-General, Sir David presided over many initiatives and esteemed conferences including being Chairman of the Preparatory Committee to establish the Caribbean Court of Justice (1999-2001); first Chairman of the Regional Judicial and Legal Services Commission (2003-2004). In 2001, for his contribution to public service, law and politics, he was awarded the Barbados Centennial Honour (B.C.H.), and Barbados' highest national honour, Knight of St. Andrew (K.A.). He is currently Chairman of the Integrity Commission in Turks and Caicos and will be appointed member and Chairman of the Commission of Enquiry into the 1990 coup attempt in Trinidad.

With apologies for my poor photograph of Sir David Simmons here, but I had to capture the helmet which he had on display in his office.

The main objective of my first visit to Barbados was therefore to identify and introduce myself to the main 'Security' players on the Island. I cannot recall whether I demonstrated the Morpho Touch on this occasion or not, because I know that I made two or three more visits as will be touched upon later. I can recall a somewhat amusing incident, however, that I know happened on this visit. It was a very hot weekend and as I was to dress down on weekends, I dressed in shorts and sandals.

My sandals, however, were beginning to rub blisters on my heels and I didn't want to wear ordinary socks with them so I decided, therefore, that I would walk into Bridgetown and purchase a pair or two of white sports socks.

The weather was so hot that I took a plastic bag so that I could carry in it, one of the hotel's small towels with which I could wipe away my perspiration. I was also wearing my sunglasses. Having purchased the socks and put them on, I began the very hot walk back to the hotel which was quite a precarious walk due to having to jump over the open drains and sewers that were regularly encountered. I had also to pass by a number of 'Rum Shacks'. These were small wooden and corrugated iron buildings much like a larger than average garden shed. Their purpose was to sell rum and not much else. They were full of locals and to be honest, they weren't places where I would normally want to be.

However, I was so hot and bothered and what with a very large cold coke machine staring out at me from within one of them, I couldn't resist going in to get one. As I walked towards the machine, a very loud Australian accent greeted me from my right but the owner was in a dark corner and out of view. I heard, "What's a 'white face one' like you doing in here matey" or words to that affect.

I turned around to find the only other 'white faced one' in the shack, drinking a large rum and coke. I wish I could remember his name but his amicable character and his persuasive techniques were responsible for me agreeing to join him. He poured the Gay Rum from a half bottle and the coke which then came in tall glass bottles. The cost was negligible and even so, I wasn't going to accept his hospitality without reciprocating. I bought a half bottle of rum and some coke and then he bought another, and so it went on. I was there for some considerable time and I began to get hungry, as I do – very often. I asked the barman if he had any food on the premises and I hoped for a packet of crisps or similar. He dived into his back room and in his naked hand, returned, holding high, a large chicken leg. "Is this OK Man"? He enquired. I would have eaten anything and with my hand, took the large chicken leg out of his hand and ate it. Hmmmn not really the thing to do, but in my condition, I had no worries. Anyway, my new found friend explained that he had earlier that day, moored a yacht at Bridgetown harbour and that he had skippered it full of young people across from Airley Beach, Australia on what I gathered to be some sort of youth 'Outward Bound' mission.

It wasn't until later, that I wondered why, only recently having arrived, he had ended up in that rum shack as the only 'white faced one' occupying it. I had no evidence at all, but suspected that he may have been drugs running. I often passed his yacht but never bumped into him again as the yacht was always deserted.

One of the many Rum Shacks along Bay Street Bridgetown which was on my route into town.

Anyway, many hours later, I managed to walk to the hotel feeling very much the effects of the rum. I can recall telling myself to breathe in and out very heavily and to watch out for those damned open drains and whoever it was that was responsible for spinning the world around. I had a vague recollection of calling into the Shell Service Station and buying a 'pattie' or two. I may well have said hello to the chap who often stood outside leaning over the fence of the Police Boxing Club but all was vague and, in a daze, it was to bed I went.

I woke with a stir and in a hot sweat which was easy to do in that heat. Something had, however, caused me to wake with a start and I immediately knew that it was my sub consciousness – I had left that plastic bag behind in the rum shack and not only did it contain the hotel's towel, but it also had my expensive sun glasses in it – those which change the level of shade with the light density. I wasn't the type that would want to lose a hotel towel, nor fork out for a new pair of sunglasses!

I lay awake for some time wondering if I could ever find that particular rum shack. Although they were all along the same road, they all looked alike and there were dozens of them. Daybreak came and it was a Sunday. My first port of call was the Shell Garage and I persuaded them that I definitely put my bag down somewhere when I bought the patties. I couldn't remember whether I had or hadn't but I thought that if I told them that I had, then they would make more effort to find it.

The main Police Station in Bridgetown, Barbados which contained the Fingerprint Bureau. Police Headquarters were almost opposite.

All to no avail and so I then came upon the Boxing Club and asked the guy if he saw me walking home that night. He actually remembered me walking back to the hotel but couldn't say whether or not I was carrying the plastic bag. I therefore began to pass rum shack after rum shack and each one that was open, I made the enquiry. I soon discovered that they were all designed almost identically – one square room with a bar across and invariably a Coke machine and a small store room at the back. After two or three, I walked into the next one and without even asking, the chap said, "Ah Mr. Humphrey. (Never said in the West Indies as Humphreys with an 'S' at the end) You left your bag here last night man". God, I must have introduced myself. Without any ado, he disappeared into his back room and presented me with my bag which was all intact.

I couldn't believe it. Whilst crime in Barbados was bad, as in most Islands, it wasn't a touch on Jamaica, but I never ever believed that such honesty would prevail as was then demonstrated. I had thought that I would have been on a fool's mission. My tour on this first visit to Barbados involved me being mostly at the local Police Station and the Police Headquarters which were in the same street but on the opposite sides of the road. The buildings were very handy to the city centre and just a few blocks behind F. W. Woolworths or at least in that direction. I also visited the Airport Immigration Section and went to the Immigration Headquarters which were near the Marina. It was then that I found the Chief Immigration Officer, Gilbert Greaves very difficult to meet. His Secretary, Ann Carter constantly told me that he was either not in or at a meeting and it was becoming obvious to me that he suspected that I was some sort of travelling salesman.

My second visit to see Sir David Simmons was not about this but when he asked me how I was getting on, I told him that everyone was very supportive but that I hadn't managed to see Gilbert Greaves who was always busy or out of his office. Without any ado, he picked up his telephone and very politely asked his secretary to get Gilbert Greaves on the phone.

I was getting a little extra hot under the collar as I was never one to cause a fuss and I wondered how this telephone conversation would go. Sir David had already given me an extraordinary length of time and was truly taken up with the concept of this Interpol Caribbean initiative. He was so intelligent that he could foresee the importance of it. He had taken pains to understand it thoroughly by allowing me to give him a full version of how I saw it rather than a summary. He was definitely on our side and he could see how it would be very useful to the Immigration Department. I later learned that he had chaired the enquiry into the attempted coup of Trinidad and Tobago and quite frankly, I could see why he wanted the Immigration procedures tightening on Barbados.

The phone rang and of course, I could only here Sir David's side of the conversation. I was thankful that he did not divulge my presence. He asked Greaves if I had visited him etc etc. and exclaimed his surprise when Greaves obviously told him that I hadn't. He was looking after my longer term interests and without any 'ifs or buts' he told him that I should be seen as soon as possible before I returned to the UK and that he should report the outcome to him "because this was something that Barbados badly needed" – etc. etc.

On my return to the hotel, I found a message on my 'Ansa phone' from Mr Greaves' secretary. I would have loved to have ignored it for a day or two but I was on a tight time scale. I was in his office the next day but sensed that he didn't want to know. He was merely bowing to The Attorney General's demands. A horrible man, I thought. His attitude was that this was work, and had nothing to do with benefitting the Island. We wouldn't be doing business with Immigration, the airport or with works permits which sadly, also fell under Greaves' umbrella.

Another interesting man I met, was the Comptroller of Customs, Captain Randolph A. Straughan otherwise known as 'Randy'. He was the challenging type, completely open and opposite to Greaves. On the down side, rumour had it that he was so ambitious, that he wanted to be in charge of the Island. Other rumours suggested that if you wanted anything imported with no fuss then you'd better get in touch with Randy who could 'organise it'.

On my side, was the fact that he was a Rotarian; not that that meant that he was 'Lilly White', though he may well have been. He took me to a meeting of his Club at the Accra Beach hotel and treated me to lunch. The first thing I thought about was, "Why wasn't I stopping here?" It was a beautiful hotel, again right on the beach but the quality of it was far better than at the Grand Barbados, where I was staying. Whilst it was further out of town at Christ Church, it was closer to the ACCP Office where I had based myself. It was also a lot closer to the airport. Tremendous reviews can be found about it on the Internet.

Randy asked me why I wasn't booked in there and I suggested that it was probably well over my daily room rate allowance. The receptionist almost jumped to attention as he approached her and he discovered that it wasn't after all, that much more expensive there. I was to stay there on my subsequent visits and indeed I showed it off to Jo when she later joined me for a holiday.

At that time, Captain Randolph Straughan was the Comptroller of Customs but since then, my search for an image of him reveals that he has almost achieved his goal of being in charge of the Island. As can be seen in the photograph below, he became a Permanent Secretary of the Ministry of Defence and Security. I found him to be a very nice chap who enjoyed a good time. So far as the project went, he was all for it. So far as the Police were concerned, the Commissioner, Grantley Weston saw me and introduced me to his Deputy Laurie Boyce and his own Staff Officer, Deputy Superintendent John Collymore. I also worked very well with the Head of the CID, Senior Superintendent Emmerson Moore who was also in charge of the Fingerprint Bureau. Barbados was to become a success and I can recount when, on a subsequent visit we held a party in the Fingerprint Bureau to celebrate their first Murder Mark Identification.

'Randy' on the left with the Barbados Prime Minister

On my final day, I paid visits to the Work Permit office, the Customs Offices again and as Sir David Simmons asked me to return for a summary report, I called in at his offices to do just that and to say cheerio. I'm not sure whether it was on this occasion or later that Sir David mentioned that they were looking for a replacement for a Chief Security Manager at the famous 'Sandy Lane' hotel and golf complex. Jo and I were taken there during our holiday and I couldn't believe what a Marvelous place it was. We got on so well and there was no doubting that I could have been living there now, if I wanted but having tasted life in the Caribbean, there would be no way that I would swap home for it, even though I had been offered a plumb job there.

Chapter 25 - CCLEC Meeting, Trinidad and Antigua Againxx

I had only been at home for 10 days when, on 11th November, 2000 I set off again on another Island hopping trip which wouldn't see me back home until 2nd December and then only for five days before I was to be off again. This time I was being based at the Hilton hotel, Trinidad and Tobago to attend an annual meeting of the CCLEC.

We pronounced it as 'seecleck'. The acronym is for CARIBBEAN CUSTOMS LAW ENFORCEMENT COUNCIL. They met on a different Island each year and this year it was to be at The Hilton hotel, in Port of Spain, the Capital of Trinidad.

It was to be a great platform on which we could hopefully 'sell' the concept of AFIS to those not yet initiated in its value. There were ninety one delegates and observers representing forty nine countries or agencies to this conference all in this very large hotel. There were delegates from Anguilla, Antigua, Bahamas, Barbados, Bermuda, British Virgin Isles, Canada, Cayman Islands, Cuba, Dominica, Dominican Republic, France, Granada, Guyana, Haiti, Jamaica, Mexico, Montserrat, Netherlands Antilles, Netherlands, St Lucia, St Vincent, Trinidad and Turks and Caicos.

However, **in addition** to these countries' normal Law Enforcement agencies, there were also representatives from all of the countries contained in the chart below. I have since forgotten the meaning of some of the acronyms but for sure, there were always more than one delegate from each and in some cases, many more.

Not only was Ray Elvy and I to have a major slot to present our system to the delegates en block, we were to set up a large presentation and demonstration stall in one of the foyers of the hotel so that we could give individual, or small group demonstrations.

I had arrived on 11th November 2000, two days prior to the commencement of this three day conference with Sagem Engineer, David Boyle and Ray Elvy. As can be seen, just about every Customs and Security agencies from most parts of the world, were represented. We couldn't believe that the

UK (Home Office)	ECDCO
US Customs Service	IADB Washington US
JIO Puerto Rico	ICC New York
CCLEC Office	IMO
ACCP	Interpol
AFR CONSORTIUM	Louis Vuitton C&E
Australian Customs	Overseas Territories Office
Caribbean Export	Project Management Office Barbados
CIFAD Martinique	
DFID Barbados British High Commission	REDTRAC Jamaica
	RSS Barbados
Digital Port Control Canada	UNCTAD Geneva
ONDCP Antigua	UNDCP Barbados

equipment we were to set up for this 'CUSTOMS LED' conference had actually been held up in a Customs shed on this very Island, Trinidad. I spent over a whole day, pleading with Trinidad's Comptroller of Customs who, of course, was himself a conference delegate, and despite his making phone calls, it seemed as though we were never going to get the equipment set up in time for their conference. In some perverse way, I was itching to apologise to the conference during my presentation that we could not actually demonstrate it because it was being held up by the Trinidadian Customs. What an embarrassment and shambles, but he didn't appear too concerned; I suppose this was typical of the 'West Indies'.

Fortunately, I knew a man!! A very good Rotarian friend in Worcester, Paul Westcott had a son Simon, who was then living in Port of Spain. (And still does). He married a Trinidadian girl and Simon was running her family's Construction Company on the Island. I knew Simon and his parent's very well and had already been in contact with him prior to me landing on Trinidad. Fortunately, that year, Simon was President of the Port of Spain Rotary Club. His father had been my club's president. We had already met and he had invited me to lunch with his club and so out of desperation, I rang him to tell him of my plight. I couldn't believe that I was getting nowhere with the host Comptroller of Customs and so Simon took me to the 'Customs Sheds' where we chatted them up and told them of our plight. I eventually got it delivered and we just managed to get it up and running as the delegates were arriving. No thanks to the Comptroller of their Customs though.

Now viewing the photographs below, I can emphasise that this wasn't a convention with several suppliers stands etc. We were the only presenters with such a display. I was to attend other similar conferences in the Caribbean but this was by far the best, so far as the 'social scene' was concerned. For a start, the hotel was very nice, probably the best in Port of Spain. The rooms, restaurants and facilities including a very large outdoor pool and stage area were great. We also made many friends of the delegates and I recall that although the Cubans had difficulty with English, they were very keen on our system and I had made tentative arrangements to visit their delegation in Cuba in the future – unfortunately a trip which did not come to fruition.

Our AFIS Stand at the 2000 Annual Caribbean Customs Conference even though Customs had held up the equipment.

Being able to chat to the many delegates who visited our display did, to a certain extent, soften the blow so far as my nerves were concerned, about having to stand on the podium and address this huge room of delegates. I felt that I had already made friends with them. Also, by now, my presentation had been given so often that I had grown in confidence. I have already mentioned that we had made the video film which more than adequately explained what the system was all about. Showing that first also helped me. I trust that I displayed my usual amount of excitement about the system and the results we had achieved thus far.

The other plus about this conference was that CCLEC had laid on a lavish party at the end of the conference. This was to be on the poolside stage and included some magnificent evening entertainment. The food and alcoholic drinks were marvellous and all absolutely free gratis. I could have paid a very hefty price to see such a show. It would have been good enough for any top London theatre. Dancing girls, audience participation with limbo dancing, just about everything, and it was very professionally presented.

The balloons were out for the show that night

The show wasn't all play for me because my job was to ensure that we engendered as much interest in our system as possible. If ever I pretended that I wasn't a travelling salesman then this was proof enough that I had been lying to myself. I chatted up the organiser of the conference and persuaded him to let me have a copy of details of all of the delegates on a 3.5 floppy disc. This was great because having printed off a copy, I was able to make notes against the names of those showing interest so that I could perhaps follow up the contacts. This meant that I would be writing to them at the first opportunity.

And so, my six frustrating but enjoyable nights at the Hilton, Port of Spain came to an end and after checking out on the day following the end of the conference. I flew to Antigua for my second visit there to follow up on the contacts I had already made. That first trip which was hastily arranged as I left Bermuda, was far too short to thoroughly investigate whether it was worthy of persevering with this poor country. It was only the new 'Office of National

Drug and Money Laundering Control Policy' building (ONDCP) which had sprung from foreign aid which made me believe that there was at least, half a chance.

The beauty of making return visits to these Islands was that, during initial visits, I could identify better hotels in which to stay. Whilst the Royal Antiguan Resort had been fine, its location was not the best and the fabric of the hotel was looking a little tired. I had eyed up a better beach location at the Rex Halcyon Cove on Dickenson Bay.

The lovely beach housed a few large hotels including 'Sandals' but the beach wasn't that commercialised or over populated. The rooms at this Rex Halcyon Beach hotel, were all similar to chalets at ground level with a veranda and little patio as seen on the photo below. The patio area led straight onto a very nice area of grass with a pool in the centre and from these grounds, the beach was directly accessed.

In addition, the approach to the hotel was at the end of a cul-de-sac which also contained some little shops and cafes belonging to the hotel. It was a nice set up and I particularly enjoyed the private patio on which I could work with my laptop.

It was a short walk to the end of the beach and I recall one evening after work, that whilst swimming in the sea, I saw on the horizon, the figure of a man wind surfing on this calm blue, Caribbean Sea. He appeared to be miles away but as he got nearer to the beach, he became more into view. I dreamed that I would love to be able to do that and I watched him from being a little dot on the horizon until he alighted his board very close to where I stood. I couldn't help commenting to him how I envied him. We started to chat and I discovered that he had a very heavy Australian accent and many years previously, he had spent a holiday at the Siboney Beach hotel which was a smaller hotel but right behind us on the beach. He must have had plenty of money, because he told me that he had enjoyed his stay there so much, that he bought the hotel!! Not to overrun my story, but I'll just say that I stopped in that hotel on my next and last trip to Antigua.

On this trip, I was to stay for nine nights until 26th November and to cut out all the drivel of exactly where I went and who I met, I will just say that my mission included me seeing all those I needed to see at The Police Headquarters, Customs, Immigration, Antigua Defence Force and the ONDCP Drugs Unit. On this occasion, I had already persuaded the Antiguan powers that be, that Antigua should take part in our 'Proof of Concept' pilot. The bureau seemed to have no system at all, so much of my time there, was spent on helping them to prepare the 10,000 Tenprints we would be shipping to Tacoma for acquiring onto our system.

I found the Commissioner, Truehart Smith a truly likeable character and I'm pleased to say, that outside our business, we became good friends. I was able to pop and see him at any time when he was free and, in his office, and we had long chats together. He would have been draining me of information and ensuring that I was 'on side'. Little did he know then, that he needed our assistance because what I found in the way of fingerprint bureau skills and systems wasn't anyway near par when compared with other Caribbean countries. Truehart had recently been married. I'm not sure whether or not this was his first marriage, but he explained that as it was impossible to invite me to his wedding because I was not on the Island, he wanted to invite me to attend a weekend luncheon at his house with other friends.

It was many years later in 2012, that I discovered that Truehart, then retired, had been subject of an enquiry that unearthed the fact that the hotel he hired for his wedding reception, had not charged him for it!! I couldn't have believed he was the corruptible type and I didn't learn of the outcome, but corruption was so easy to unveil in such countries, anyway, the garden party / dinner he laid on was very enjoyable. I felt honoured to be invited.

The Bureau staff consisted of just a couple of officers with Inspector Henry Christian in charge. I may been wrong but there seemed to be no exact system of filing and although they may have been taught years ago about the 'Henry' system of classifications, the piles of Tenprints I saw strewn around a small room among exhibits from crime scenes etc. made me pretty convinced that they required a system.

I had arranged for our fingerprint 'Coffins' to be shipped there and filled with their 10,000 quota of tenprints so that they could be acquired to our system and have their serious crime marks searched against them. I couldn't help wondering how they were going to sort them out. My help would have been absolutely useless in that sort of area because, of course, I was not a trained fingerprint expert. I was there mainly to look after the logistics of getting them packed and shipped to Tacoma.

This photo shows just three of the hundreds of silver metal boxes we used to ship tenprints to the Central Site in Tacoma from the Caribbean Islands. We referred to them as 'coffins'.

Henry Christian was once again very helpful to me and frequently acted as my chauffeur. He had his own vehicle but I think he was paid a mileage allowance.

It was necessary for me to walk past Antigua's Fire Station where I saw many fire engines which had been built by Carmichaels of Worcester. The Carmichael family was a well-known to me and I associated with a few of them. Derek Carmichael was a member of our Rotary Club and his father; John was once a respected Chairman of Worcester Magistrates. Readers may recall that it was from Derek Carmichael's car hire business that I hired the van to convey us to IBM Warwick to retrieve the DODs containing our data.

The Fingerprint Officers busy in their Fingerprint Bureau which is just an annex office to Insp. Christian's Office which can be seen through the door below

When in charge of West Mercia's Operations Department, I also commissioned Duncan Carmichael of the 'Fire Engines' part of the family business, to design a prototype police personnel carrier for use in riotous situations. It had been the era of Liverpool's Toxteth riots. I felt a little sheepish because by the time they had completed a very good prototype Police Support Unit (PSU) vehicle to demonstrate, the riots going on in the UK at that time, had seen their course – 'Riots, what Riots?' (Another Story)

Anyway, I decided that Derek and his family might appreciate a photograph of their Carmichael Fire Engines outside of the St John, Antigua Fire Station.

Henry Christian had, in fact, been looking after me from the minute I arrived. The next day was a Saturday and Henry rang me early to ask what I was doing.

My bewildered non-plussed answer was good enough for him to offer to take me out for the day and evening. I didn't know what was in store for me when he told me that on Saturdays, officers of the Force would be carrying out firearms training. He asked me if I would like to go to the firearms range to have a look. I was in the middle of writing my report on what I had been up to but was bored to death with doing that so I gladly accepted, but obviously didn't know what to expect. I had retired from a police force which possessed perhaps the most modern Firearms Training School in the world, I knew that I wasn't going to experience anything quite as good but I had no idea how poor it was going to be.

Off we went into the countryside where we eventually reached a field. I was absolutely amazed at what I was to witness. The range was just how I have described it, a field. At the one end of it was a man-made hump of earth which was obviously designed to stop the bullets that missed, or went through the targets. There were no buildings in the field but at the side of it, against a high hedge had been erected an awning so that the waiting officers could benefit from some shade. A few cars, some with Police livery, were parked around this awning and there were about twenty officers all in their weekend gear – jeans and other casual wear.

The area around the awning housed a few empty wooden cable reels which, when turned on their sides, made tables. Crates which had contained bottles of Heineken beer, were also used as seats and the contents of them had been placed in a tub of iced water. On the makeshift tables, they played dominoes and drank the beer at the same time until it was their turn to shoot. Yes,

SHOOTING practice during a domino and beer session!!! I couldn't believe what I saw.

Anyway, who was I, to make any sort of judgment or comment? I was being taken out by one of their senior officers, in fact as the photo shows, they gave me a gun to have a go. (After a few drinks, naturally!) Yes, I was firearms training with the Royal Antiguan Constabulary during a boozing session – heaven forbid! We spent two or three hours on the shooting range and then we took off in Henry's car. I had no idea where we were going but my stomach was beginning to rumble which told me that it was about lunch time.

I suppose we had travelled ten to twenty miles when Henry pulled up on the side of the road adjacent to a wooden shack type hut which had been built in the shape of a roadside cafe. Benches and a few tables were outside the main structure and obviously many locals were there partaking in the lunch that was being served from within. We were in the countryside in the middle of nowhere, so burners were being fired by bottled gas. These were being used to cook rice and very large chickens – none of the 'force fed' young chicks killed for Tesco after a few weeks, here! These were fully grown chickens, of the same sort and size as I could remember having for Christmas when I was a boy. The cardboard plates were filled by the traditional half chicken, rice and peas. It seemed like their West Indies 'rice and peas' was tantamount to our fish and chips.

If you were on holiday, you probably would not have found this place, but if you had, you would have just driven by. However, I was with Henry and I experienced the fullest and tastiest of piping hot delicious meals for what was just a few dollars. The banter came for free. Henry eventually dropped me back at my hotel and told me that he would pick me up again in the early evening for a surprise trip? The due time arrived and we drove down to the St John's marina where he had arranged with the owner of a tourist Pirates' ship to take us out on that evening's voyage.

I had thought that it was the 'Jolly Roger' but my search of the Internet reveals that it must have been the 'Black Swan'. This was all good fun. Basically, as much 'Rum Punch' as you could drink, plenty of singing along with the crew and the usual tourist's fun and games. It was a great evening and with him hosting me earlier in the day, Henry had looked after me all day and evening and even collected me again on the following morning, this time accompanied by his wife. They drove me all around the island, stopping at the usual tourist locations such as Shirley Heights and Nelson's Dockyard National Park. There are said to be 365 Beaches on the Island, one for every day of the year. I wonder who had counted them. What a great weekend I had. Thanks Henry.

So, it was back to work on the Monday morning for the week. I put quite a lot of hours in, helping the bureau staff record the prints being sent to Tacoma. In addition, I managed to fit in visits to the Immigration Department and the Ministry of Labour. To repeat myself, I had discovered that most Caribbean Islands had just given up on policing the issue of 'Work Permits' or ensuring that visitors left the Islands when they should have done. They went through the motions alright, but stamps in passports or slips of paper would invariably be ignored and never policed. With Morpho Touch, they would simply need to take a set of fingerprints when every work permit was issued and then checks could be followed up by simply checking a print on the Morpho Touch portable machine which would instantly verify whether or not, a work permit had been issued to them.

I also visited Camp Blizzard, the barracks of the Antigua Defence Force. Colonel Trevor Thomas was a fine man but despite their personnel being able to operate the Morpho Touch handsets, unlike policing scenarios their use in military operations was probably not feasible. I visited the Airport Security Department on the same day. This was when I discovered the boxes of entry tickets which had never been followed up to see whether persons entering their country on Tourist Visas had in fact left when they should have done.

The following Thursday proved to be a huge eye opener for me. I needed to visit the Legal Affairs Department and as the Attorney General was also the Minister of Legal Affairs, this was another department which fell under the same wing. The not so popular Dr Errol Cort, was still in office. It may be recalled that he was one of those who had attended my presentation at The Royal Antiguan hotel during my first visit. He was an extremely ambitious man and I was a little surprised when he asked me to call by his office. We started off with a pleasant chat, when all of a sudden, he swivelled in his chair and picked up what was a letter from a side desk and handed it to me. He asked me if I had heard of the company who had sent the letter from London. There are many 'pockets' of all kinds of 'Law Enforcement' or so called 'Security Experts' in the UK who perhaps saw the Caribbean as rich pickings in their offer of training, reviews and the like.

The British and Commonwealth office also had a big part to play in supplying such expertise through the Foreign Office. I glanced through the letter and I did not recognise the author company through its letter head. Its contents, however, made me believe rightly or wrongly, that this was from a small gathering of retired Metropolitan Police Officers who had set themselves up to conduct such training or reviews.

I smiled and politely informed Dr Cort of my beliefs. He explained that he wanted a review conducted of the Royal Antigua and Barbuda Police Force being carried out and during his explanation to me, he mentioned that he was not happy with the Commissioner, my friend, Truehart Smith. He said that he wanted to ensure that those who would conduct the review, needed to be the right people and that was why he had shown me the letter. I couldn't resist in telling him that that, was the very experience in which I was engaged in, when I worked with HMI Sir John Woodcock. He had been Her Majesty's Chief Inspector at the Home Office. I continued by informing him that at that time, I was working as a Self Employed contractor and that I felt sure that Sir John and I might well be attracted to conducting a 'one off' Inspection together on similar lines as we had inspected UK Police Forces.

Errol Cort's eyes lit up and he snapped back at me, "When can you find out from Sir John whether you can do it"? The time then was probably just after lunch time and the time difference was such that Sir John would have been up and about. I said, "If I can use your phone, I'll call him right now"? I rang the number immediately as we had always kept in touch and I knew it without having to look it up (0121 453 1122). Luckily Sir John answered the phone. I told him where I was and who I was with. (The Attorney General and Minster of Defence for Antigua must have had him believing I was pulling his leg!) I explained the proposition and from my knowledge of the force I suggested that a couple of weeks fact finding on a Pre Inspection and about 2 weeks Inspection proper, would probably be sufficient. I did not want to talk money in Dr Cort's presence but said to Sir John that I would initially negotiate on his behalf. He was quite excited about it and quickly suggested to me that I include the presence of Lady Kath and Jo on such a venture.

Having terminated the call, I explained to Dr Cort how I thought the process could be explored. The Force as a whole, wasn't as big as many Police Divisions I have experienced. The difficult bit would no doubt, revolve around the budget and the 'Organisation and Structure' especially how the force interacted with the political stratum of the country. My experience of their firearms training, their fingerprint bureau and the lack of resources at Headquarters, were not only indications that the force was ripe for review, they indicated that as a performance indicator, we would be just at the tip of an iceberg. The seed in my head had, however, been intentionally planted by Dr. Cort about his view that it was about time that a new Commissioner be appointed. Whilst the outcome of an inspection may well have led to such a recommendation, I knew that neither Sir John nor I would be swayed by the fact that that, was Dr Cort's observation. I too felt quite excited about the whole deal. With my current duties for the AFR Consortium and for SMI, it wouldn't have been ideal for me to take a month out, but it was far from impossible. I would definitely be up for it.

At that time, I was being paid £200 per day by SMI and so I suggested to Dr Cort that to employ Sir John for £500 per day and me for £300 wouldn't be unreasonable. I cannot now, honestly remember the exact numbers but it would have been around that region and subject to Sir John's agreement and for all our expenses and wives' travel and accommodation to be added. He had no trouble with that but as I had emphasised, I needed to discuss these things with Sir John on my return. He was left in no doubt that perhaps those figures were provisional.

Having visited the other security agencies on the Island again, (ONDCP, Customs etc) I took Henry Christian out to dinner on the Friday evening. It was always in my own interest to catch up with my administrative duties whenever I could and so I fitted as much of this in as I could during the following weekend until Henry collected me and took me to the Airport on the Sunday for my onward flight to Bermuda.

Chapter 26 – Second visits to Bermuda and The Bahamas.

It was on 26th November 2000 when I arrived at Bermuda to once again, enjoy the luxury of the Hamilton Princess hotel. Fingerprint Expert Ray Elvy was to join me this time. The plan was that now we had gained the confidence of all the agencies from our initial visit, and the lavish meeting and dinner we sponsored with Sir John Hoddinott, we would now re-visit with the demonstration kit and with approximate costs, so that the deal could hopefully, be closed out. We also needed to organise their 10,000 Tenprints to be shipped to Tacoma for the free 'Proof of Concept' pilot.

The prices for the Bermudian agencies had, in fact, been remodelled by JCR but I felt that compared with those in England and Wales, they were still a little high and very much interim because the printed cost models had yet to be produced. These meetings with all the different agencies carried on all week and it wouldn't be that exciting if I went through each of them here. Suffice to say that their interest level, remained high. Howard Cutts (Cuttsie) was again our link man and as a thank you, Ray and I took him out to Dinner. He had not only fixed up meetings for us, but also driven us around the Island. It was on this same day that I felt generous and so I bought Jo a ring at A.S. Cooper & Sons Front Street, Hamilton.

This was a short trip to Bermuda and I left there during the evening of 1st December for the overnight flight to Heathrow and home. I had been a long time away and naturally; I was still quite excited about the proposition to conduct an Inspection of the Antigua and Barbuda force. My week at home gave me time to agree fees and costs with Sir John and, we discussed our wives' presence and perhaps the inclusion of an odd game of golf. I recall that he was happy with what I had negotiated and so I began to send Dr Errol Cort e-mails outlining our proposal.

Following that week at home, I spent the night at Gatwick Airport Travel Inn before my early morning flight to Orlando, to meet Pat and Ron Wright. I was a little concerned that Dr. Cort hadn't responded to my e-mail but, I realised that he was a busy man. I arrived at Orlando on 8th December 2000.

The fact that I had commenced working in the Caribbean alone, (apart from brief help with Sir John Hoddinott, Ray Elvy and John Sims in Bermuda) bewildered me a little, although I think Pat and Ron had probably done the work for the Cayman Islands when we first started this project. I was certainly not involved in it but conscious that there were numerous countries making up the Caribbean and that It would have taken me an absolute age, to visit every one (on at least two occasions for each), just to roll out our 'Proof of Concept' pilot. This was the reason why Pat wanted to meet with me and Ron in Orlando, so that we could split the task.

I checked into the Orlando Airport Marriott hotel where I was to meet them. The idea, however, was that it would be Ron Wright and myself who would complete the whole project between us. Before I left, I purchased a very good map of the Caribbean, showing all of the countries we would be required to work in. I still have the map somewhere and it stretched across two coffee tables. Following many hours of debate, Ron and I started to bid for the various countries in which we would work but our first job was to identify the countries where we thought that a visit might be viable. We eventually listed thirty six countries which we thought would be possible contenders for a visit.

I would naturally, retain those countries I had already visited but the division as a whole, was quite bizarre because after a preliminary discussion, I recall drawing a pencil line vertically through the Caribbean region, so that it represented approximately, a 50 x 50 split. It indicated that Ron would work on the one side and me the other. Yes, it took our three flights and two days accommodation at this very expensive hotel for us to end up drawing that line ---hhmmmmnn. We ended up having dinner at Fish Bones in Orlando which was to be the first of other visits I was to make there in the future. It became my favourite restaurant.

From Orlando, I caught a flight to The Bahamas where I landed at Nassau and booked into The Holiday Inn, Junkanoo Beach hotel where I was to spend six days doing the rounds of the main security agencies. I wasn't to know it at that precise time, but The Bahamas was to become one of my favourite locations and was another place, where I was later to take Jo on holiday. I suppose this was because the country was far more westernised than other Caribbean countries and whilst I enjoyed the simplistic rustic countries which in fact, made up most of the Caribbean, The Bahamas was far closer to the US mainland and it was a lot easier to deal with them. For a start, I could easily understand what was being said to me as opposed to me wrestling with the broad thick Caribbean accents of Jamaica, Antigua and many other less contemporary countries.

The Bahamas was also far wealthier than most other Caribbean countries and also, they were more advanced than others in fingerprint expertise. They operated a proper fingerprint bureau and indeed, they possessed a 'stand-alone' AFIS system but it was not networked to any other location for sharing purposes.

Plane loads of US citizens would fly in every night to gamble in the 24 hour casinos on the Bahamian Islands, primarily on Nassau and rightly or wrongly, I gained the impression that apart from tourism in general and off-shore banking, much of their riches stemmed from their closeness to the USA. Indeed, 80% of their tourists were American.

It would be easy for the bureau to convert to our system but so far as the Immigration Department was concerned, I was to discover they had an absolute nightmare of a problem with illegal immigrants floating over on makeshift rafts and small vessels from the very poor country of Haiti. So much so, that on a monthly basis, they chartered a Jumbo Jet to take them all back. They even constructed a special detention centre for them. What used to happen was, those deported Haitians would return time and time again, more often than not, using other identities. A simple solution to this would be to fingerprint every illegal immigrant caught and deported which would go a long way to solve the use of those false identities. The 'Morpho Touch' was just the job for such operations.

The other reason which made Bahamas a favourite location, was that my contacts in all of the agencies were very positive and friendly. The Police Commissioner, Paul Farquharson was to become another person I could call a friend. He and I dined together and in a later private visit on holiday with Jo, he tucked us under his wing but more on that later. The Comptroller of Customs, John Rolle was another great chap and he did his best to facilitate all that I required on my visit. Similarly, Vernon Burrows was the Director of Immigration and like the others, he was able to readily identify the benefits of our system. I'm not at all racist when I say that it was far easier to educate these more 'westernised' people than with some of the others in the emerging Caribbean countries, many of whom, believed that I was just a travelling salesman. It was the likes of these Bermudian and Bahamian heads of agencies, who were of sufficient intellect to see through that and were more willing to examine what exactly the benefits were.

Claudia Williamson was Commissioner Paul's Secretary and Inspector Wayne Millar was his Staff Officer. Through them I arranged my first visit to Police Headquarters on the day following my arrival, 11th December 2000.

My visit to Police Headquarters happened to be around coffee time and I was quickly ushered off to the equivalent of The Officers Mess where we were not served coffee but a bowl of what I could only describe as fish soup. It seemed to me to be hot water in which was boiled large white fish, bones, fins and all. It wouldn't be my 'dish of the day' but it tasted OK.

Paul Farquharson – Commissioner of the Bahamas Police

The Head of the fingerprint bureau, was Inspector Paul Rolle, also a nice chap and we were to work closely together. His Bureau was out of town at The Criminal Records Office, Thompson Boulevard. I'm not sure if Paul was any relation to John Rolle, the Comptroller of Customs and Excise, but this name was a very popular one in The Bahamas.

The only difficulty I had in The Bahamas concerned their existing 'Stand-alone' system to which they were already signed up. They had naturally built up a good relationship with the company supplying the system and I could well have been seen as someone who might want to upset that relationship. The idea of a networked system bringing in all other Caribbean countries and their other Customs and Immigration agencies was, however, a very strong influencing factor which I think they were willing to accept.

192

This first visit to The Bahamas was very much exploratory and as a consequence, I had little time to get around all of the agencies. I spent successive days with The Police, then Government Buildings, then Customs House and on my final day, I visited the Immigration Department. It was on this day that another of those generous feelings took a hold of me and I popped into the Columbian Emeralds Shop in Nassau to buy Jo her silver twist bangle. This and the ring and necklace I bought her in Bermuda, is an indication that I was probably receiving a financial income, more than I had ever experienced in my past career.

My stay at Nassau was for only a full six working days and so I returned and landed at Gatwick during the early morning of 17th December. Christmas was approaching, and I had been away from my family for far longer than I would have desired. Mum was a priority and she was still in hospital and was beginning to slide more into frailty. I suppose in hindsight, I should have seen this coming but she was always such a strong lady and, apart from her falls, I had automatically assumed that she was doing fine. It all came so suddenly.

In addition to domestic chores at home, I was still unable to make contact with Dr Errol Cort, in Antigua; he with his strong desire that Sir John Woodcock and I should carry out an Inspection of the Royal Antigua and Barbuda Police Force. Where was he ? And why hadn't he replied to my e-mails? I sent him some more e-mails and, in the end, decided to telephone his office. I spoke to his secretary who, by the way, I was unable to strike up a friendship with. Without and warmth in her voice, she was very cold and kept saying that he was either engaged in meetings or out of his office. I recall that on one occasion she said he was at the prison attending the Christmas Party. As Minister of Justice, he was also in charge of the prison system.

As Christmas approached, it became clear that something was wrong. I couldn't understand that a man of such standing as the Attorney General could not just tell me that he had changed his mind or whatever, it was not like him to want to 'hide' from me. I was later to learn, however, that there was some investigation into the fraudulent use of funds belonging to the Country's Medical Benefits Scheme. I cannot find reference to Dr. Cort's direct involvement but although unsubstantiated, I heard that he had been suspended from office as it had been alleged that he had travelled to the US mainland on private visits when fraudulently using the schemes funds. I have found the following extract on the Internet which makes reference to a Scotland Yard Enquiry:-

SCOTLAND YARD CALLED TO INVESTIGATE MEDICAL BENEFITS FRAUD. Lester Bird, Prime Minister, has ordered the Director of Public Prosecutions to pursue a criminal investigation into a twenty-year misdirection of funds within the Medical Benefits Scheme. Opposition politicians have accused key officials of depriving citizens of proper drugs and medical care as well as receiving huge kickbacks from certain contracted drug suppliers. The entire Board of the Medical Benefits Scheme, the Attorney General, and the Health Minister has been fired and appropriate legal action has been requested by the Prime Minister (Fraud Info Newsletter (The Evening Standard), May 24, 2001, summary by Marg Reynolds).

GOVERNMENT TO BE PRESSURED TO INVESTIGATE ALLEGED MEDICAL BENEFITS CORRUPTION Opposition United Progressive Party spokesman, Mr. Spencer, stated he would request a commission of inquiry into alleged financial wrongdoings in the Medical Benefits Scheme (MBS). Further, he plans to mobilize the people of Antigua and Barbuda for a protest if Sir James Carlisle, Governor General, decides against a public inquiry. (Cana News, Apr 8, 2001, summary by Marg Reynolds).

I am unable to find anything about the result of this investigation but it appears that a Commission of Enquiry was also held because the following extract found on the Internet refers to Dr. Cort's Office in particular. The announcement was made by Lester Bird, the Prime Minister over two years later but I can confirm that Dr. Cort remained suspended when I made a further visit to Antigua in 2001.

On Wednesday 7th August 2002, Prime Minister Lester Bird made a special broadcast to the nation concerning the findings and recommendations made by the Commission of Inquiry. The following are excerpts from that broadcast:

"There was no finding by the Commission that the Prime Minister or the Cabinet acted in bad faith, fraudulently or corruptly. There are findings against two former Ministers of Health and the former Minister of Justice and Attorney-General, but it is clear that these former Ministers acted on their own and without Cabinet's knowledge.

So, even though I had taken an instant dislike to Dr Cort as described above, what sort of luck was that? I had been lucky enough to have been asked by the Attorney General to arrange an Inspection of a country's Police Force, then that Attorney General gets himself suspended pending a corruption investigation. I just love that protest placard in this photo below – 'BUSTED! CORT GOT CAUGHT'. Now I knew why he wasn't taking my calls.

Whilst Dr. Cort never impressed me as a popular politician, I could not, in that era, find out what happened to him though I do know that he must have been either forgiven or absolved from blame because my research later in 2011, found that once again, he was then an important member of the Antiguan Cabinet Office. In March of that year, there had been demonstrations against the police routing of political parades around election time and the demonstrators were accusing the authorities of intimidation. The riot squad had been called in to quell public disorder. In addition, he was once again accused of corrupt practice. Perhaps his suspension was a very good omen for Sir John and me.

"An angry ALP Chairman Gaston Browne said the march route had been approved by police, in writing, and they would be acting in accordance with that written permission. They have deliberately changed the route in order to frustrate our march," Browne said. "We will not be intimidated under any circumstances."

The riot squad was deployed to block the planned route and was booed by protestors. The officers, in full gear, stood their ground as the demonstrators taunted them and declared that they too would not back down. The confrontation lasted for about 15 minutes before the riot squad was ordered to withdraw and the march continued along its planned route, ending in a rally where several ALP speakers addressed the crowd about the incompetence and shortcomings of the ruling party.

Earlier in the day, ALP picketers outside the office of National Security Minister, Dr Errol Cort had minor scuffles with police in another dispute over where they could and could not protest.

The picketers, who'd gathered at 9 am, initially marched up and down one side of the building, waving placards with messages for Dr Cort to step aside until questions are answered about whether his law firm paid taxes on the EC$3 million (US$1.1 million) in retainer fees which it allegedly received from fraud-accused Allen Stanford. The ALP's call follows a US$1 million lawsuit filed against Dr Cort, a former Finance Minister, by Stanford investors last month.

The protestors loudly chanted 'Errol Cort must go right now' as they walked along the street but at one stage decided to change the direction of their picket.

WOW. This Dr. Cort was certainly walking a tight rope but wait!!!

Could this man be the one and same who was honoured in the last (2023) King's honours list????? Oh No!

ANTIGUA AND BARBUDA

ORDER OF THE BRITISH EMPIRE

Commanders of the Order of the British Empire (CBE)

Dr. Leon Errol Cort. For services to National Development.

Well, suppose the King's judgement must be far better than mine!

My return to the UK and the end of the millennium year saw me writing up reports on what I had achieved so far in the Caribbean. These were for both the AFR Consortium and Sagem who were in effect, my joint employers.

Things at work looked good. If we were to be consumed by the Home Office's PITO in June 2001, then this Interpol Caribbean initiative might just be the project to keep us going, but as I've said before, how on earth could we keep going if we were not going to be in control of our fingerprint data? I couldn't see how we could continue with our English and Welsh forces service, but it might have been another story if we could develop the Caribbean initiative apart.

The countries I had visited so far, were very enthusiastic though it always had to be remembered that the 'proof of concept' pilot they were enjoying, was a free service. Would they be so enthusiastic when they were asked to pay for it? However, the lack of skills possessed were such that I could not foresee us installing very expensive workstations in these countries – or at least in most of them. Indeed, a decision was made, perhaps later on in the process, that we could operate a scheme involving the posting or scanning of tenprints and marks to the central site where our records databases would be acquired and searched there. That would be my favoured system.

My final duty of the year was to meet up with Pat Pitt at The Hilton hotel, Heathrow. He had flown in from Seattle and we held a breakfast meeting which involved my explaining in more detail, the Caribbean prospective. I returned home during the same day.

Chapter 27 – It's 2001 and only Six Months to Go?

The new millennium had started very well so far as myself and my family were concerned. I had embarked on what was to be, one of the most exciting chapters in my life. There I was, thanks to Pat and his start up team, having whizzed all around England and Wales, playing quite a pivotal role in the introduction of the first computerised fingerprint identification service and now, I was continually travelling, not only to the US and France but to all of the Caribbean Islands spreading the digitised AFIS concept far and wide.

I was working very hard but I was thoroughly enjoying what I was doing and I was being paid far more than I received as a Chief Superintendent of Police. The sun, sea and sand was that added bonus but naturally, it was overshadowed with Mum still being in hospital. Among almost weekly visits to our family homes in Hereford, I had spent every Christmas day travelling there, to collect our two widowed mothers to spend Christmas with us. Both had now slid into old age surprisingly rapidly and to be honest, I never expected my Mum to return home. No doubt our Christmas was spent in the usual way with the family but now, I suspect, I had been too busy to record the event on camera, at least, I'm unable to find any photographs of that Christmas.

I didn't know then, but any 'perceived' domestic problems would pale into insignificance on 11th September 2001 when the mass murder of those poor innocent souls were to perish in the twin towers of Manhattan resulting from a cowardly act by terrorists. However, as I have already alluded to, Mum's failing health and her inability to look after herself, causing her admission to hospital in December 2000, never to see her return home. She was to be discharged from hospital to a Care Home in March of this 2001 year.

The AFR Consortium was officially to wind up on 30th June 2001 but we still thought that perhaps there was a chance that we could continue to provide at least a Livescan Service to Police Forces or maybe the replacement service could involve us. All these happenings were to form additional chapters of my 'Life Story' so far as 2001 was concerned, so let's look at it in a little closer detail.

No sooner had we planned the splitting of the Caribbean countries between my colleague, Ron Wright and myself, then shortly following the New Year, Ron suffered a heart attack at his home in Northumbria. We had only just commenced our research into the individual countries we were to manage and I received the news from Pat who asked me to scoot up to Ron's home and collect his lap top. In short, his condition was such that Pat wanted me to take on the whole of the Caribbean, by myself. As I've said many times, "Oh well, someone had to go!"

So therefore, 2001 commenced with me searching Ron's computer for any research work he had completed in respect of the Islands we were to divide between us. Neither of us had time to do a lot of research but my job at that time, was to simply 'cream off' what he had done and convert his work into my style, to eventually produce 'Operational Requirements' for each country.

I was due to work again at the Central Site in Tacoma but before I departed, I managed to complete Operational Requirements for Work on Granada, Turks & Caicos, St. Lucia & St. Vincent. My memory tells me that these were the Islands that Ron had visited because I had not visited them at that time. We thought it advisable that although I hadn't actually visited them, it might be better if I explained the situation with regard to Ron's illness and send them the draft operational requirements with a nice accompanying letter. This would also act as an introduction to me as Ron's replacement.

Unfortunately, this work was interrupted by me having to travel to the Solent hotel, Fareham, following the financial collapse of our hardware company, Protocol Solutions. There was obviously nothing we could do to help this company, but we needed to guard against their demise having any detrimental effects on what we were doing. There was a need to ensure that the equipment we had installed was safe from seizure by creditors and such like. I had little to do with what actually went on, so thankfully, Pat agreed that I could revert to what I had been doing so that I could get on with it before I set off for Tacoma.

Mum was still in hospital at this stage and it took some explaining to her why I needed to fly to Seattle on the next day. I felt guilty in leaving her as I was the only child but in fairness to her, she made it easier for me in her usual, kind manner, by trying to convince me that she would be fine. Jo was a tremendous help, as was a cousin I had in Hereford.

My trip to Tacoma included the period when, through Pat, I wrote the below article for publication in the magazine distributed to the members of the Association of Caribbean Commissioners of Police from their office which I shared in Barbados.

The AFR Service Bureau

The proposed Automatic Fingerprint Recognition (AFR) Service Bureau is providing ACCP members with the opportunity to acquire, at reduced cost, the services of a worldwide Automatic Fingerprint Identification System (AFIS). This system would enable Interpol members to search tenprints from suspects and scene of crime marks (latents) against their own fingerprint database as well as the databases of co-operating countries

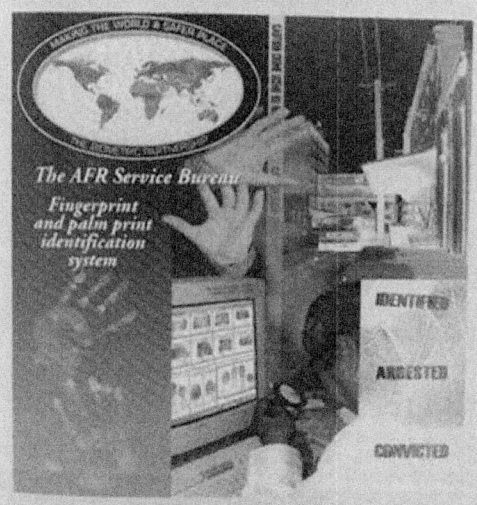

For the first time member countries have the powerful tool needed to apprehend criminals who operate locally or internationally. Under the auspices of Interpol, ACCP members will be able to identify their own and international offenders by reference to a world database of fingerprints and scenes of crime marks.

What makes this possible is a central facility that benefits from efficient fingerprint technologies, secure data networks and workstations staffed by some of the most skilled, experienced fingerprint officers available internationally. The system is proven and currently provides an average of 500 scenes of crime mark hits a week.

Organisational Structure

Each participating country is able to populate its own database while having search privileges across other country's databases with their consent. They can select only those technologies and services that meet their particular requirements and are also able to remotely search the central database from workstations within their own jurisdiction.

As a low cost option, countries may also elect to send their fingerprint cards and scene of crime mark (latent) exhibits to the central site via secure transmittal by air (referred to as the 'Fed-Ex Option'.) Upon receipt at the central site, they will be searched and the results will be forwarded in real time to the country. In accordance with 'Interpol Operating Rules' it is proposed that the participating countries will have access to each other's databases to search suspects' tenprints for identification. The member country will also be able to search scene of crime marks against the central database of criminal tenprint sets.

Once the database is populated, it will be managed in accordance with member country's data protection guidelines and the overarching principles established by Interpol. The database is however freely accessible by other member countries for search according to their operational requirements and with the written consent of the member owning the database.

In addition, member countries would benefit from the availability of central site facilities able to manage tenprint acquisition, provide 24-hour tenprint identification and specialist mark searching expertise. The central site also provides operational management of the system on behalf of the member country.

Multi-Agency Concept

Other Law Enforcement agencies such as Immigration, Customs, Defence Forces, Prisons etc. will be able to share the benefits of the system through a 'Multi Agency' server. In conjunction with the British Police Forces, AFRC Consortium, Sagem will operate the system.

Sagem systems are the most successful crime scene latent mark identifiers in the business. Sagem provides systems and algorithms to more than 150 countries and agencies in the world including Interpol and the FBI. Their system has already identified almost 110,000 crime scene marks, just for the AFRC since it commenced searching their fingerprints in

April, 1996. The system has been constantly upgraded and is maintained to the leading edge of the technology. It is also in compliance with all relevant standards thus enabling the electronic movement of fingerprint images between other compliant systems in the world. An International Help Desk operating in up to six languages on a twenty-four hour basis, uses sophisticated tools for ensuring continued service without on site intervention.

Individual member countries can select the acquisition system(s) that best meets their operational requirements. Some may choose the sophisticated real-time livescan solution capable of producing provable evidence of identity while suspects are still in custody. At the other end of the scale, some countries may elect to use the 'Fed-Ex Option.' Indeed, countries may mix and match their technical solution according to their operational need. Flexible service options are provided to suit the budgets of any country with a migratory path to more sophisticated solutions as budgets permit.

The Service offered is available immediately and requires no effort from the country other than the provision of the records for back record conversion (BRC) and search. If required, the country may elect to receive start-up assistance, training in fingerprint management and assistance with the bureau management. The system is managed with 'whole life cycle' support, which is included in the service fee, 24 hours per day, 7 days per week.

Central Site

Over time and with experience, the facilities of the Automatic Fingerprint Recognition Consortium (AFRC) central site have grown from management of the central AFIS system and acquisition of inked tenprint records to providing fingerprint expertise in real time, around the clock. Members of the present consortium have realised the operational benefits of central site expertise in four ways.
1. The use of livescan equipment requires real-time confirmation of identity by a fingerprint expert as provided by the central site.
2. The real-time acquisition of tenprints allows a simultaneous search of the marks database and the communication of results while the suspect is still in custody.
3. AFRC fingerprint experts have accumulated valuable knowledge of the AFIS system and the central site allowing them to focus their expertise on serious crime marks that are of particular immediate importance to member countries.
4. Operational and management experience of 24-hour day operation of a leading technological AFIS solution is immediately available to Interpol member countries.
Interpol members will benefit from a fully functional central site that can deliver expert fingerprint services. There is no start-up cost and the service is immediate.

Proving The Concept

Caribbean countries are being used by Interpol to "prove the concept" whereby all participating countries are able to search the fingerprint databases of all of other participating countries through one shared but segmented database.

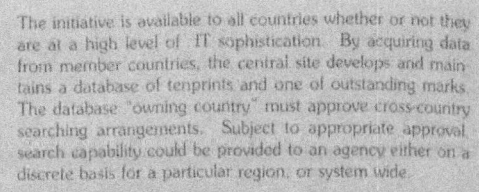

The initiative is available to all countries whether or not they are at a high level of IT sophistication. By acquiring data from member countries, the central site develops and maintains a database of tenprints and one of outstanding marks. The database "owning country" must approve cross-country searching arrangements. Subject to appropriate approval search capability could be provided to an agency either on a discrete basis for a particular region, or system wide.

Currently, hundreds of fingerprints of persons already deported from Caribbean countries are being loaded onto Sagems system to form a Pan Caribbean 'Deportees database'. This database, is perhaps an excellent example of how the system can be of use to other agencies forming a 'Multi Agency' alliance. It is intended, for example, that Immigration Departments will have equipment installed within Ports of Entry, so that any suspected illegal immigrant can very quickly be identified against this database by the simple scanning of one finger into the system. Should such checks be desirable at any other location or any mobile environment e.g. at Cruise Ship terminals, then up to thirty thousand (30,000) fingerprints can be downloaded from the Multi-Agency database to one of Sagem's hand held MorphoTouch units. This system, almost as small as a mobile telephone, is battery operated and has a built-in finger scanner which can be used to check anyone's fingerprints against those held in the unit.

Already many Government Departments are interested in converting their Work Permit schemes to this technology. 'Smart Cards' can be produced from the equipment which contains not only a description and photograph of the owner but a chip containing that persons fingerprints and which can be authenticated by the insertion of the card in the MorphoTouch unit.

Is It Working?

Cayman Islands was the first ACCP member country to have its fingerprint database converted to the system in February 2000. The second mark searched resulted in the identification of a murderer.

The success of the Cayman Islands experiment led to the system being demonstrated at the ACCP Conference in May 2000. Since that time a further seven countries have now joined in the free 'proof of concept' pilot and a further four countries are in the process of having their records converted. Through this initiative a total of 727 crime scene marks have been identified up to January 2001.

The success of the concept is due to:
- System accuracy
- Operational discipline of fingerprinting each prisoner
- All prisoners fingerprints being loaded and searched against the databases. This can identify a person from the same or another country.

The project so far has achieved no less than two-hundred and forty three (243) cross-border tenprint identifications and eighty-five (85) of those have been records where the fingerprints were from persons using different identities. This, in itself serves to prove that criminals know no national bound-

201

aries, and as far as the Caribbean is concerned, they operate in more than one country. Given its geographical nature one of the areas of crucial importance to the Caribbean is the ability to identify criminals who operate in countries other than their own, particularly when using false identities.

Successes

The last country to have their fingerprints loaded was Barbados. They submitted 2,252 crime scene marks to be searched against their own 9,200 Tenprints and against a further 35,115 Tenprints belonging to eight other countries. In one case three separate marks found in an abandoned stolen vehicle identified three different individuals. All have since been arrested and charged and are awaiting trial for several armed robberies.

The first wave of electronic searches produced no less than 290 'Hits'. All these were achieved in a matter of a few days. The six 'hits' obtained through manual searching during the previous year is no criticism of the Barbados Fingerprint Bureau but it demonstrates that manual searching cannot hope to compare with the modern technology now in place.

Future Development

A new round of visits to Caribbean countries will be made in the coming months. Any country wishing to register their interest or require any further information should contact the AFR Central Site Offices in Tacoma. An important aspect of the system is that it continues to evolve, not only in respect to the AFIS itself, but also in the operating procedures, managerial practices and fingerprint expertise.

This system will put ACCP member countries at the forefront of AFIS technology and it is anticipated that the Caribbean initiative will be the first of many similar regional initiatives to be conducted under Interpol's umbrella. This must surely lead to the building of a 'world wide' fingerprint searching system. Quite simply, we are about to make history in the Caribbean.

Conclusion

The AFRC Service Bureau makes available to ACCP Interpol members the most modern AFIS system, supported by a modern data network capable of remote interrogation throughout the world. It can be readily tailored to suit the needs of individual countries and the overall objectives of Interpol. The operational central site facility ensures competent system and database management. It also provides oversight of tenprint acquisition, together with a world-class fingerprint examination resource, providing specialist mark searching and speedy responses to participating member countries. The service is offered at a cost lower than a capital procurement with immediate implementation. As operations are provided as part of the service, there are no overhead costs, only one price for the total service.

Most importantly, the members of the ACCP can be confident that the concept works and has been proven. The system includes the latest state of the art matching technology capable of incremental implementation and provides excellent value for money.

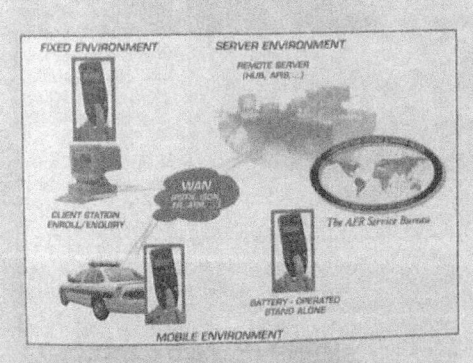

INTER-AGENCIES TRAINING
- Inter-Agencies Package
- Tenprint Operator
- Immigration
- Latent Expert
- Livescan Operator

ORGANISATION & FINGERPRINT EXPERTISE
- Latent Expert
- Establish Fingerprint Bureau
- Accuracy and System Testing
- Fingerprint Bureau Management
- Backlog Conversion
- Expert Data Protection Advice
- Conversion Support/QA
- Security of Premises and Data
- Fingerprint Remedial Work

AFR Consortium
Tacoma Financial Centre
1145 Broadway Plaza Suite 830
Tacoma WA 98402

Contact:
Mr. Patrick A. Pitt
Tel: 001 253 207 4000
Fax: 001 253 207 4026

There was no way that we were going to be distributing the AFIS equipment for them to operate independently, the idea was that we would continue the 'Bureau Service' option we incorporated during our earlier 'Emergency Service' days.

This ACCP magazine article was as a result of Pat persuading Jean-Claude to sponsor the magazine in the sum of $1,000. It was also a thank you for their office putting up with me when I worked in Barbados. It obviously very much worth our while because it would doubtless be read by the Commissioners of all the Islands and amounted to some cheap publicity for what we were trying to offer. I have retained a copy of the magazine in which the article is printed. It is naturally attributed to Pat Pitt as our leader though I, and possibly Ray Elvy wrote most of it other than the technical details and the images which SMI added.

This period in Tacoma was also the time when I was writing a proposal for each Caribbean country. That indeed, was my primary purpose for being there. It was quite important and involved me working in close co-operation with our SMI colleagues. The CEO, Jean-Claude Richard (JCR) was again to work closely with me but he had specifically hired a previous employee, Pam Steiner to work with another of their employees Ron Wholleben, to write up the technical aspects of what their hardware could do.

Ron operated Sagem's special software which would transform our basic 'word' writing into their 'special effects' productions. Assisting me with the writing was my old mate Ray Elvy, the Head of Bureau for Surrey Police who had been seconded to us to deal with the fingerprint science aspects of the proposals we were to write. Together, we were a team and our individual efforts would eventually be embraced together to form the finished proposals which Ray and I would be delivering to the various countries.

So far as my employment as a consultant or contractor was concerned, my efforts were gradually being appreciated more by Sagem and the situation became awkward. I believed that much of my work I invoiced to the AFRC, was being re-charged to Sagem, so this led to the question being asked as to whether I should also be contracted to Sagem for the work I was doing for them, though it wasn't me who asked the question. I hadn't any reason to think of these matters at that time, but on reflection now, I had accidentally become a very important cog in their wheel. If I failed to persuade Caribbean

Countries to join in this project then their investment in AFRC, particularly with me, would be wasted. I had an excellent relationship with all of the Sagem employees and Chief Executives, including those at their Paris headquarters. Thankfully, their confidence in me was shown by them offering me a contract. I had no idea that was coming as all I did was what I was told. Pat was pulling all of my strings and as he and Jean-Claude were good business mates, then so far as I was concerned, it didn't matter who directed me to wherever. I just went.

The time was about right because every one of the days I had been researching and writing up Operational Requirements for the Caribbean countries at home, I was being paid for at an enhanced rate by Sagem. My writing all of the proposals in Tacoma was similarly paid for by Sagem. Pat and the AFR were on to a good thing because whilst they could retain my services, they were having me paid for by Sagem for a great deal of the time which obviously reduced AFRC costs. However, I was to learn that at the final hurdle, the AFRC was to turn its back on me.

For the sake of what I was to discover later, I will add here, that on the same day as I had signed my contract with Sagem Morpho, I took Jo's car to Startins of Ombersley Road, Worcester to have a new exhaust pipe fitted. The reason why I mention this will be made known later.

I had completed the thirty page 'Operational Requirement' for Jamaica and it was a day later on 18th February 2001 that I travelled to Gatwick Airport to fly to Kingston, Jamaica. I was to visit several more countries before eventually arriving back home almost a month later.

This time, I had been booked into the Hilton hotel, Down Town Kingston and after checking in, I later took a Taxi back to the Airport to collect Pat and Sir John Hoddinott. All senior management in the Consortium had been desperately trying to make contact with the Commissioner of Police of Jamaica, Francis Forbes. (Frankie) This eventually came about during my last visit to the Central Site in Tacoma when I had written to him with a draft of the 'Operational Requirement' for his Fingerprint Department. We had all been making various telephone calls and out of the blue, his secretary, Joan Golding made contact with me in Tacoma. I arranged that I would call her straight back and whilst I can't recall the excuse I gave, I needed time to set up the tape recording of our conversation.

Chapter 28 – We Catch the Jamaican 'Big Fish'

I was ecstatic at having caught 'The Big Fish' and when I eventually spoke to him, I can recall his very quiet but precise voice, "Ah Mr. Humphrey, (no-one in the Caribbean would add the letter 's' to my name) just what is it that you want us to do"? Those were his exact words.

My telephone call to Jamaica's Commissioner, Francis (Frankie) Forbes created quite a bit of excitement. Jamaica's absence from inclusion in our Caribbean initiative was bound to prove a disaster.

I answered his question then explained exactly what we wanted him to do but that it would be far clearer to him if he afforded us time to explain in person. He agreed and before arrangements could be made, I discovered that he had a penchant for Chinese food, so I booked a large table for dinner at The Jade Garden Restaurant for 21st February, which gave me three days after our arrival, to take Sir John and Pat around the various Policing establishments on the Island.

Apart from giving Frankie a presentation and explaining to him face to face, exactly what we were trying to do, the main purpose of my presence there, was to conduct further research in their Fingerprint Bureau and hopefully to instil some confidence in those that operated in it. I had planned that Ray Elvy join me again. It would be Sir John, Pat and myself who would be attending the meeting. I had previously met the Jamaican personnel responsible for their fingerprint bureau so I took Sir John and Pat to the Criminal Investigation Bureau, (CIB) East Queen Street where the bureau was located. This was the same station that had been attacked with guns by Jamaican gang members sometime after my first visit.

I introduced them to the management team and among them was the Assistant Commissioner for Crime, Mr Dyer who proved to be a very good contact and we became friends in so much as our work was concerned. He was later to personally speak to the driver, Fraser I had hired, for the purposes of vetting him, to ensure that he was to be trusted. I hadn't thought of him being a problem but I had been lucky in having picked up a good taxi driver. He became my full time driver and so I booked him for every trip I needed to make. It was much later, during my last visit to Jamaica and following me receiving from him, some of his wedding cake, that I was to learn that Fraser was his surname. His full name was Radcliff Adolf Fraser and he gave me all his contact details. It was such a coincidence, that just like Truehart Smith, Commissioner at Antigua, he wanted to invite me to his wedding but as I was absent, he had saved me a slice of his wedding cake.

Fraser was the 'king pin' of all Kingston's taxi drivers and he had never left the Island. I constantly heard his fellow taxi drivers asking him many questions over the radio, about policy and how much certain fares should be charged and what routes to take etc. etc. I was just lucky to have selected him when I first needed a taxi on Jamaica. He gave me so much local intelligence.

It was just before I returned from my last visit to Jamaica that Fraser passed comment about how he liked my shoes. They were an ordinary pair of Clarkes shoes which apparently were then most fashionable in Jamaica. His size was far smaller than mine, else I had been prepared to give him a pair. However, I came by an opportunity a year or two later to send him a pair. The story is as follows:-

The Hilton hotel was used by British Airways to accommodate their Captains and First Officers. They operated a system whereby the UK flights would land at Kingston where the Captains and First Officers would be replaced by a pair who had had a four or five day layover at the Hilton. The Cabin crew would stay on board when the plane took off again for the short flight to Montego Bay where they would also, be replaced by a fresh team.

At the Hilton, we were able to take advantage of their upgraded breakfast room where we were to meet the BA Pilots and their First Officers. It was here, during my first or second stay that I was asked by a First Officer, Mike Carr, if I played golf. Apparently, because they were members of their BA Sports Club, they were entitled to take advantage of two sets of clubs at all of their 'stop over' hotels and two memberships of a local golf club. Mike Carr was a golfer but unfortunately for him, his Captain, David Parkinson didn't play. Now who was I, with my soft, generous nature, to deny a poor golfer, the chance of having a game when he had nothing else to do in Kingston?

I got very pally with them both and on one of my days off, I joined Mike in a game at a local Kingston Club. It was ironic that although I played with Mike and that he lived at Welford-on-Avon, about half an hour away from my home, that it was David Parkinson, his Captain with whom I developed a longer and lasting friendship. David had a very nice wife and a small son and they lived at Ringwood Hampshire. His son was mad on trains and on one of their visits to us at home, we took them for a ride on the Severn Valley Railway. It was also during one of these visits that I dashed down to town and bought Fraser a pair of Clarke's shoes. David was still flying Boeing 777s into Kingston and he kindly volunteered to give Fraser a ring on his next visit and to hand over of the shoes to him.

How fantastic it was that during our conversation over breakfast at the Hilton that I discovered that Mike and David were actually going to be the pilots who would be flying me back home. As I've said, I'm not really sure whether it was the first or second stay at the Hilton when all this happened, but whenever, I was invited by them to sit in the 'Jockey Seat' with them during take-off and landing at Gatwick. That was a really memorable experience for me.

It was David who insisted that I provide him with my British Airways 'flying itinerary' and miraculously, all flights on BA from then on were upgraded to Business Class. This was also extended to Jo when she came out to Tacoma for a holiday with me later in the year. More on that later.

So, back to work – where was I? I recall that my trips around Jamaica included a visit to a court where a murder trial was in progress. This was at Half Way Tree and was right next to the prison. Sir John, Pat and I arrived by taxi at The Jade Garden Restaurant. I think that Ray Elvy was yet to arrive in Jamaica. We were a little disappointed that the commissioner could not attend and he had sent his deputy, Sydney Brooks and the Assistant Commissioner Crime, Mr Dyson. To repeat, it was that evening that Mr Dyson spoke to Fraser as I could sense that he was a little worried if I had got a good or a 'dodgy' driver. I saw him take Fraser aside and he spoke to him for some time and in effect, had vetted him. On his return to us, he whispered in my ear, "That man will die for you, he is OK".

Our meeting with the Commissioner was planned for around lunch time on 21st February. It was a sweltering hot day and we booked into the Reception area of Police Headquarters in Old Hope Road. I had prepared several acetates and was in possession of the Operational Requirement which would form the basis of our discussions.

As another aside, I can recall that a huge marquee had been erected on the lawns of the headquarters except that there were no sides to it. It was just the roof that had been erected to provide shade. Beneath it there were rows of chairs on which were sat numerous Jamaican's all waiting to have a police certificate completed so that they could get a passport. They ran a 'shuffle' system because when the queues of people had subsided within the main building, their seats were filled by the appropriate number from beneath this marquee roof. We had been told that many of them had been deported from other countries back to Jamaica and they would try to seek passports under different identities. This was the very problem we could assist them with.

I forget now, what time our appointment was for but I do remember that we were kept waiting for a very long time. I kept enquiring and was told that the commissioner had some important meetings which were lasting longer than anticipated. He was, in fact, in discussion with the Permanent Secretary to the Minister for National Security, Mrs Elaine Baker and the Government's Director of Finance, Mrs. Y. Cooper. I was to meet these ladies several times in the future but they were not present at our meeting then. My memory of the occasion was that we were mainly sat around Francis Forbes' office on large comfortable settees.

It was following that initial meeting that the conversation became more relaxed, and Sir John broached the subject of the crime situation in his Hampshire Force and related the times when he had authorised several of his senior detectives to make the trip to Jamaica in their investigation of 'Yardie' gang influenced murders in Hampshire, undoubtedly being linked to the Jamaican drugs trade.

He suggested that perhaps he could be shown the 'Trench Town' area of Kingston from where these gangsters operated. Trench Town is mentioned by Bob Marley in his famous song, 'Don't Worry'.

Without much ado, Frankie picked up his phone and ordered a car to take himself, Sir John, Pat and me on a tour of 'Gangland'. The car arrived and it contained Bullet Proof helmets for all except one and you've guessed it, as I was the most junior in rank, that one was going to be me. I have seldom been so frightened. We drove around Trench Town and the driver wasn't going to stop for anything, even road 'stop' or 'give way' signs. We were glared at by the local people and as we passed the Trench Town Police Station, I could see that it was barricaded by numerous sheets of corrugated iron all of which sported dents caused undoubtedly by the throwing of heavy missiles.

I hadn't realised how this gang warfare had grown over years, but seeing this type of environment demonstrated how easy it would have evolved. It was a real eye-opener and I shall be very surprised if the degree of lawlessness will ever reduce in Jamaica. It was no wonder that the decision had once been made for plain clothes patrols to operate in plain vehicles with automatic machine guns. No thanks, not for me. Thank God we live where we do!

Having completed our presentation and tour, Sir John returned to the UK and Pat to Tacoma. I think that this visit by Pat and Sir John was more of an introduction than anything else. I remained in Jamaica for a longer period sorting out the Tenprints to send to Tacoma for the 'Proof of Concept' pilot and for the gathering of more information with the other agencies. We had been joined by Ray Elvy who was a 'Godsend' for me because naturally, he was another fingerprint expert and a very good one who could speak the fingerprint language with his Jamaican 'expert' colleagues. We spent the whole of a day conducting a tenprint throughput audit at East Queen Street, for the whole of the year 2000, in each of their Parishes.

This was to provide an indication of how many tenprints were being produced, though we guessed that a serious under production of them might apply to an Island such as Jamaica. It was a wonder that I was ever able to calculate their requirements because I can recall that they were unable to tell me how many Tenprints were held in each of their slots on the numerous shelves that completely filled the walls all around the Bureau. They were covered in dust and as I've commented on before, many were years out of date.

It was obviously necessary for me to count the number being sent to Tacoma and so I counted out a good number, say 100 and then weighed them on some primitive scales I found in the Bureau. These were the spring type usually found hanging up in market stalls to weigh vegetables. They were very old and rusty but they helped me to roughly count 100 at a time.

Chapter 29 – The Dutch Caribbean

Ray and I finalised our Tenprint Audit and on the following day, I took off for Miami to catch a connecting flight to Aruba. I was quite looking forward to this visit as I had not yet been to a Dutch Island. The three Dutch Islands of Aruba, Curacao and Bonaire are located close together in the 'Dutch West Indies' or the 'Netherlands Caribbean', as that area is sometimes referred.

They are situated not far from the coasts of Columbia and Venezuela and are south of Jamaica and the other Caribbean countries. I thought it peculiar that I needed to fly north from Jamaica to Miami so that I could fly south again, probably over Jamaica, to reach Aruba but that's the way it was.

The 24th February was a Saturday and I could not have expected what was to greet me. This little Island was buzzing and I soon found out what it was all about. I arrived fairly early in the morning and booked into the Raddison hotel and was quickly told that today, was the day of the 'Grand Carnival'. The Caribbean was noted for Carnivals on most of the Islands but this was to be the Carnival of all Carnivals. I have often vowed that I would love to take Jo to Aruba to witness it. You never know!

I changed into casual clothes and headed off on foot a short distance where I could see crowds beginning to gather. I was not wearing a hat and I was soon told by more than one local, that I had better get one because I was going to be subjected to some very long and intense heat. I'm not one to shrug off such advice and I was so very pleased that I didn't. It wasn't just the extreme sunshine, but I was soon to learn that having got my position sorted out, there was little chance that I could move away to perhaps find some shade. I soon bought a hat and at the same time, the atmosphere was so vibrant, that I bought a disposable camera in the mistaken hope that I could capture the atmosphere. Although I know I took plenty of photographs, unfortunately, I just cannot locate them now, but also, whilst they were very nice and colourful, it was impossible for them to record the sounds of the vibrant rhythm of the music. It was a fantastic experience. I guess that just about everyone on the Island was there, watching this very long carnival, full of colour and music. The floats were bedecked with various presentations, much like the carnivals in Somerset I experienced as a boy, but far more exotic, colourful and vibrant.

For some reason, I had booked to see Alwin Nectar, the Commissioner of Police on the following day. Why they should agree to see me on a Sunday, I don't know, but it may well have been because I had planned an Island hopping exercise. I duly arrived at the Headquarters and was given strange reactions when I told people that the Commissioner was to see me. "Why man, don't you know it was the carnival only yesterday"? Of course, I knew, and when I told them so, they exclaimed that the Commissioner would most likely not be in office on the Monday either.; they needed to get over the hangovers of Carnival. Sure enough, that was what happened. I had been enjoying myself on this little Island for almost three days and had not been able to see anyone, despite my making appointments to see them. This was typical Caribbean culture.

My flight schedule dictated that I had to leave Aruba on the Wednesday, 28th February and so, I was going to have to present my proposals to the Police, Aruba Tourist Authority, Airport Security and the Immigration Department in those two days prior to then.

It was on this day that I received an unexpected call from Jo. She told me that she had been contacted by Lloyds Bank and she had been asked that I telephone them on a number which clearly wasn't the normal Worcester number. In those days, your local manager was actually at the bank! Because the call concerned my business account, they were not inclined to talk to her about it. All sorts of things went through my mind but before calling the number, I laid all of my bank documents and computer print outs on the bed so that I could quickly refer to whatever documentation they may have wanted me to refer to. After all, a call to the UK from Aruba was one of the most expensive calls to make!

I rang the number to be asked all sorts of questions about my most recent card transactions. Had I purchased some surfing equipment in a Cornwall resort, was one question I can remember. The purchase was supposed to have been made on that same Saturday that I had taken Jo's car to Startins to have a new exhaust pipe fitted.

From my answers, they quickly deduced that my Gold Account Debit Card had been 'skimmed' or 'cloned'. They hinted that it had most likely happened when I had called into the Clackett Lane Service Station, just outside London to fill up with fuel. Fortunately for me, I was now in possession of my American US Bank Debit Card and so this enabled me to immediately destroy my Lloyds Gold Card and for them to cancel the account so that the card could not be used again. They issued me with a new card and refunded all the purchases that clearly, I had not made. All was well.

I made some very good friends in the Dutch West Indies and Aruba was no exception. The huge problem, was that all three Islands were governed by the Dutch authorities in Amsterdam. They didn't have such good equipment as ours, even on their mainland, Netherlands where Aruba were required to send their fingerprint requirements, but even if they wanted their Islands to have it, they would have sourced the equipment themselves.

In addition to the Police Commissioner Alwin Nectar, I saw Marvin Peterson, the Head of their Fingerprint Bureau. I also saw Trudi Hassel, Mikela Werleman and Wilfred Howell, all Chief Immigration Officers at the Airport. I also met the leader of a special anti-Illegal Immigrant squad who all sang from the same hymn sheet concerning their masters and decision makers being in Amsterdam. It seemed that they had discounted being hit by criminals from other Islands because the Amsterdam databases were not going to keep tenprints of such people. I also met the Director of Public Order and Security, Mr Andres E. Paulina who also dealt with Work Permit Authorisation.

Whilst I knew what to expect on Curacao and Bonaire, I took off from Aruba and landed on Curacao on the Wednesday, 28th February 2001. I had booked into the Sheraton hotel for the one night as I knew I needed to be in Bonaire the following day. Luckily, I had arranged a joint presentation at Police Headquarters to representatives of the same organisations as I had presented to, on Aruba. Whilst they were all very interested, their response was bound to be the same, and it was. I was going through the motions and quite frankly, had I not already booked my flight and hotel the next day, I wouldn't have carried on to Bonaire. The Bonaire experience, however, turned out to be some good fortune at least, from a selfish point of view, because Bonaire and Aruba turned out to be among my favourite Caribbean Islands.

I also discovered that whilst Aruba and Curacao were very expensive Islands, Bonaire was to be extremely expensive. The lack of many hotels on this small Island meant that Sagem were required to book me into one of the most expensive hotels I was to lodge in. I learned that flights to Bonaire were few and far between and most people arrived there on very expensive yachts. My hotel was indeed, equipped with moorings for such yachts and their passengers would frequently be residents at the hotel. It was aptly named The Harbour Village hotel.

It was on Bonaire that I was probably best entertained. My stay was to last two nights and very quickly, I was contacted by one of the youngest Commissioners of Police, I was ever to meet. He was Gerald Daantje who insisted that he take me out for dinner that night. He was very interested in what I had to show him but when realising that I was on a fool's errand, he took time out to entertain me for the rest of my stay. He arranged a joint meeting with the Heads of the other agencies on the Island so this gave us a little extra time together. He insisted on taking me to his home where he gave me a cherished Police cap which I still have in good condition. He then drove me all around the Island on the second day, showing off the tourist locations and the salt flats for which the island was renowned. It is apparently the number one 'diving location' in the Caribbean where the sea is so blue and clear. A great visit but sadly, no interest so far as our Interpol / Sagem project was concerned. I should add that the administration of these Dutch Islands being in Amsterdam was always in our knowledge, but I was advised to go, on a 'just in case' initiative. It made sense due to Amsterdam's failure to generally hold other Caribbean Islands fingerprints.

My tour of the Dutch Caribbean and the experience of their wonderful hospitality was to come to an end on 3rd March 2001 when I left Bonaire for the Island of Puerto Rico. I was to stay the night in a hotel there purely so that I could catch a plane the next day for the small Island of Dominica. Once again, I needed to fly out of my way due to the small number of flights leaving Aruba and none at all, apparently flying directly to Dominica. I spent the night on Puerto Rico followed by a flight to St Lucia and then transfer planes to get to Dominica. Three planes to travel such a short distance!

As I was not to court Puerto Rico with our wares, I had not researched it, so I didn't know what to expect. It's one of the largest Islands in the Caribbean nestling almost at the head of the Caribbean Greater Antilles chain of Islands between the Dominican Republic and the British Virgin Islands. I had thought that with such a name, it would be a Spanish Island and so I was most surprised when I was greeted by American Immigration Officers. When I quizzed the lady officer who checked me in, she was proud to announce to me that I had landed in an American State! I knew that that wasn't the case but when I challenged that, I was told that it was an unincorporated territory of the US. The Spanish apparently ceded the Island to the US in 1917 following the Spanish-American War. I suppose it was much like being in one of our British Protected Islands. The US and UK arms stretch some considerably lengths but, in this case, Spanish was the main language.

My surprise was to be continued because once outside the airport, one could be forgiven for thinking I had been placed in central Manhattan. With all of the tall sky rise buildings with glitzy shopping arcades, we could well have been in New York or Los Angeles. It being an off-shore Island also led to it being a 'gaming' paradise Island with a Casino in most hotels, including mine.

My taxi took me to the Intercontinental hotel and although I'm not usually taken by the razmataz of these buildings, I couldn't avoid being impressed. It was the sort of place that you could spend a great two weeks holiday, but I wouldn't want to live there. Having checked in, it took some time to explore the hotel with its five restaurants and then I wandered down the long two mile beach and then the main street where the hotel was located. It seemed that all of the shopping arcades were interlinked. I was really in the USA.

The San Juan Intercontinental hotel: A High Rise Monster from the outside but inside, a five star luxury hotel located right on the two mile beach and among a row of very high class shopping arcades. A good 'one night' experience.

Chapter 30 – Dominica and Guadelupe

The morning saw me taxi back to the airport to catch my plane to St Lucia. I there boarded another very small prop shafted plane to the tiny air strip on Dominica aptly called Canefield Air Strip. This had obviously been an airstrip carved out of sugar cane territory and was built by the British in 1979 shortly after Dominica achieved its independence. It served the capital Roseau.

Canefield Air Strip and its only Arrival / Departure Building

It is one of those Christopher Columbus Islands now close to the French Islands of Guadeloupe and Martinique and although sometimes referred to as Dominique (French) it is actually pronounced Dom-in-ika and is not to be confused with the Dominican Republic.

Dominica is a very green island full of nature and loved by naturists and hippies with great diving to be experienced around its shores. It is often referred to as the Nature Island of the Caribbean. It's only twenty-nine miles long and 16 miles wide but is recognised as one of the top eco-tourism destinations in the world.

The terrain seen in the background of the airstrip is typical which means that roads on the Island were mainly very narrow, winding and dangerous coastal roads with just a couple crossing through the mountains.

I was to learn that the Immigration requirements and duties of the Island were carried out by the Police because I was checked into the Island by PC 136 Pellam John-Baptiste. I was quick to educate him of the reason for my visit and if the decision could have been made by him, he would have signed up for the fingerprint checking system for Immigration Departments, there and then.

Having landed at this tiny airport, I was a little confused as to why Sagem had booked me into the Castaways hotel which, although was only 6 miles from the airfield, took about a 30 minute taxi ride to reach. It was north of the airfield whilst Roseau was about four miles south of it. This meant that the people I wanted to see who were located in Roseau, were about 40 minutes away from the hotel. It didn't make sense and travelling to and from it would become very expensive.

I did my usual trick of obtaining the taxi driver's mobile telephone number and off he shot whilst I booked into this very rustic hotel. It was, however, very close to the beach and I was told that breakfast would, in fact, be served on the beach. All good so far. It was a very hot day and I was shown to my room. I couldn't believe that there was no air conditioning unit in it. The room looked shabby and it only took me a few seconds to come to the conclusion that I wasn't going to spend two nights there. I marched straight back to reception and handed them the taxi driver's telephone number asking them to cancel my reservation and to get the driver to return.

This obviously caused a fuss and I was questioned as to why I wanted to leave. I told them that I couldn't stop in a room without air conditioning and then the manager slowly stuttered out that actually, they did have a newly refurbished room with air conditioning but that it was yet to be used and would need making up with bed clothes and towels etc. I asked to see the room which, as was stated, was in brand new condition. I told him that I thought I could manage a beer whilst his staff made up the room. It obviously took no time at all and I found that I was in a great room in a great 'rustic' hotel. There were many tourists there, plenty of young single people who were on diving holidays. I chatted to them and discovered that this was one of the diving pearls of the Caribbean. Oh well, I had to get on with my work!!!

My first job, as always having booked into hotels, was to get my laptop plugged into the local telephone network so that I could search for the nearest 'dial up' location for the Internet. I needed to check my e-mails. Oh dear! My arms had been metaphorically amputated when I realised that my laptop would not fire up. I was stuck in one of the most rustic of Caribbean Islands and there would be no chance of me getting the damn thing fixed here!

It was 5th March 2001 and I enjoyed breakfast on the beach and summoned my taxi driver to take me to Roseau where I had a preliminary meeting with the Police Commissioner Matthius D. Lestrade. Although the Islands dependence on Agriculture had been vastly assisted by tourism, especially the visits of Cruise Liners, one couldn't help but notice that the infrastructure was very poor, as was the Island in general. The Commissioner, however, was quite excited about the project but my first impressions of the island was an indication that there was no way that they would be affording to buy into it. Hopefully, there was always a chance that I may be wrong, but I always tended to back my senses.

The state of my laptop was soon brought into our conversation. I had brought it with me just in case someone on the Island had the knowledge to fix it. Matthius thought for a while and suggested that there may well be someone located in a room on the first floor of a building in Kennedy Avenue, one of the main streets in the centre. I needed my laptop also to show off some slides and to demonstrate aspects of our entry / exit system. As this was a preliminary meeting, I hot footed it to Kennedy Street to try and find this man who Matthius had thought had done a Microsoft Course in computer technology.

It took some time to find, but I eventually saw a very small IBM or Microsoft sign at the foot of some old wooden stairs leading to a couple of small rooms occupied by a company called Burgcom Inc. It was at 42 Kennedy Avenue and by the look of the main room there, and the one man occupying it, my impression was that this was a one man operation and I doubted whether I would leave it with my computer fixed. I found the chap there to be a very pleasant lad who told me that he had received training. I cannot now remember whether this was Microsoft 'software' training or it could have been IBM training in 'hardware'.

I have a sense that it was the latter and the stroke of luck was, that my Laptop was an IBM variety. My level of confidence began to rise as his fingers rippled over the keys like a wave petering out on a Caribbean beach.

He fiddled around with it for a while and eventually he started it up in 'Emergency' mode. This was a procedure which I can do myself now, but at that time, I hadn't a clue. There was obviously a problem that needed fixing in the long term, but knowing how to fire it up in 'Emergency' mode suited my requirements at least for the remainder of that trip. I was eternally thankful to him and I paid him the modest sum for his time that he had requested. I had been given the use of my arms again.

The rest of my day was taken up by demonstrating my kit not only to the Police, but to the Ministry of Labour, a Mr. Matthew George, concerning the usual illegal immigrant problem they suffered with Immigrants working without work permits. To repeat, the immigration requirements fell beneath the Police's umbrella and so I was able to include the illegal immigrant subject with the Commissioner and his Inspector in charge of Immigration, Charles E. Cuffy. I also saw their Head of the 'Scenes of Crime Department', Alec Bazil and the Comptroller of Customs, Mr David Adolphus and his Senior Executive Officer, Mrs Nora Williams, during the following day.

Whilst this was an independent country and although being filled with their excitement for it, I left the Island with little doubt that the finance involved, would preclude them from enjoying it.

Guadeloupe and all that French

My next port of call was to the French island of Guadeloupe. My departure from Dominica was, however, to be an experience in itself. As I've explained before, this airfield was nothing more than an airstrip and the plane I was to be conveyed in, was a little propeller driven thing which from memory, carried only about 8 to 10 passengers. I was amused as I climbed into it. There was no flight attendant and it was necessary to just find any spare seat. I couldn't stand up in it because of the lack of headroom and so I crouched down and shuffled my way to a seat.

The cockpit was separated from us by a shabby curtain and it contained just the one pilot. I can vividly remember that when the pilot reached his starting place on the strip, he started to rev the engine up until it reached a high pitched squeal. The whole thing began to shake and vibrate and I wondered whether it was going to collapse onto the airstrip in little pieces. The pilot pulled back the curtain and stared at us passengers. He raised his thumb in a gesture which no doubt was intended to convey the message that we were about to take off. He was unable to speak to us because of the engine noise. Nobody objected and so he increased the engine speed even more when all of a sudden, we jerked forward very quickly. It was as if he was holding it back on a hand brake which he suddenly released. We began to increase speed along the runway.

The planes vibration never stopped and because the pilot had left his curtain open, we were able to see the airstrip in front of us. Whether this thing would ever take off, was probably the question all of us passengers were inwardly considering. My doubt increased when I couldn't help noticing that the plane's nose appeared to be facing to the side of the runway. Miraculously, we appeared to continue in a straight path along the strip even though the nose was aiming to the left. Was the chassis bent, or was the plane crabbing along? For some reason, when one is in the hands of someone you imagine to be fully trained and competent, much like a surgeon who has power of you when he operates, one's confidence is totally given over to that person and sure enough, that confidence was rewarded when this load of metal slowly rose into the air to make the short trip to the neighbouring Island of Guadeloupe.

Guadeloupe is something vastly different. For a start, it is controlled by the French and for all intents and purposes, you may as well be in France. Everything about it was French. The car registration numbers were French, we drove on the right hand side, all road signs and indeed other signs were in French and everyone spoke no other language other than French. If you had been in a coma and suddenly awoken from it, you would definitely think you were in France.

I recall the airport being quite a posh affair, it was an International Airport and obviously quite modern, far different from that at Dominica. I introduced myself to an Immigration Officer who made contact with the Regional Police Director's Office to tell him that I had arrived. I must have made arrangements to visit the Immigration, Police and Customs Heads prior to my arrival but I can't recall exactly what the arrangements were. I was taken to my hotel, The St John hotel, Anchorage, Pointe a Pitra, the Capital City and then to Police Headquarters at Morne Vergain, Les Abymes, not far from the airport.

The huge problem I faced, was that no-one appeared to speak English. That included Claude Destampes, the Director of the region's policing. We were in his office, pleasantly nodding, shrugging shoulders and making noises but quite frankly, neither of us could understand what the other was on about. Thankfully, he eventually introduced me to Francois Thierry and I think he had probably been lifted off the shelf because he spoke English, though not very well. Whilst Claude Destampes was the Director of Police Operations for the whole Region, the Commissioner was in fact Francois Thierry - Ooops, he hadn't been dragged off that shelf after all.

I sat in a comfortable chair and the Commissioner loaded a cassette or a disc into a player and began to show me a film on a monitor, naturally, it was all in French. The film was a publicity film made all about the policing of Guadeloupe. They appeared to want me to watch this but then, they left me alone in the office. The gesturing of them to their watches and the odd English word spoken made me understand that they were waiting for another person I had arranged to see. This was Bernard Foucre. I was to learn that he was aptly named!!

When Bernard arrived, I went through the motions of showing them our film and demonstrating our kit. As anticipated, I was to learn that just like the Dutch Caribbean countries, Guadeloupe and the other French Islands were also controlled by their motherland. I cannot blame any future reader of this for wondering why on earth we had chosen these countries to visit. It seems quite obvious now, as I write this that an awful lot of money was wasted. I recall we discussed this at the time we planned to take on the Caribbean, but as well as Sagem being a French Company, we did wonder how much influence these companies had and we weren't completely sure what the relationships were between the Islands and their mother countries. There was only one way to find out.

From a selfish point of view, I had a great time on Guadeloupe. We quickly wrapped up the business side of things and we were off to a very fine restaurant for lunch. The French certainly know where and what to eat. I have in my notes that we went to Lolla Palooza but whilst I can find plenty of references for Lollapalooza on the Internet, I cannot pin down a restaurant of that name in Guadeloupe. We went through the lunch hour and most of the afternoon. One course, after another, and I don't know how many bottles of wine were consumed.

It was late afternoon and I suspect that these three senior position holders would be driving straight to their homes. I say this because, I had been handed over to Bernard Foucre, to give him his proper rank, the Principal Commissioner / Director of the Department of Frontier Police of Guadeloupe. He was the loudest of them, knew little or no English and had had far too much to drink to be driving me back to my hotel. From what I could gather through the odd word and his gestures, he was going to show me a little of Guadeloupe. I imagine he was single or most likely divorced because it was plain to me that he was taking me around the 'Red Light' area of whatever part of Guadeloupe we were in. In addition, he was showing off by driving at break neck speeds. I recall resting my hand on his right sleeve to indicate to him to slow down as we sped along the roads. It is fair to say that I was quite frightened. We didn't stop once and I was very relieved to arrive at the hotel. As I said, FOUCRE by name and FOUCRE by nature!

Chapter 31 - Barbados Again and Bermuda stalls

I left Guadeloupe the next morning and arrived at Barbados again after having to swap planes again at San Juan, Costa Rica. Having been introduced to the Accra Beach hotel on my previous visit by the Comptroller of Customs and Rotarian, Randolph (Randy) Straughan, I booked to stay there for three nights. It was quite close to the ACCP Secretariat Offices and so that was very useful.

My mission was to massage acceptance to our proposal. I paid another visit to see Grantley Watson, the Commissioner and have a note that I made some other presentations but I can't now recall to who they were made. I do know that once again, I met up with the Attorney General, Sir David Simmons during the evening of 9th March 2001. He was a real supporter and I had high hopes that Barbados would be included in those countries who would join our system. If Sir David had anything to do with it, they would be 'on board' for certain. On a personal note, he was also encouraging me to think about living there and to consider a vacancy at the Sandy Lane Golfing complex. Whilst appreciating that, I was sure that Jo would have none of it.

My room was one on the left overlooking the pool and beach

It was on a late afternoon after finishing my business, that I decided to get my shorts on and nip down to the beach bar at the rear of the Accra Beach hotel. This being a little further south than Bridgetown, the sea was a rougher with relatively much higher waves being blown in, than was the case higher up near to the Grand hotel where I had stayed previously.

It was 'Happy Hour' which meant that the Rum Punches were going at half price – two for the price of one. Not wanting to pass over such an offer, I sat on a stool at this open air beach bar, gently sipping the Rum Punches and laughing my head off at a gang of mainly girls, trying to get themselves on board a few canoes which they had hired from a beach trader nearby. The one would get in and as another tried, the waves would tip the canoes over, spilling any who had managed to get in. Their antics were hilarious and much to the delight of us all at the bar, their attempts to get properly afloat went on for quite some time.

They eventually gave up and walked up to the beach bar and I explained what fun they had given us. We got chatting and were all taking advantage of the 'Happy Hour'. I'm pretty sure that this was a gang of British boys and girls but I cannot remember anything further about them although they did their level best to persuade me to go out with them to some club later on. I was very much older than them and I think they took pity on this old Granddad who was out in the Caribbean all by himself. In the end I agreed and following a few more rum punches, the time came when we needed to go to our respective rooms to change. That's when someone must have pulled a switch to make the room spin!!!

I hadn't realised how easy those drinks had slipped down. All I can remember about being back in my room was that I had tried to put my foot into my trouser leg and failed miserably when my toe got caught up somewhere in the waist band area which caused me to tipple forwards. (Should that be 'topple' but it was tipsy that I was!)

I can recall the clatter of all the coins spilling out of my pockets and rolling across the cold, hard marble floor of my room. I can also remember saying to myself, "Oh sod it". The coins stayed where they had landed and I slumped on top of my bed and that's where I stayed until awakening at about 3am feeling very cold, as the air conditioning was still on and I was semi naked lying on top of my bed. My apologies were given at breakfast the next morning and I never saw them again.

On my last night in Barbados, I took John Parker and Keith Renaud, the Heads of the ACCP Secretariat, out to dinner at the Shak Shak Restaurant just up the road from their offices. This was a 'thank you' dinner for allowing me to use their facilities once again.

I left Barbados and arrived back at Gatwick early on 11th March. Mum had spent too long in hospital and most of my time spent at home was in finding her a decent care home. I recall many that I wouldn't have lodged a dog in. We eventually found a decent one and by coincidence, she moved into it from Bromyard hospital on the same day as I had to travel from Nassau to Bermuda. I was gutted that I couldn't be in Hereford to see mum settled, however, Jo did a very good job.

Just over a week had elapsed since I left Barbados and now, I was off to the Bahamas again. I booked into my favourite hotel in Nassau on 18th March. It was the Colonial Hilton which was nearer the centre of town and had its own beach area and a very nice pool. Pat was due to arrive later that day and so I booked a dinner table at 'The Poop Deck' which was Commissioner Paul Farquharson's favourite restaurant. During the next day, we were again to meet with Paul and the Permanent Secretary to the Minister for Law and Order, Mark Wilson. During the final day, I took Pat to Force Headquarters and their fingerprint and Criminal Record Office which was a short car drive to the outskirts of the city.

Having left the Bahamas, I was back at The Hamilton Princess hotel, Bermuda for four nights and had fixed up a dinner date with Howard Cutts, the head of Bermuda's fingerprint bureau. Pat was due to join me from Tacoma, a day or two later. Our purpose was to hopefully reap the rewards of a very hard slog in putting together the final proposal to the Bermudian Government. We were to jointly present it during the following day.

We held a more casual meeting with the Commissioner, Jean-Jacques LeMay during the day prior to our presentation. It was obvious that he would push for acquisition of the system but we needed to strategise concerning us persuading the government that it was good value. This was to be made even more difficult when I saw the costings and almost fell off my chair. They were delivered to us in Bermuda behind the actual proposal which we had already completed and had with us.

I had gathered a rough idea of what the system was going to cost and what the various countries could afford. Even with my lack of knowledge, I had worked with British Police forces and I knew the sort of prices that each were paying. They were calculated on a cost per record basis. The Bermudian throughputs would probably equate similarly to the smallest forces in the UK. The only additional costings involved would be shipping and acquiring the records, but these prices I saw, seemed comparatively massive to me. I discussed my concerns with Pat and he eventually made contact with Jean-Claude in Tacoma. The end result, was that Jean-Claude faxed revised pages dealing with the costings which we needed to insert into the proposal before we made the presentation.

We presented our proposal during the following day at the Bermuda Police Headquarters. Pat and I knew how important this presentation was going to be. They had assembled all of the top Government Officials including the Permanent Secretary to the Minister for Home Affairs and his colleagues who would be holding the Government's purse strings. The room was full of Senior Police Officers and Howard Cutts and a few of his colleagues from the fingerprint bureau. In addition, Jean-Jacques Le-may had arranged for his successor, Jonathan Smith to be present.

I have already mentioned the huge push in Bermuda, (and in other past Colonial countries) to fill important positions with their own indigenous people. This followed a general inclination to rely on British or Canadian expertise in Governmental spheres in connection with the training and expertise within their various agencies such as Education and the Police. We weren't to know, until a late stage, that Jean-Jacques secondment to Bermuda was to end and he would be returning to Canada. He was to be replaced by a white 'home grown' man, Jonathan Smith.

Jonathan had received some rapid promotions and I felt they had pulled a 'fast one' because he was born in Bermuda of white parents and had received a good education. Whilst there were plenty of white people on the Island, many were from companies with roots in other countries and it was otherwise quite unusual to see white people on the Island in such influential positions other than in those Banking or Insurance Companies ensconced on the Island, from abroad. It was sensible to have Jonathan at our presentation, because he would be inheriting the system for the force.

The presentation went very well. Pat and I once again did our double act with him addressing the technical issues involved and the way we would handle the process of acquiring tenprints and crime marks via FedEx submissions to Tacoma. I did my usual operational 'enthusiasm' bit about the successes already achieved by Bermuda and all other Caribbean countries taking part in the 'proof of concept' trials. We knew that the fingerprint bureau and the Force's 'Big Wigs' were all anxious to receive the service and so, the only remaining hurdle to clear was to persuade the Government officials of the operational and financial values.

Everyone was so enthusiastic that Pat volunteered me to stay on for a couple of extra days so that I could be used to set up and chair a press conference. We hadn't, however, counted on Jonathan Smith wanting to gain a few 'brownie' points by later suggesting to the Government that as he was soon to be inducted into the Commissioner's Office, he ought to review the proposal in more detail. This was entirely sensible for him, but we did think that he could have accepted the advice of his predecessor and the fingerprint experts and all the literature and information that we had provided. As much as I liked Jonathan, I personally thought that he was out to impress his new masters by displaying an over cautionary approach. But after all, the Government would need to find the finances and they wouldn't have thanked him had they signed up for something he knew little about, especially if it had proved to be a 'flop'. He was holding the aces.

This procrastination wasn't apparent to us immediately afterwards and I did stay on to handle the press as I've said above. I had been used to holding press conferences when in the force and to be frank, I was quite looking forward to doing it. (Much like when I once launched a National Motorway Speeding Campaign on TV and then got booked for speeding not so long after!!)

The procrastination slowly extended and although I was to receive plenty of apologies, the decision for Bermuda to be the first country to sign up for the service was not decided upon before I had to return to the UK on 25th March 2001.

Chapter 32 – Turks and Caicos and on to Jamaica Again

Interpol was really pleased in the number of hits (matches) we had achieved in fingerprints found at serious crime scenes throughout the Caribbean. My job was in effect, an easy one because although I always made sure that I was enthusiastic about the system and them buying into it, the results we had achieved through our 'Proof of Concept' pilot had, in effect, sold it to them. But there wasn't a lot of consideration involved because the 'Proof of Concept' initiative was free of charge, so no cigar yet!

April was to bring along the annual meeting of the Caribbean Overseas Territories (COTS) Police and Customs Representatives. This was an important security meeting not only for the British protected overseas countries of Anguilla, British Virgin Islands, Cayman Islands, Montserrat and Turks and Caicos Islands, but for the whole of the Caribbean and representatives of many of the other countries would also be invited to it.

My short six day period at home involved writing up the Operational Requirements for the countries I had visited, to prepare for further presentations and demonstrations in the Bahamas, and for further visits to Jamaica. All this, in addition to planning for the COTS conference, which was to be held on the Island of Providenciales, Turks and Caicos. This was a huge ask and I worked from very early mornings until very late nights each day to complete these 'at home' tasks. I also needed to give some time to family which included plenty of visits to Mum. I needed to tie up some loose ends with her and her new abode at Bodenham Road, Hereford. Jo had taken the brunt of her move whilst I was absent.

And so, it was off again to all that sun, sand and glorious sea, in yet another country I had never visited. My passport admitted me to the Island of Providenciales on April fool's day, 2001. Despite Cockburn Town on Grand Turk being the Capital of the Turks and Caicos Islands, as mentioned above, the conference was to be held on the more populated Island of Providenciales. The total population of the Islands was about 45,000 but around 50% of them had settled on Providenciales. The Allegro Resort hotel was to host the conference. Although I'm jumping ahead a little, it is interesting to note that about eight years after my visit, the United Kingdom suspended Turks and Caicos' self-government following allegation of ministerial corruption. However, they continue to be a British Overseas Territory.

Although the conference was due to last for several days, I was to give my presentation on the first day (the day following my arrival) and then leave on the following evening for an overnight stay at Miami before an onward flight to Kingston Jamaica for my 3rd visit there.

I was alone on this visit to Turks and Caicos and so needed to cover the areas that Pat used to cover. I used a Multi Media Power Point presentation and also by then, our excellent film had also been made. In addition, I was once again very lucky to have David Thursfield in the audience as one of the delegates. David was then, the Commissioner for the Cayman Islands Police and we had been close in West Mercia, and more importantly, he and his wife, Linda were a couple we could call friends. We have remained friends ever since. He was only too pleased to endorse my comments on the system's operational successes by relating to them from his first-hand knowledge of our first undetected murder hit by use of the 'Proof of Concept' initiative. This was yet another of our 'double act' performances and everything went well.

So, on 4th April 2001 following my overnight stay at The Crown Plaza hotel, Miami, I was admitted to Kingston Jamaica for another eleven day stay at the Hilton hotel. With the fingerprint bureau staff, I was to explore how we could capture the fingerprints of all the Jamaicans who had been expelled or deported from other countries and returned to Jamaica. The US in particular deported numerous of these during every month and many of them would simply provide false details to acquire another passport under a different name. It was a real headache. The joke about this, was that if all illegal immigrant Jamaicans were to be deported back home, the Island would sink!

I also wanted to see if Livescan machines would be a viable proposition for them and if so, where they should be located. I had a meeting with Commissioner Frances Forbes and we agreed that I should perform a Tenprint 'throughput study' in the north of the Island at Montego Bay. I made arrangements to fly up to meet the Officer in Charge of that Division, a Superintendent Owen Ellington. I will always remember this day for a couple of reasons. The first concerned the fact that during my flight, I realised that I had left my reading spectacles in the hotel. I only needed reading specs in those days. I wondered if I would be able to purchase some simple 'ready read' type specs but I had no idea how easy they would be to find.

The plane landed at Montego Bay and taxied up to its parking place. From the windows of the plane, I was a little bemused to see a police car parked up almost at the foot of the steps from the plane. I instinctively thought that we must have been carrying a prisoner under escort. This made sense because the road route between Kingston and Montego Bay was tortuous even though it was only a trip of 112 miles. It was my driver, Fraser who advised against that option.

However, as I began to descend the last steps of the plane, a Police Officer marched up to me and threw me the best salute I had seen for a long time. "Mr Humphrey Sir!" The letter 'S' had once again been omitted from the end of my name. This was the trait during most of my Caribbean encounters.

The proverbial penny, had been dropped. Being the only white person on the plane and carrying my briefcase, I must have stuck out like a sore thumb. He had been sent to collect me and had persuaded the powers that be at the airport, that he should do so on the 'air side' of the airport as opposed to waiting with all of the others on the 'Public side'. I couldn't believe it. My head swelled with a little pride and I bet my chest had expanded an extra inch or two! I had been treated with red carpet treatment, but my instinct was that this was possibly the result of another little touch of corruption or unnecessary display of 'police power' that existed on these islands. I was not asked for my ticket and it being a domestic flight, there were no immigration issues.

I hoped that this officer was so resourceful that he would be just the chap that could help me solve the problem with my reading specs. "Of course, Sir!" he said, "That will be no problem, I take you to the pharmacy". We drove into the town to find the retailer choice of my driver. The shopkeeper was, however, a little apologetic because the only ones they had were of the tinted variety. We were on a very sunny Island and tinted 'ready read' glasses would be just the job for most who sought to buy them. I was actually delighted, because had I the choice, I would have selected the tinted ones anyway. I tried the first pair on and they were just the job so far as their magnification properties were concerned. I was absolutely delighted. I had been saved thanks to this resourceful officer.

I reached for my wallet and the shopkeeper used his hands to gesture to me that there would be no charge. "My gift Sir!" Oh, here we are again then? A Police Officer accompanies a smartly dressed white man into a shop to make a purchase and he's offered the goods free of charge! Would that have happened to me if the police officer was not with me? I thought probably to the contrary, I would have doubtless been charged more than the going rate! The price of the glasses was on the ticket and I withdrew the appropriate amount of dollars from my wallet, handed it to the proprietor and did not stop for any change.

As minor as it might appear, here was yet another example of the corruption I had encountered and even though, perhaps, it represented 'small change' compared with others, this reflected the attitude and culture that existed. I couldn't help thinking that this culture was endemic, certainly in Jamaica, but perhaps throughout the whole of the West Indies. I was not going to get sucked into such states of affairs!

We arrived at Montego Bay Police Station where I was met by Superintendent Owen Ellington, his deputy and I think the head of their CID, Deputy Detective Superintendent, Roy Boyd. No sooner had we met and swapped niceties, the four of us shot off in a car to a local Chinese Restaurant. I was a little surprised at this because the time then, was very early for lunch; so early in fact, that the restaurant was closed.

Whether our arrival had been pre-planned, I cannot be sure, but a few taps on the door saw it being opened by the staff who seemed very pleased to see us. I sat back to let the locals order whatever, and before long, the table was festooned with many different Chinese dishes and we tucked in. It was a long time before members of the public entered the restaurant for lunch and whilst I didn't see anyone pay for this meal, that doesn't mean that it was provided gratis, but I would have gambled that it had been. My offers of payment were greeted with all sorts of talk about me being their guest. Was this another display of corruption? I wasn't sure, but I suspected it was.

Time for me was tight but luckily, even with this elongated lunch period, their processes at the Police Station made it easier for me to conduct a Tenprint Audit and record sufficient information to write up a 'Business Case' when I returned to the hotel at Kingston. I was able to catch my return flight without any problem.

I had been looking forward to the arrival of a certain Roy Penrose who would arrive during the next day, 7th April. Roy had retired from the Metropolitan Police as a Commander. He had held the post of Commander of the South East Crime Squad and had been appointed the first Director of The National Crime Squad. This was a very prestigious appointment and it would have been when, in this role, that he would have met Sir John Hoddinott who had been the Chairman of the ACPO Crime Committee. They had evidently remained friends. As I have said before, when Sir John retired, the Consortium would not hesitate in paying him consultation fees. His Policing experience and his Knighthood and with him being our AFRC Chairman, would undoubtedly open many doors and with Jamaica being overrun with crime and criminals, it had obviously been felt that Roy would feel more at home there and with more credibility, in such an environment than I.

Like Sir John, Roy had been hovering around the Consortium, and this trip was to be a 'one off' consultation, but no doubt designed to impress the powers that be, within the Jamaican Constabulary Force. The idea was that Roy and I were to reinvestigate a few murder enquiries which involved the hits we had made on our system and which had hitherto remained undetected. As I have intimated before, Jamaica was seen as the 'key stone' of success for our Interpol Project as most other islands encountered travelling criminals from Jamaica.

The idea, put very simply, was that we would prove that our system was a much cheaper and more efficient way in which to detect crime. By reviewing a few murders, we could perhaps calculate the approximate cost of the investigations compared with a detection through an early identification of an AFIS scene of crime fingerprint. However, the cost of a full scale investigation, would not, in every case, always guarantee that the crime would be detected. Anyway, having settled him in, I gave Roy a briefing and used the rest of the day, and indeed the following day, to show him around Kingston. (Excluding Trench Town) We got on very well.

I had arranged an appointment to meet the Head of the Homicide Squad, Detective Superintendent Calvin Benjamin at Police Headquarters in Spanish Town. I'm not sure what resources he had, but suffice to say, with the number of murders taking place on a daily basis, he would be a very busy man. Unfortunately, Calvin wasn't immediately available and so we were sat in a kind of anti-room near his office to wait for him. We both instinctively began to sniff at what can only be described as a queer smell in the air. I think it would have been Roy who first mentioned this and asked if I thought it was the smell of Cannabis? I had smelt cannabis before but my limited experience was such, that I was no expert. Anyway, following our initial introductions when Superintendent Benjamin finally appeared, Roy dropped it right on his toes by asking him why we could smell Cannabis. Asking him this way left him no room to manoeuvre by debating whether or not it was, in fact, Cannabis.

Neither Roy nor I appeared surprised because the reply received was so 'matter of fact' that whilst it deserved us falling off our chairs, we both instinctively knew that we shouldn't have been expected to have been surprised. Calvin responded by telling us that the 'Seized Property' store was nearby and that when suspected cannabis seizures were made, his men were expected to try it to confirm their suspicions!!!! WHAT??

We were given a couple of murder files to go on with and I repeat that these had been undetected cases until we had cleared them up by use of our fingerprint system. We were anxious to discover why they hadn't solved the murders through traditional investigative methods. All this to prove that it would be more cost efficient to have one fingerprint expert search thousands of fingerprints automatically than to spend money on teams of detectives, perhaps unsuccessfully, working for months on such cases. The first thing we noticed was that the files were very thin for murder enquiries. I will recall one of the cases here: -

A young attractive woman had flown to the US mainland to visit friends or relations. She had, in effect, gone on holiday. She was known to have returned to Jamaica because the last sighting of her, was at the airport shortly after her arrival. From that time onwards, however, she had disappeared from the face of the earth. She had not returned home to where she lived in Jamaica, so the thought was, that she had been abducted either at the airport or during her journey home. I cannot now remember whether she had her own transport there at the airport but, whatever, many weeks later, her decomposing body was found several miles out into the countryside, in a shallow sandy grave in a dry river bed.

Roy and I began to plot what would have been the courses of actions had this murder occurred in the UK. Obviously, preserve the scene, call in the Forensic Pathologist, get the body identified, and arrange for the post mortem examination to be carried out. Have teams of detectives conduct enquiries at the airport – modes of travel, buses, taxis etc. Question passengers on anniversary flights on subsequent weeks etc. etc.

In effect, we sighed and failed at the first hurdle. Yes, we were dealing with a murder that had been treated almost like a minor complaint. So far as the scene was concerned, the body had been removed prior to any forensic investigation. Ah yes, but what about the post mortem examination? What post mortem examination? The undertakers had seized the body and so far as they were concerned, all that was left to do would be to deal with the family for the funeral arrangements.

We ascertained that mortuaries do exist in Jamaica but they are all privately owned and the owners charge a fee for having bodies rest in them and to have post mortem examinations performed. What they will not permit is having decomposed or as we know them in the UK, 'dirty' bodies in their mortuaries. We were to learn that a doctor attended the scene, took one look at this decomposed body and certified that she was dead. That was it. I cannot now recall what the cause of death had been attributed to, but whatever it was, was made without having the benefit of a post mortem examination. The point was, our cunning plan had failed at the first hurdle because how on earth could we come up with a cost comparison when no costs at all seemed to be afforded to such investigations? We briefly scanned over the other files but eventually, called it a day.

Our 'cost comparison' tactic would be doomed to failure as it became quite obvious to us that these investigations were not conducted with anything like the same sort of resources as expended at home. In fact, it should have been obvious to us because how could any force be capable of making thorough investigations into homicides when the national newspaper, 'The Gleaner' carried a daily tally of murders in each issue. Very rarely did this tally remain the same from day to day and more often than not, multiple murders would be added. They could not possibly, conduct anything like meaningful investigations but surely this was a very good reason why they should invest in AFIS equipment?

It was Roy's job to write up his report on all this, which, after all, was the reason for his short contract. However, without relying on the comparisons, the benefits of the system was obviously apparent. More murders would be detected and hopefully, the detection rate might also affect the rate of homicides being committed.

The Finished Product

I recall that we both had long periods in our separate rooms at the hotel with Roy writing up his report and me writing up my reports on the 'Deportee' initiative as well as the business case for a 'Livescan' machine being introduced at Montego Bay. It was so hot that our work was interrupted now and again to share a cool drink together. I also recall that during this period, I had the local radio on quietly in the background and that as I wrote there was quite a long chat or 'phone in' programme on air about the appalling murder rate in Jamaica. Although any contribution from me would have been excellent advertising, I resisted making a phone call to the programme in case that would ruffle feathers.

My enquiries necessitated making the odd visit to other Police Departments in Kingston. I visited 'Corporate Affairs' and spoke to an Inspector Ansel Dwyer regarding police budgets and the 'Statistics Department'. I also held meetings with the Minister for Justice again, a Mrs Elaine Baker. My 'Business Case' was to develop into a firm proposal which would be added to by the Sagem boys and girls who would insert their various images etc. Finance was, as ever, a huge issue and I had further meetings with Mrs Cooper, Director of Finance. These two ladies, Mrs Baker and Mrs Cooper would have a huge influence on whether the country would accept our proposal.

The 13th April was Jo's 55th Birthday and here was I stuck in the sun in Jamaica in a sweltering hot room writing up a 'Jamaican Business Case'. All this was to take me three full twelve-hour days of writing between 8am and 8pm. I left Jamaica for an overnight flight to Gatwick where I was met by 'Mercia Private Hire' to deliver me home on 16th. April. My idea of being taken to and collected from airports had paid off. The return trip had cost £200 which would have been far less than it would have cost in mileage claims and airport car park fees and what's more, I could have a nap on the way home!

I was to get 13 days at home now and most of this was to be taken up with me finishing off the Jamaican proposal and also working on the proposal for The Bahamas Immigration Department.

Chapter 33 - Bahamas Immigration and Jamaica again

We needed to make a presentation to the new Minister for Immigration in the Bahamas. This included Sir John Hoddinott, Jean-Claude Richard, Pat and myself. I arrived at Nassau on 29th April and booked into the Colonial Hilton. The other three were arriving from Seattle and I met them at the airport later. I had prepared a presentation for us, and Jean-Claude had prepared a mock-up of an identity card for Immigrants. We felt sure that we had a solution for them and we were pretty confident that they would want to play ball. The identity card would naturally be a biometric one carrying a photograph and a finger print of the holder. The idea was to issue each immigrant with a card which could double as a work permit, if appropriate. It was a great idea and foreign workers who would provide their prints to register, could so easily be checked out by use of a mobile, hand held, 'Morpho Touch' unit which would preclude any card holder from passing themselves off as someone else.

Our presentation was to be made on the following morning, and so we took the opportunity to take the Commissioner, Paul Farquharson out to dinner at 'The Poop Deck' again. The Chief Immigration Officer was Vernon Burrows, another important official who was a very nice man. His new Minister for Immigration was an Earl Deveaux and his Permanent Secretary was Thelma Ferguson Beneby. They were all present with the Attorney General and Minister for Justice, a Janet Bostwick. In addition, Mark Wilson, the Permanent Secretary to the Deputy Prime Minister and Minister for National Security, Frank Watson was present along with a number of senior Immigration officers. As normal, Sir John, Pat and Jean-Claude gave their pieces of the presentation and I followed up with the operational side and enthusiastically recounted some of the best 'hits' we had achieved. I also demonstrated the use of the identity card / work permit. (Smart Card) The whole presentation was very well received and we spent quite some time after it, answering 'follow up' questions.

Early during the next morning, Pat and Sir John flew off to Jamaica and I was to catch them up later. Meanwhile, Jean-Claude and I remained as we had been invited by the Commissioner to attend his monthly 'COMPSTAT' meeting at Police Headquarters where we would be able to give a presentation. This was a monthly management meeting of all the senior officers. They discussed management issues and their crime detection rates. It reminded me of my old days as a DCI and a Detective Superintendent when we similarly met to discuss similar issues. They would all be able to see how the proposed system would assist in their endeavours to improve crime detention. It was just the right audience to preach to.

I knew there would be one problem with our presentation. I could understand the Bahamian accent quite well as they were all very much more westernised than most other Caribbean countries. Their problem would undoubtedly be Jean-Claude's very thick French accent. He had stayed on in Nassau for this presentation and so easily could have gone back to Seattle with Sir John and Pat. I wished he had and my fingers were crossed as he started and I prayed that he would not go on for too long. We showed the film which, as I have said before, was a huge success and showed exactly what our system was all about. I demonstrated the 'Morpho Touch' hand held equipment and then Jean-Claude started. What was so vastly different to our monthly meetings was the fact that the room was so packed with officers that most were standing and I could see some of them shuffling on their feet.

Thankfully, Jean-Claude didn't go on for too long and, in any case, I sensed that the audience was a little sympathetic to his problem. After all, he was French and had done very well to master our language, a task that not too many French nationals bother to attempt. Without wanting to appear 'big headed' I was always thankful that my part of these presentations got down to operational matters. That is, both on the street and in the fingerprint bureau. That was their language. If I had been a recipient, I wouldn't be too bothered about how successful the company had been and how much all this was going to cost. My interest would have been in my subject, 'how many more criminals will we be able to catch'? Mine was the easiest job of them all.

Jean-Claude wasn't due to catch his plane until early evening and so I took the opportunity to take him out to Thompson Boulevard on the outskirts of the city where the Royal Bahamian Police Criminal Records Department was located. Inspector Paul Rolle was the Head of Bureau within this Department and we had already made good friends. As I have said before, they operated an American 'Stand Alone' system in their Bureau. It worked well for them but obviously, they would have given their right arms to have a system which linked up with a Central Database covering the whole of the Caribbean.

It was following this visit that Jean-Claude started to ring alarm bells in my head. He treated me to lunch at the Colonial Hilton where we were staying and he broached the subject of my dealing with follow up visits and presenting the various proposals to countries I had already visited. He was to suggest that savings could be made by my dealing with much of this by telephone. I must say that this shook me down to my heels. I had several problems here, and the one that hit me first, was the fact that Sagem was one of the biggest defence companies in the world and I couldn't believe that my expenses around the Caribbean were going to be of concern to them in any way whatsoever. However, this was entirely unexpected though it did cause me to cough and splutter and defend my position.

Jean-Claude had, in fact, not taken into account the 'Building Blocks' approach that I had been taking. It would have been no use me flying into a country like a travelling salesman, showing the customer the wares and hoping for an order. I saw my job as a 'softly, softly catchee monkey' type. I needed to build up the confidence and relationships of those who would be purchasing the system and indeed, those who would be using it and benefitting from it. In addition, short visits gave insufficient time to meet all of the important people who I knew should see and learn about it. There were always additional people who should have been shown it. I told him that to have all of the various agencies on each Island, join forces and work together using compatible equipment and database resources was no simple matter. Hearts and minds needed to be won over and although I didn't say it, I knew that my chatting ability was already paying off in that context.

We were now at a very critical stage with many proposals already completed. I could see the whole lot going down the drain if we simply abandoned them and made 'follow ups' over the telephone or just posted the proposals. The other obvious problem I had, was that now that I had signed the contract with Sagem, Jean-Claude was, in effect, my boss. In theory, he could have told me to change my practices to what he was proffering and I would have had to comply. However, I felt that we both knew that my old boss, Pat Pitt who I still regarded as my 'real boss', was pulling many of Jean-Claude's strings. We concluded our little discussion over lunch by my suggesting that as Pat was such an influential project manager, that we might discuss the issue with him.

He agreed and we concluded our very nice lunch amicably although he would have known that, so far as I was concerned, I was dead against his idea. We both went to the airport together and he returned to Tacoma and I went to Jamaica to catch up with Pat and Sir John.

We were once again, staying at the Kingston Hilton hotel and I wasted no time in telling them about my conversation with Jean-Claude. They too, were flabbergasted and I knew that with pressure from them, Jean-Claude would eventually 'give way'. However, what we hadn't perhaps then taken into account was whether Jean-Claude had been directed from his Sagem bosses in Paris. It was now creeping very close to 30th June, our supposed 'Exit' day and in retrospect, I now consider that that scenario might have indeed played out. If Sagem had already intended to continue operating our system with the Home Office and its PITO quango then spending lots of money on me and air fares, was going to be a complete waste of money. I don't think we had properly considered that a possibility, at least then!

During the following day, 2nd May 2001, the three of us went to the Jamaican Police Headquarters to meet with Francis (Frankie) Forbes, and the two very important ladies, Mrs Baker and Mrs Cooper. All the signs there were positive and later Pat and Sir John flew off to Cayman and I was 'volunteered' to stay in Jamaica again. There was still much to be done in the East Queen Street Bureau and I needed to prepare an operation order for how we were to 'Back Record Convert' their fingerprint collection into our system. This would involve the weeding out of the over age and otherwise, 'nonsense' tenprints that they were holding. My job was still very much a PR one and I desperately needed to bring some modern day thinking into a very old fashioned Fingerprint Bureau. For example, if there was a test cricket match on, the whole of the bureau staff would down tools and watch it on TV. My 'brick wall' was to get a very old fashioned Superintendent 'on side', he was the man who was failing to accept that keeping Tenprints of criminals now over 100 years of age, amounted to a waste of valuable space in the bureau.

I have mentioned this before, but the only fast way to approximate the number of Tenprints they held, was to weigh a batch on an old fashioned and rusty 'spring' scales. This missionary visit, however, only continued for the next two days during which I also arranged for the Montego Bay tenprints to be acquired ready for Livescan implementation.

I arrived back at Heathrow during the early morning of 5th May 2001 and was to spend the next week working from home, preparing for the Annual ACCPO Conference in St Lucia. I also had to prepare a talk to deliver at a Drugs Commander's Course at The Hyatt hotel, Gros Islet, Pigeon Island Causeway, St Lucia. This course was to be attended by all Chief Officers, their managers and supervisors of all the Caribbean Island drug squads. Our system would doubtless be extremely useful to them especially at times when drugs raids were held when the portable Morpho Touch unit would come into its own.

At the conference itself, here would be senior police and government officials for all the police forces in the Caribbean. What an opportunity that would be and poor Jean-Claude Richard, whether with pressure from his parent company, Sagem or not, was going to have to spend an awful lot of money on personnel and equipment costs to persuade hearts and minds that they could not refuse to be dragged into the 20th century so far as fingerprints and crime detection was concerned.

So, what with my continual mentioning of meals, nice hotels, indeed, beach hotels, ocean swims and rum punches, I'm beginning to wonder whether any reader of this might be coming to the conclusion that my travels were all about enjoying myself. This may be an ideal opportunity to let me clarify the situation. The fact that I am a type of animal that will enjoy himself in most any environment in foreign lands so long as the inhabitants are not hostile, is absolutely correct. I will talk to anyone and usually make them believe that black is white, if that is my goal. The fact that if given a task, I will move heaven and earth to obtain the objectives concerned, is also very correct. Oh yes, I enjoyed myself whenever the opportunity arose but don't get mistaken if you think that my eye was off the ball.

Putting the hours in when I should be asleep has been with me for many years and 5.30am is the time when I can write with greater speed of thought. It is also the time when I can often reflect and cause many a penny to finally drop. I have never been a clock watcher and have never relaxed until the end of the job has been successfully arrived at. I think Pat was of a similar disposition. For example, I cannot understand people who do not immediately respond to emails but allow them to lay in their in box for several days. What is the point of that when you can get rid of it as soon as possible?

Chapter 34 - The St Lucia ACCPO Conference

The annual conference of the 'Association of Caribbean Chief Police Officers' (ACCPO) was to be held at The Bay Gardens hotel, Rodney Bay, St Lucia, just a short distance from a very nice beach. It was to be held for a complete week commencing Monday 21st May 2001.

I needed to make a few trips to the airport to pick up some of our delegates, including my old mate David Thursfield who had also brought his wife, Linda along. Also, I was to pick up Francis (Frankie) Forbes, the Commissioner of Jamaica. This was convenient as I was able to deliver Jo to the airport before collecting Frankie from his flight soon after. Frankie was always a very smart dresser and it was on the journey from the airport that I asked him how he always managed to look ultra-smart even after alighting from a flight. He told me that whenever he got to a hotel and unpacked, he would hang his creased clothes near to the shower so as to let the steam take the wrinkles out. So, with all of my travelling, that was a tip I shall always remember, though I have never tried it.

With every Commissioner and other chief officers of every Caribbean Country and with many other very important observers present, it was a golden opportunity for us to plug home the system we were hoping they would accept. It was so important that Jean-Claude arranged for a new generation Livescan machine to be installed at the venue for demonstration purposes.

On the selfish side, I had seen the conference to be a golden opportunity for Jo and I to take a holiday over in St Lucia before the conference started. We had flown out together via Barbados and as we were Jazz enthusiasts, we stayed at a more convenient hotel nearer to where the Annual 'Out Door' Lucia Jazz Festival was to take place on Pigeon Island Causeway, the day following our arrival. The festival was to boast many famous jazz groups and singers and the star attraction this year was Luther Vandross though I confess to never hearing of him until then.

My deal with SMI was, that as they had asked me to do the drugs conference presentation during our holiday on 18th May, they would pay for my accommodation from the night previous to the drugs conference which was when we moved into the Bay Gardens hotel. This saved me having to pay for another night's accommodation at the Auberge Seraphin hotel where we had stayed for the Jazz Festival.

For now, I could forget about both conferences until 18th so we were to enjoy our holiday on St Lucia but before it was to end, I had to deliver my talk to the 'Drugs Commanders' conference at the Hyatt hotel. We took an early taxi and we enjoyed ourselves at a table alongside their glorious pool. At the appropriate time, I left Jo to enjoy the pool while I changed in a room provided and delivered my talk. My lasting memory was of the enthusiasm shown by all these drugs squad chiefs who couldn't wait to be able to use our AFIS systems.

All went well. However, the inevitable happened again when Jean-Claude wanted me to stay on St. Lucia after the conference, to include a trip to Antigua, which was, in any event, to have been included on my agenda. He was obviously in a hurry but the inconvenience to me was that the usual 'fallout' from this conference would take me an age to work on. I suppose keeping me at the hotel at St Lucia for a week or two to do that, would still have worked out a lot cheaper than flying me back to London and then returning to Antigua later, on a return trip.

Our driver would have been waiting at Gatwick to take us home. However, Jean-Clause agreed that Jo could use it without me, to return to Worcester as planned. It therefore cost them to provide me with the same transport on my eventual return. Surely this multi-million pound corporation wasn't penny pinching again as I thought that issue had been overcome; or could all this be connected with our possible 'Exit' from this project on 30th June? It made me wonder. The below list of attendees proves how important this conference was going to be.

It will be noted that in addition to Douglas Bell the Sagem engineer who had installed the Livescan machine, that it was only Sir John and myself who were from 'Sagem'. Sir John had evidently been sponsored by Sagem and not the AFRC which then seemed appropriate.

It is also interesting to see the presence of Interpol delegates who were hoping to eventually benefit from our system, whoever would be operating it. It was because I was to spend a few extra days there writing up the 'post conference' notes that I spent some time with them.

Presenters/Observers/Exhibitors

His Excellency Sr. Lazaro Cabezas	Ambassador – Republic of Cuba
Honourable Velon John	Minister of Legal Affairs, Home Affairs and Labour – St. Lucia
Sir Denis Byron	Chief Justice – St. Lucia
Sir John Hoddinot	SAGEM
Senator Professor Ramesh Deosaran	Director, Centre for Criminology and Criminal Justice UWI Trinidad
Mr. Ronald Noble	Secretary General – INTERPOL
Dr. Edward Greene	Assistant Secretary General – CARICOM
Mr. John Anderson	US Depart of Justice – ICITAP
Mr. Dave Byrom	Project Management Office, Barbados
Mr. Stuart Cameron-Waller	Director Regional Co-ordination & Development – INTERPOL
Mr. James Collardeau	Permanent Secretary – CCLEC
Ms. Susan R. Chainer	Legal Attache, U.S. Embassy, Barbados
Mr. Larry Covington	U.K. Overseas Territories – OTRCIS
Ms. Ann G. Duncan	Caribbean Regional Co-ordinator, International Association of women Police
Mr. David Evans	U.K. Overseas Territories – Adviser
Senior Superintendent Novelette Grant	Jamaica Constabulary Force
Mr. Graham Honey	U.K. Drugs Liaison Officer – Barbados
Mr. Barnard Humphris	Law Enforcement Director – Caribbean Anti money Laundering Programme (CALP)
Lt. Col. Fairbairn Liverpool	CARICOM
Mr. Paul Mathias	U.K. Regional Police Adviser
Mr. Flavio Mirella	United Nations Office of Drug Control and Crime Prevention (UNDCP)
Col. Jose Manuel Perez Cernodo	DGPNR (Police) Cuba
Mr. Alan Reid	Adviser-ONDCP-Antigua
Mr. Brian Reynolds	Programme Director – CALP
Mr. Giles Sabatier	European Commission Drugs Control Office – Barbados
Mr. Richard Sauve	Royal Canadian Mounted Police – Jamaica
Ms Terri Swann	President – International Association of Women Police
Mr. Gary Tuggle	DEA – Us Embassy – Barbados
Ms. Marilyn Williams	US Embassy – Barbados
Mr. Gary Allen	Caribbean Media Corporation

Mrs. Patricia Brandon	Pan American Health Organisation
Ms. Cheryl Corbin	President – Caribbean Council of Forensic Laboratory Heads
Mrs. Bernice Dyer-Regis	Quality Tourism for the Caribbean
Professor Clifford E. Griffin	North Carolina State University
Mr. Norman Heath	Consultant – Neheath & Associates
Mr. Shaun Mallinson	National Training Centre – U.K.
Mr. Christopher Nuttal	Consultant to Government of Barbados
Ms. Nelcia Robinson	Co-ordinator – Caribbean Association for Feminist Research and Action (CAFRA)
Mr. Douglas Bell	SAGEM
Mr. Bill Branan	Director, Motorola
Mr. Charles Briggs	Sales Manager, Cable & Wireless
Ms. Karen Dorans	AFR, Consortium
Mr. Andrew Gray	Vice President, Motorola
Ms Peggy Haynes	Account Executive, Cable & Wireless
Mr. Brian Humphreys	SAGEM
Mr. John Magee	Manager, Caribbean markets, Motorola
Mr. Mark Pickett	Director, Second Change Body Armour Inc
Mr. Patrick Pitt	AFR Consortium
Mr. John Rich	President, Intech
Ms. Antonia Saul	Account Manger, Fujitsu-ICL
Mr. John Shaw	Vice President, ABM
Mr. Steve Somersall	Account Executive, Cable & Wireless
Ms. Kerry Ward	Account Executive, Cable & Wireless
Mr. Ronald Wright	AFR Consortium
Mr. Billion Young-Chin	Lock, Stock and Barrel - Jamaica

I had been taught how to operate our 2nd generation Livescan machine by the engineers who had installed it and thus, I was to 'show it off' to those present. Our three handed presentation would only take about an hour and a half on one of the days and so there was plenty of time to introduce myself to those attendees who I hadn't previously met.

Meeting and greeting these important people was very often done at the bar during the evenings or around the 'Livescan' machine and the 'Morpho Touch' equipment that I was demonstrating to them, sometimes, as individuals.

The conference was not unlike other similar large scale conferences where various sponsors would host evening dinners; I suppose they were advertising their businesses. On the evening when it was Sagem Morpho's turn to sponsor the evening dinner, we went to JJ's Paradise Restaurant, on Marigot Beach. This was some huge, very 'up market' Beach Restaurant and it had arranged it so that we ate there on their special 'sea food' evening.

I recall that it was necessary to hire a fleet of buses to take us the 13 miles or so along the coast to Marigot Bay and as one descends down the hill into it, the scenery simply takes one's breath away. I had also been lucky to see it from the sailing ship that we had been on during our holiday.

There had been many famous films shot at this location including Dr Doolittle. We had a great night and meal and it was voted the best sponsored dinner of the week. However, the conference had concluded and I had three clear days to write up the conference business rewards and to start a mini tour of St Lucia to reap in any stragglers who may have had second thoughts about our system. My first port of call was to the Police and Customs Departments in the capital, Castries. We were now just two months away from 30th June 2001 when the NAFIS project was due to take over from us and commence operations. My job now was to stop these government departments from 'pussy footing' around in St Lucia and elsewhere and to get them to prove their good intentions by getting their signatures on 'letters of intent' signifying their intention to sign up to our 'Post NAFIS' solutions as I've hitherto described.

The Deputy Commissioner of St Lucia, a Neal Parker was a white British Subject on loan from a British Force. There would be no problem here and he was confident that St. Lucia would be 'on board'. After seeing the customs officials and working on post conference business at the hotel, I eventually flew out of St Lucia landing on Antigua during the night of 28th May 2001, almost a month to the day before our 'EXIT' was due from this project.

Chapter 35 – My Alarm Call in Antigua

I booked into the Siboney Beach hotel; this was the hotel that I had stumbled across whilst chatting to its owner after he had finished a long windsurfing session. It was a small hotel but it had a good homely feel about it. My check-in was quite late and I retired to bed.

I had two full days in which to whizz around all of the similar 'Security' type agencies on Antigua. (Police, Customs, Immigration, Airport Security, Defence Force and the Drugs Agency – ONDC) They had all received their proposals from me, so in hoping that their appetite had been whetted, it would be a quick visit to each to obtain letters of intent or to encourage their compilation if they hadn't already been prepared. This may read as being quite a simple task, but the laid back culture of the Caribbean made what should have been a straightforward task, very often, quite frustrating.

My first visit was to Police Headquarters. I had tipped off my friend Truehart Smith's secretary that I would be calling in and as I walked along the corridor towards his office, Truehart dashed out with cap in hand. "Hello Brian, what are you doing here"? Here we go – his secretary obviously hadn't told him!

Before I could adequately respond, he continued, "Come with me". I followed him and we got into his car. I hadn't a clue what was happening. He then told me that we were going to see the Home Secretary, Cutie Benjamin, (Steadroy Benjamin) – him with the high pitched voice. My absolute delight thinking that this was perhaps the positive culmination of their decision was quickly shattered.

I wasn't to know that there was one hell of a political eruption taking place on the Island. Cutie had been made the Home Secretary and my old mate; Dr. Errol Cort had been suspended pending the investigation into his involvement in the alleged corruption allegations surrounding the private medical scheme. There was also that million dollar question about the non-payment of tax allegation against him.

We arrived at Government Buildings and quite frankly, the signing of a letter of intent was the last thing on both Truehart's and Cutie's minds. We went into Cutie's office and I had to pinch myself in the realisation that here I was, sat in the Home Secretary's Office with the Commissioner of Police and all three of us listening to a radio on Cutie's desk. We were listening to the live broadcast of the inquisition into these alleged corrupt practices. The Home Secretary was just the man I would have prayed to see, but I knew that this was no time to start talking about a 'Letter of Intent'. Although I briefly mentioned it, at that time, they were in no mood to even think about it. That would have to wait until later.

It was fascinating to hear these two commenting on what was happening at the enquiry. I was also fascinated to understand that such a procedure was being broadcast on live radio, although as I write this, a similar inquisition is being broadcast at home concerning the lessons to be learned from the Covid Pandemic. Little did they know, that I had been asked by Dr Cort, who had been the Attorney General before his suspension, to complete a review of the force with Sir John Woodcock and that it was Dr. Cort who had suggested that Truehart needed replacing. There was clearly no love lost between the two and naturally, I kept my silence.

By the time that day had ended and during the whole of the following day, I completed my business with these agencies. I wasn't going to get much further towards a decision from this Island. I decided to have dinner out on the beach in the Siboney Beach's own beach restaurant. I opened the menu and in the front inside cover, the hotel had placed a press cutting from the UK's Sunday Times, extolling the virtues of this restaurant. It was described by the author as the best Caribbean Beach Restaurant! I was in the process of reading the write up when from the corner of my eye, I noticed what I thought was the unexplained movement of a rug which drifted right over the entire floor.

Although we were on the beach, the floor of the restaurant was on a wooden deck and as I looked up, I saw that there were no rugs on the floor. What I had seen was the mass movement of numerous rats that moved across the floor as one unit, just like a moving rug. There was a young lady and others in the restaurant but this young lady who was alone, yelled out an ear piercing scream which would have been heard from miles away. I decided to tuck this experience of the 'Caribbean' section of my memory into my brain's 'trash box' and carried on with my meal. It was with Jo in Castries, St Lucia that we had both witnessed a similar blanket of rats running across a busy road.

Perhaps this wasn't going to be my favoured hotel after all. As I've said many times before, there's plenty of rats in the Caribbean, including two legged ones and nothing much else other than sand, sea and sunshine! I had been tempted by a very lucrative job in Barbados but whatever, there was no reason at all that would have tempted us to leave our family in the UK to live there. As they say, "There's no place like home" and the Caribbean surely wasn't home nor could it ever be.

I went to bed that night content in the knowledge that although it wasn't the most successful conclusion I had achieved in the Islands, I had finished my business on Antigua. My memory suggests that all were quite happy to at least sign up for our 'proof of concept' pilot and the 'New Deal', but some, including Antigua, had yet to produce written evidence.

I was looking forward to taking off for St Vincent and Grenada, Islands which were places I had not hitherto visited. We were 'behind the clock' with the UK and so I was rudely awakened very early in the morning by the voice of one of my UK AFRC colleagues on the telephone, Dave Moffat. The news he gave me was to shake me to my roots.

He said, **"SMI have pulled the plug on the whole project. No Caribbean and no Interpol project. Just cancel all flight plans and your itinerary and get a ticket back to the UK as soon as possible".**

I was half asleep and asked Dave several times to repeat and explain. I was more than wide awake by now, though still in denial. I could not believe that SMI would have spent those thousands of dollars on me, my expenses and more so, the cost of the conferences we had just attended and much, much more. The thing that now strikes me, which didn't at the time, concerns the fact that this was a call from Dave Moffatt of the AFRC who were not now my employers. Things were now falling into place and I'm now sure that Jean Claude had simply fallen between a rock and a hard place between Sagem's and AFRC's designs. I had indeed, been having my strings pulled by both and at the same time, though Pat had obviously been pulling them harder and it was he who had briefed Dave to call me. So, who was it indeed, who had been employing me?

The efforts of Jean-Claude Richard in nudging me to follow up business on the telephone instead of making personal visits and flying directly to Antigua instead of returning home from the ACCP conference first, was all now burning back into my mind. With the benefit of hindsight, I could almost guarantee that the decision to withdraw from the project had been under consideration by Sagem, Paris, for some time.

My worst thoughts involved the possibility of them negotiating with NAFIS to continue with the UK service and Livescan but were preventing from making this public until negotiations had been finalised? All conjecture in my mind but I didn't know, nor could I be concerned about the reasons: They had pulled out and that was that! Nothing I could do or say was going to change that.

I was totally shocked that no-one from Sagem or SMI had the decency to speak to me directly. Indeed, they have never made contact with me at all since. I was supposedly under contract with SMI and therefore, I suppose I could have sued them for breaching my contract. I never gave it much thought at the time but I really wasn't bothered. My sadness then was that we had really reached a point when the system worked very well and Livescan would have certainly proved to have been successful in the Caribbean.

None of this had made sense to me, because even if NAFIS had taken over from us in the provision of our domestic fingerprint service for England and Wales, they wouldn't, so far as I was aware, be in a position to offer a Livescan service to the Caribbean unless on the off-chance they had been similarly negotiating behind curtains with Interpol. I later learned that Sagem 'Defence' were indeed to have linked up with Identix.

Most of the Caribbean agreements had been secured already. We had in effect 'bagged' all of the big 'keystone' forces such as Bermuda, Bahamas, Jamaica, St Lucia and almost Antigua. We all felt sure that others would follow suit. If that wasn't immediately apparent following my visits to the smaller countries, they would soon want to 'play' when the results would come rolling in. There was no rhyme nor reason to all this, it was so weird.

Chapter 36 – What now?

I was such a small cog in this wheel at this point and I did as I was told and cancelled my Grenada visit. I left Antigua on a 9.50pm over night flight back to the UK arriving early morning on 1st June 2001. I took the family out for a meal, maybe it was to celebrate my premature arrival from the Caribbean! My Interpol business was ended but there was more involvement to come.

Many balls were now being juggled in the air. I hadn't even noticed that I had left the AFR Consortium and I had never asked for a contract with SMI. Just to confuse things, I was like a shuttlecock being pinged from one corner of the court to the other to suit the whims of whoever it was holding the racquet. Just to confuse things, I was now working for the Hampshire County Council due to its Police Authority connection.

The collapse of the project meant that in any event, we lost most of our clerical staff and some part time consultant contractor colleagues of mine. With Pat's world collapsing, I felt a little sympathy for him. There was no doubting that he was a workaholic and even as undiplomatic and 'bullish' as he could be, he had been pulling many strings within SMI. But they had now completely pulled the mat from under him. Loving to control, he was now without those he used to influence, but could do nothing except perhaps, work on an 'attack' strategy. There were, after all, many UK and foreign forces who had been promised at least a Livescan service within their 'New Deal' contracts, many of which, were to extend beyond 30th June 2001. They were now, to be left 'high and dry', at least until seeing what NAFIS had to offer.

Pat, as I came to learn, had a propensity for 'firing from the hip' and he also had 'form' for litigation. It wasn't long before rumours started about another bout of litigation, this time against SMI for breaking contractual promises. True, they must have spent an awful lot of money in promoting our 'dream' systems for the UK and Interpol in the Caribbean but, after all, this was seen as an investment to them which might well have resulted in vast profits. What about me? Well, as I've hinted above, let's take the family out to dinner! I could at least look forward to spending more time at home with them and enjoying my pension.

Bearing in mind that this so called 'Story' is probably the last chapter of my already written 'Life Story', on the domestic side of my life, there has been a mountain of words I have omitted in it concerning the hassle I was enduring from the Wychavon District Authority's refusal to grant me planning permission. My plans submitted involved the almost doubling it into the land I had acquired from a neighbouring farmer.

Having hired a professional who failed, I took on the job myself and won. It was only a matter of a few days before I got a contractor to start work and I was to now able to project manage the job myself. Little did I know that torrential rain was to play havoc with the progress of it and large diggers would get bogged down on the job. However, life was great and what a difference this completed work was going to be to our already rather smart garden. This was all thanks to Jo, my gardener. I was excited and couldn't wait for it to be finished.

The grandkids also enjoyed the job as can be seen by the photographs below.

Exactly one week into the Project and Jo and I take time out to share our 35th Wedding Anniversary with the family.

On 12th June, 2001, the inevitable happened when I received an e-mail from Pat confirming that the SMI / AFRC project was now dead and of all things, he wanted me to make a telephone call to Jonathan Smith, the new commissioner of Bermuda, to offer our apologies to him, especially as we had, by then, received a letter of intent from him. His procrastination hadn't help matters, indeed, had we signed them up before Jean-Jaques LeMay ended his secondment from the Canadian Royal Mounted Police, life might have been entirely different because Bermuda would have been seen as a star worth following by other Caribbean countries. Such is fate.

I had been the only contractor who lived a short distance from the Project Office and it was only because I got on so well with Jonathan, that I agreed. Surely, Pat wasn't minded to continue with the Caribbean project? That was a rhetorical question because I instantly knew what he was up to. Pat could have made that call himself and this was just a rouse to get me on board.

So, the greed of being offered good fees and I suppose, some loyalty towards Pat and the AFRC, overtook common sense and off we were to go again with what was to be the start of a series of very short term contracts involving my services. I thought it was folly but I didn't like to let him down.

Grandson Oliver gives the builders a hand

Ramp wall and start of gate pillar

Whilst our consortium of police forces was now defunct, there was the business of winding up, which we called the 'Exit Strategy' to take care of. Once again, we had to arrange for all of the equipment placed in fingerprint bureaux all over the country to be removed. This was to be a repeat of what we did six years previously, so now, we were obviously very efficient at this type of work. We also had two very large suites of offices at The Business Centre, Roman Way, Droitwich to wind down. All files needed to be properly recorded and archived but one couldn't expect Pat to just 'roll over'.

It wasn't long before the wheels started to turn and more litigation was to follow. Our assets remained large and with the concurrence of the police authorities concerned, we could use those financial assets to take part in another bout of litigation, this time, against Sagem Morpho Inc. for breaching the many promises and contracts that had already been put into place. Whatever they had, or hadn't done with NAFIS, they had certainly upset many police forces and other agencies around the world and we had been made to look proper fools. Our garden project was only four days old and already, I had been contracted to sit on the end of a phone at Droitwich, not only to make contact with Bermuda, but all of my other contacts in the Caribbean to 'sweet talk' both those who had produced letters of intent, and those that hadn't.

It could only have been Sagem (SMI) who could facilitate the continuation of what we intended in the Interpol project, so this, to a certain extent, absolved the Interpol with being complicit in a conspiracy with NAFIS. Also, what about Sagem? They had pulled the plug on our project, so being service providers, how on earth could we expect them to reincarnate that Caribbean part of our deals? It was either me who was confused, or had Pat gone completely mad? Had anyone thought about the Government ceasing paying out the Home Office Grants towards the AFRC members costs of joining the Consortium during its interim solution?

Sir John had by now, relinquished his chairmanship of the Consortium and had subsequently retired from the force. He was busy elsewhere and as we know, sadly, and way before his time, died suddenly earlier in this year. I was thinking to myself that we could have really benefitted from his guidance, but alas!

On the other end of telephone lines, I was now speaking to confused Commissioners, high level politicians and heads of security industry agencies to put them fully in the picture – at least, as fully as I could make the situation out to be. For the few who had not responded regarding sending us their letters of intent, then I was to encourage them to do so. In my own mind, I thought that the whole idea was futile. Whilst obviously not disclosing my inner feelings, I was being paid to do my best and that is what I gave the situation. I just couldn't see how we could hope to provide any type of fingerprint service. But, on the other hand, the resultant picture would no doubt enhance our civil claim, but I was never privy to all that was going on behind the scenes.

It would have been a horrific job for SMI to back record convert all forces Tenprints and Marks onto fresh databases with a different company, and even if they desired to do that, how would it be achieved and with whom would the service be contracted? I suspected that their work behind the scenes with Sagem and maybe, Interpol, may have played a part. On the other hand, they may have even offered AFRC and / or Sagem, compensation to take over the existing databases. To be honest, the situation was so unreal and confusing, I became detached from wanting to know, and it was only whilst writing this book that I learned that Bureaux staff were sent to Preston for a short course on the new system and I have a sense that maybe, as identified earlier, the American TRW company became the service provider for NAFIS, but I cannot be 100% sure.

However, I since learned that in December 2004, on behalf of the Home Office, PITO placed a $244m contract with Northrop Grumman for the delivery and integration of an 'IDENT1' system and were also responsible for the maintenance of that system. They were also to add Scotland into it. The installation of forty new Livescan terminals for the Scottish Police Service was completed in April 2005. That IDENT1 system was also integrated with the criminal records on the Police National Computer. I also believe that due to data protection laws, there was no alternative other than to destroy the data we had been responsible for keeping. Again, I cannot guarantee that but if true, with all that effort expended, what a sad day that would have been.

On a more pleasant note, the idea of having an 'End of Consortium' dinner was fully supported and this was held at The Raven hotel, Droitwich on 20th June 2001. I was, by then, working under a contract which employed me at the Droitwich Offices on 'SMI Litigation' work and one of the first jobs I became involved in, concerned the archiving of all documents. We called it 'Document Control'. My employers were not now the AFR Consortium. As the Hampshire Constabulary was always the 'lead force' in the Consortium and we had used the services of their force solicitor, Ted Mason, my contract was now with the Hampshire Police Authority as they had taken on the mantle of tidying everything up in accordance with the 'Exit Strategy'. I had never been a member of the Hampshire Constabulary, but I must say, that there wasn't many forces that I would have happily transferred to but Hampshire was from what I had witnessed, was a very good force.

But first, there were the many fingerprint machines and computers to decommission from the fingerprint bureau all over England and Wales. With Pat's blessing, I recruited my old West Mercia Dog Section Inspector, Keith Rowland to give us a hand. I was also later responsible for recruiting him to help us in Tacoma and I knew by then, he was liked by all. Also, one of the newer contractors, Alan Hammond worked on it as well, as did the lad from the Droitwich office, Ian Duggan.

We were also kitted out with protective clothing and industrial style boots. £155 per day wasn't to be sneezed at and we had some fun. Most other employees and contractors had all gone. Luckily, I lived in the right place and that saw this opportunity come my way. It wasn't for the first time that I had been in the right place at the right time.

Chapter 37 – Letting Sleeping Dogs Lie

Whilst all the pieces of the 'Exit Strategy' were being put in place, Pat and Karen Dorans were still resident in the US because that is where they now lived and continue to do so. Pat was in constant contact with us regarding the Hampshire Police Authority (HPA) Exit Strategy and often made UK visits. However, he briefed me to join him in Tacoma yet again, to assist with the ongoing SMI litigation. I found it hard to believe that I would be returning there again.

Paul Young of Mercia Travel picked me up on 23rd July 2001 and I took off once again from Birmingham Airport for a flight to Newark where I changed for Seattle. I stayed in my old Apartment No 211 at Cliff Street Lofts. My contractor colleague, Tony Grace, an ex-Detective Superintendent from the Hampshire Force was in another apartment on a higher floor. My trip was to last until 10th August.

On the next day, Pat and I went to the luxurious offices of probably one of the best lawyers (and the most expensive) in the State of Washington, possibly in the US. This shouldn't have come as a surprise to me because with our reserves and the support of the old Consortium forces, we were bound to hire the best lawyers possible, as we had done with the IBM litigation. This firm was Preston, Gates and Ellis whose suite of offices were on a very high floor of one of the tallest 'high rise' buildings in Seattle, the Bank of America Tower.

The views from the offices were magnificent and overlooked the Puget Sound. We were that high, that I noticed small planes flying beneath us or at least, that is what it looked like. The offices contained a law library which I swear was bigger than the old Worcester Library; but boy, weren't these lawyers expensive! It was later on in the process when we were to give a presentation to them and during my discussions on the phone, they suggested that there was no need to bring a slide projector as they had one there that we could use. You've guessed it. Not only did they charge a fortune for hiring their equipment, they even charged us the time to discuss it on the telephone!

The name 'Gates' in the firm's name, related to the father of Bill Gates, who had founded Microsoft. This briefing was an all-day briefing and apart from exclaiming how much this day cost us, I promise not to mentioning it again.

Whilst we could afford to put the whole matter of evidence gathering in their hands, they were in a unique position to have, on their side, Pat, Tony Grace and I, some very experienced Detectives who had spent their whole careers in the 'evidence gathering' world. What's more, it was us who had been involved in this whole issue and who best could be employed to do the job for them?

Our meeting ironed out a strategy for this and so, by being employed as 'para-legals', we were able to considerably reduce costs by us doing the donkey work with them conducting the strategies and holding the reins. So, just a few of us were kept on and most of the work would be done by myself and Tony Grace. Although Tony and I were actually being paid through Hampshire Constabulary, we were in effect employed / directed by Preston Gates and Ellis as their 'Para-legals'. This was a term more frequently used in the United States for unqualified lawyers doing the footwork for the qualified ones, as I had been experiencing in the UK.

We also had Pat and Karen there, though Pat was very much the conductor. Dave Moffat, a fellow regular contractor, was also kept on. I recall that one of our first jobs was to catalogue and index every e-mail that had been sent between AFRC staff and SMI staff. This was a massive task and I suggested to Pat that I could get Keith Rowland back again who we could use to do some filing and indexing. He agreed and so I telephoned Keith who had also helped us with decommissioning the UK sites. I was not only his boss during my last posting as Chief Superintendent, Head of Operations in West Mercia but he had also been a close neighbour. Keith was a likeable character and I knew he would do a good job and would get on well with the rest of us. I rang him and he was obviously delighted to join us even though I warned him that the job was pretty mundane.

Going through all those emails and documents was a boring but necessary function in our evidence gathering phase. As an aside, there had been consortium talk of a loyalty bonus payment for AFRC personnel but I had never been officially told of that, it was just talk in the office. Indeed, only four weeks before Sagem ended our project, I had been informed in a memorandum from Pat, that as I was now under contract by SMI, I would not qualify for it. This was very peculiar because, on the one hand, I had never been officially told that there was a loyalty bonus and surely, I wouldn't have accepted any forced transference from AFRC to SMI if I thought that that would have caused me to lose the bonus if it existed. To this day, I don't even know how much was paid out to others if indeed, that was the case.

Also, I had probably done more than most other of my colleagues in an effort to get the job successfully completed. However, I was then receiving a daily rate which was higher than most, if not, all others so, on the one hand, I wasn't too concerned, but on the other, I knew that my change of paymaster made no difference at all as to what I was actually doing. I had never applied for this transfer to SMI and indeed, I was never formally asked to change and I continued to receive my taskings from Pat. So far as I was concerned, nothing had changed at all. A contract was produced with a slightly higher day rate and I walked into that blind as there was no reason not to do so.

My assumption had been that it just became more financially convenient for Pat to have me being paid directly by SMI instead of the AFRC making continual re-charges to SMI. If there was a bonus and I had no official notification that there would ever be one, then I would have believed that I had earned one, indeed, probably far more than many others. Who knows, maybe the others would receive an enhanced share now that I wasn't to receive one?

It didn't really concern me that Pat was eventually to tell me that my SMI contract would preclude me from receiving the bonus. I must admit that I was just 'peeved' because I knew in my heart that I deserved it probably a lot more than some who were to receive it. It was only very much later when I was to learn that another contractor, Terry Smith had muddied the waters by asking Pat some questions about it as to whether or not I would be qualifying for the bonus because apparently, he didn't think that I should be. He also told him that from what he understood, I was expecting to be paid it. WOW! This sounds as though I had discussed it with Terry and for all I know, I may have done but I can't recall doing so. However, he was correct in one thing and that was that I would have expected to have been paid it.

Colours were eventually nailed to the mast when I also learned that Terry had asked Pat if I had yet signed my SMI contract. He was also worried if he was

259

able to let me into the Droitwich Project Office or able to continue using the facilities?? This was nothing to do with him. Whoever reads this should just pause for a while and ask why these question should be asked by a fellow contractor. You see, if I hadn't signed the SMI contract, then maybe I hadn't yet been converted from AFRC's books and I would be similarly rewarded with the loyalty bonus. It was ironic that on that date, the contract wasn't valid because although I had signed it, JCR hadn't!!

Whether I should be allowed in the consortium premises or not is a complete joke. I would still have been expected to have permission to be in the Project Office, no matter whoever was paying me. To me, we were all there as a team and my paymaster was insignificant. I was doing the same job. It was like telling school pupils that when they leave, they shouldn't be allowed back again. In my mind, there was only one reason for such an exchange and that was Terry's desire that he should lead Pat into actions which he knew would result from his mischievous communications with him. I recall that Terry's justification for asking these spurious questions was that he was going to have to brief me on my upcoming evidence gathering roll. That was another joke. I did that role and he was never required to brief me. Indeed, it was Pat who was the ringmaster and the jobs I did in that role were all for him. Tony Grace and I were working at Pat's direction, not for Terry, indeed, I also found evidence of Pat telling Tong Grace that I was his resource in that particular project. (NOT Terry!)

However, apart from not believing that such sneaks existed and now the joy of me being able to confirm those suspicions I had previously been made aware of prior to me actually joining the consortium, after all these years passing, I would rather smile and let that sleeping dog lay in the happy knowledge that the information I had been warned about, was indeed, correct, after all.

I had always made myself aware that by jumping over heads, in particular, the head of he who turned out to be the 'snitch' would cause some problems. My work at categorising emails was, low and behold, to turn up the answer and well and truly identify that 'snitch'.

Anyway, as I've said above, I let sleeping dogs; or should that be 'snakes in the grass' die! The information I received just prior to my AFRC contract about 'the snitch' had proved to be spot on!

Chapter 38 – Goodbye Sir John and Nightmare in Seattle

At that time, it had been just over a year ago when I finished para legal work with local solicitors, so continuing working on 'Litigation Support' was just fine by me as I could just plod along. It was whilst still in the UK, that on 13th August 2001 we were to hear of the tragic death of Sir John Hoddinott, our retired Chairman, the man who had given birth to the Consortium and the man who I really admired and enjoyed working with in the Caribbean.

As mentioned in early chapters, he was a true and very respected leader and a proper gentleman who earned the total respect of everyone who worked for or with him. I had the honour of often working with him alone and I will always remember him once asking me how I got on with Pat. I was obviously not going to be disloyal to Pat and as what might be expected, I 'hedged' an answer. It was then that he told me as his chief constable, he thought it wise to take him off CID and put him in the Computer Department where he might not get into trouble. I was hitherto oblivious as to how Pat became head of the Computer Department until then. I asked no questions and told no lies.

In a similar vein, it had been another Hampshire CID man I came across who, in that era when most officers working in local CID offices, knew who was committing the most crimes on their patch. He mentioned that one of his supervisors came up with a brilliant rouse to make it easier to obtain search warrants. This involved making a call to Crimestoppers as an anonymous member of the public to suggest who the culprit was. Naming the suspect, made it easier to obtain a search warrant to execute on their suspect's address. Maybe not a bad tactic, but I hadn't heard of that before. This was obviously prior to the implementation of The Police and Criminal Evidence Act 1984. I'd better not name the instigator but he will know who it was when he reads this, and he is bound to be one of the first!!

Returning to Sir John's death, Such was the man, and one of my biggest regrets was that because I was to be in Tacoma on the day of his funeral, I would not be able to attend it. I dearly wanted to pay my deepest respects to him.

I spent my 57th Birthday at home and we had a huge family barbeque before I took off once again for Seattle via Birmingham and Newark, on the following day. I was to continue my SMI litigation work for just a week. This work mostly involved finding witnesses and recording their witness statements. I was never briefed by Terry Smith and the jobs were always going to be ongoing for months to come, so I couldn't understand why I would be required in Tacoma for just a week and then six days later, fly me back on a flight to Tacoma again, for a tour of over a month until 5th October 2001. However, during that longer period, following my three weeks assignment, I took a week's leave to extend my stay so that Jo could come out and join me for a holiday. The rent for the Cliff Street apartments was still being paid whether it was occupied or not, so my staying on there, didn't cost anything. It would have been empty had I not been there and so, I just needed to pay for Jo's flight.

The outward trip for Jo was to be exciting in itself, but little did we know then, the inward flight back home was to prove to be a nightmare. We had learned that our good friends, Mike and Mair Aston were flying out to Seattle from Heathrow in order to visit Mike's Nephew who worked at Boeing in Seattle. We knew the flight they were catching and so Jo booked a seat on the same BA flight without telling them. She would obviously bump into them at Heathrow. It must also be remembered that my friend David Parkinson was still flying BA planes around the world and he had always insisted that I e-mail him with details of all my BA flight itineraries of the future. He had never failed to get me upgraded into business class. I told him of Jo's flight details but obviously, she wouldn't know if this little perk would come to fruition until she got onto the plane.

Anyway, first things first. She was dropped off at Heathrow and sure enough, after making her way to the 'booking in' queue, she spotted Mike and Mair and crept up on them to surprise them with her presence. She quickly described what was going on and all were naturally very excited about the surprise. Once on the plane, she was asked over the intercom system to identify herself to an attendant and so, the magic had worked once again. Regrettably, she waved cheerio to Mike and Mair as she was ushered into the business class compartment. Her male companion sat next to her, insisted that she ask for champagne and generally looked after her.

My holiday planning included a short flight to Phoenix and by hire car, we would spend some time in the Grand Canyon. Sadly, on our arrival at Phoenix, despite having pre-booked a car, the Budget Car Hire desk, informed us that they had run out of budget size cars and so the clerk apologetically asked us if we would mind taking a bigger one for the same price. So having agreed to suffer this inconvenience, we walked out onto the car park to search for our bright shiny red Ford Mustang Sports Car. Woooow!

One of the highlights of this trip concerned us taking a flight in a small fixed wing aircraft which took us in and around the Grand Canyon. However, suffice to say that we enjoyed a wonderful few days at the Grand Canyon hotel. But now, I must remember that in addition to this book being an annex to my life story, its primary purpose should concern the progress made in the world of digitised fingerprint searching. So, back to work.

Jo was due to leave Seatac to return to Heathrow during the next day, 11th September, 2001. No one was aware what the 11th September 2001 was to bring. We were eight hours behind UK time and so when those two planes were flown into each of the twin towers of the World Trade Centre in Manhattan, most of us residents in Tacoma were asleep. New York was three hours in front of us and so morning was tragically, well under way for them.

Jo and I were sound asleep when the telephone rang. It was Tony Grace, my mate who was in another of those apartments above us in Cliff Street Lofts. The conversation went like this:-

Tony: "High Brian, did you say it was today that Jo's flying back?"

I wondered what the hell he was on about because he knew only too well that she was to go back that day. I said, "Yes, of course". He said, "She won't be going back today. Switch your TV on". I can't remember now what he said in his brief description of the events that were unfolding but we lay in bed watching the horrific scenes unfolding in New York. One thing was for sure, and that was, Tony was right. No one would be flying anywhere over the US that day and probably for days to come. All aeroplanes had been ordered to land and they were grounded for an indefinite period. If you weren't in Manhattan at that time, I guess that almost the whole of the rest of the population of the US were off the streets, watching that terrible incident unfold. All I could think of was the word, 'Cowards'.

I had arranged to drop Jo off at Seatac Airport and recommence my working life in Tacoma. The few of us contractors there from the UK, were speaking to each other on our phones and it wasn't long before Pat decreed that there would be no working today. We could, and should, stay where we were to watch this terrible news as it broke. Keith Rowland had yet to arrive.

The huge leaps of progress that had been made in telecommunications and TV pictures being capable of being beamed all over the world in such short times, now meant that we were to experience such a huge horrific chapter in our lives, almost at first hand. Oh, those poor people who died such horrific deaths for no reason at all.

I'm sure that there is no need to describe this terrible terrorist attack on the USA, as just about every aspect of it is now so widely known. Suffice to say here, that at the time of writing anyway, it turned out to be the most horrific terrorist attack ever, and I shall never forget those live TV pictures of those poor people, who, to avoid being burnt to death, were throwing themselves out of the buildings for what they thought would be a more acceptable death. Jo's problem of getting back home, paled into insignificance.

However, we went to the airport later but it was obvious that none of the airlines could give any useful or meaningful information. They had been ordered by the US Government not to fly. I suppose we were lucky in a way, because accommodating Jo at the apartment was not a problem. Many visiting passengers would be required to find their own accommodation in and around Seattle. The air around Tacoma and Seattle was always very busy with air traffic. It was an eerie feeling to see the sky empty of planes. We needed to visit a shop in Tacoma, I think for food and it's fair to say that the nation had been numbed. People appeared not to be talking to each other. There was a sort of silence, most definitely in the air but also on the ground. The shopkeepers would mumble things like, "terrible isn't it", just a few words to convey to others that the magnitude of what was happening, was just too big to warrant detailed analysis through speech. Every member of the population was at one. There was no side to be taken, to discuss or to argue about. It was just terrible and everyone knew it, so I think that that situation was responsible for this weird silence.

The other thought that passed through my mind, was that with the time bands being what they were, those terrorists would have boarded the planes during the early morning in New York. If they had boarded the planes at about the same time on the West Coast and at Seattle, then they could well have been on Jo's plane. I know the chances of this happening would have been so remote, but what were the chances of Jo making an Atlantic crossing at the same time. It makes you think.

Suffice to say that Jo spent a week travelling on the bus back and forth to the airport trying to discover how BA was eventually to get her back home. She understood that I was expected to carry on with my work but she has often said that she doesn't ever want to land at Seatac again! She had been delayed for a total of six days and she eventually took off on 17th September, arriving back at Heathrow on 18th. I received the confirmation in a message from our daughter Sarah.

The 30th September 2001 fell on a Saturday. It was my day off and so I drove down to Anacortes and took a Ferry from there to Friday Harbor, had a walk around and then caught another Ferry to Orcas Island. This was just nineteen days after the atrocities of the World Trade Centre Disaster and America, and the rest of the world, were still reeling and counting the cost. No doubt the celebrations of those Al-Qaeda cowards who had planned to kill all those innocent civilians, had not yet waned. I had received my share of good luck and fate often blessed me. This was one of those peaceful afternoons, I couldn't have wished to be anywhere more beautiful or serene, when all of a sudden, my pager broke my silence.

I was to learn that Sarah had just produced our third Grandchild. It was another girl, Georgina Phoebe James!! Both were doing fine but unfortunately, I couldn't be there, however, their health was far more important than my presence, so long as they were both well. I eventually made my way back on the Ferries to my car at Anacortes. I'm sure the thought of little Georgina Phoebe being blessed by being a part of our family, made my journey pass far quicker than it otherwise would have done.

I had to work for another week in Tacoma before I could fly back to the UK again to see our new granddaughter. We were still operating from the suite in the Tacoma Finance Centre, Broadway and it seemed ironic that our software company, Sagem were also in that same building and that we were there now, in the process of suing them. Life does, however, go on in many mysterious ways. I returned home on 5th October to continue working on the Hampshire Police Authority litigation project but once again, after only nine days, I was back on a plane again for Seatac. I and others were simply collating the evidence, mostly by recording witness statements, to be used to to sue SMI.

However, on my arrival, instead of the normal banter I was used to having with Immigration Officers, on this occasions I was taken aside and questioned regarding my continued visits into Seatac and the US in general. They had been used to many British Subjects coming into Seatac when we were in the process of Back Record Converting all our Tenprints to create our emergency database. As I've said before, we employed numerous fingerprint experts in the UK to perform duties in Tacoma on a rota basis, including our daughter Sarah.

So far as myself was concerned, my repetitive flights to and from the US were beginning to be noticed by the US Immigration system. It was deemed necessary that I should get an 'A Class' Visa for Government workers. The following was copied from Wikipedia:-

A visas are issued to "*representatives of a foreign government traveling to the United States to engage in official activities for that government.*" *The A visas are granted to foreign government ambassadors, ministers, diplomats as well as other foreign government officials or employees traveling on official business….* Etc. etc.

All this caused a bit of a fuss which meant that Pat needed to have letters drafted concerning the importance of my presence in America etc. It was necessary for me to fly back to the Passport Office in London personally, to be interviewed and either have my application approved or not. I received a memo from Pat to return to the UK for that purpose and to do an audit of the archives for our litigation purposes.

I therefore returned home a little earlier than expected and Paul Young picked me up to take me home. I had a very short time to get this Visa on my passport sorted out. So, two days later on 5th November, still suffering from Jetlag, I took the train to London to visit the Passport Office. The application had already been sent ahead but I was taking a huge gamble as my ticket to return only six days later, had already been purchased. I didn't know what would have happened had there been a hitch in the process of my visit. Thank God there wasn't and I came away with it safely tucked into my pocket.

Wow! What a difference that 'Class A' visa had made. I was now a Government agent or employee and I remember telling the rest of the crew in Tacoma, the exaggeration that they almost threw me up a salute as I was waved through Immigration this time.

Once again, now that I look at all these dates, I cannot help but wonder why my periods in the US were relatively short. I had just returned to Tacoma on 11th and only after five days work, I am on a plane again returning to the UK on 17th November in compliance with a Memo from Pat. I was to be tasked with obtaining additional witness statements from many other UK ex-employees of the AFRC and UK Fingerprint Officers. I travelled all over the country and on this visit, went to South Yorkshire, Thames Valley, Bedfordshire, Lincolnshire and Hampshire by arrangement to record many witness statements, mainly from fingerprint experts. This was a job I enjoyed because I had always prided myself in recording good witness statements. If my trip back to the US was to finish off what I was doing there, I could have understood, but I would again be returning to the US on a further occasion in the future. I emphasise that every trip back home, my jetlagged brain was eight hours behind. It really was screwing my head up and I often wonder if that was the reason, I now enjoy only about 5 hours sleep per night.

Chapter 39 - A Dude Ranch and the Last Chapter

I'm not at all sure how the various parties of our litigation against SMI were actually linking. Hampshire County Council, the AFRC and our lawyers Preston, Gates and Ellis were all involved and naturally, once again, Pat was the ringmaster of the effort at least between the Hampshire Police Authority and us, the remaining AFRC staff and contractors. We were getting paid by Hampshire County Council who presumably was being compensated by Preston, Gates and Ellis. And there was Pat ostensibly pulling the strings as if the AFR Consortium was still in its original format.

I'm not sure what it was but I emphasise again, that I had not got a clue as to who was paying who and for what but I was darn sure I could have organised personnel and taskings in a manner a lot more efficiently than that experienced. There appeared to me to be two centres of effort that required attention - The Project Offices in Droitwich and at Tacoma. There were tons of documents and witnesses living in both places. Why we were flying so frequently between the two, I could never fathom.

I once again returned to Tacoma on 5th December 2001, to receive the same rapid transit through the US immigration thanks to my 'Class A' Visa. This trip was to prove a bit of an enigma because when I arrived, the rest of the team were already there. Pat and Karen were residents in the US but in addition now, was Keith Rowland, Dave Moffat Tony Grace and Peter Jones, the retired Assistant Chief of Hampshire. In addition, Ian Duggan our Droitwich based 'Clerical Assistant' was also there. I hadn't a clue how we were to be occupied, but, on my arrival, I was told that we would all be travelling to a ranch in Montana in two, 4 x 4 vehicles. The trip was over 500 miles and would take about eight hours depending on our progress over the Rockies which would, by now, be covered in snow. So, why were we all going there, I wondered?

Apparently, unbeknown to me, some time ago, Pat had taken other business people / contacts to this 'Dude Ranch' and it appeared to me soon after we arrived, that this trip, as pleasant as it was, was a bit of a 'Team Building' exercise. We did take some documents with us and to prove a point, we spent about half a day reviewing them.

The journey there was an experience in itself. As I've said, we were in 4 x 4s and as we rose in height to go over the mountains around Spokane, it became a legal requirement that winter tyres or snow chains had to be fitted to the vehicles. As we dipped down the other side into Montana, we were met by quite heavy snow and I wondered whether we would find the 'Dude Ranch' at all.

We eventually arrived at what was, a great holiday ranch location. However, it was in the winter season, when it normally did not operate. It appeared that Pat had befriended these people, Mr and Mrs Leo and Ellen Hargrave who were lovely 'God Fearing' people. They had laid on their facilities, out of season, especially for us. Leo had been a Bombardier on Super Forts (US aircraft) during World War 2.

We learned that one of the Michael Palin's travel series, 'Michael Palin's The Hemingway Adventure', was filmed there when he stopped for a televised stint at this same ranch. The book on that series was there in the ranch and I believe I bought it when I returned home, but I cannot now find it.

The ranch was a massive affair. There were numerous buildings scattered about. The main ranch house had obviously been there for some time as did many large outhouses where cattle and horses could be penned, or to be worked on. In addition, there were newer places designed to accommodate guests. They were in the form of log cabins but with all modern conveniences. I was to bunk down in the main ranch house with our hosts, Leo and Ellen and one or two of the others. They were a lovely couple and very religious, so we said grace at the long table in the huge, well equipped Diner / Kitchen. They cooked us fantastic meals and I had never seen such big steaks on a plate before.

We were to be staying at The Hargrave Ranch for five nights and the highlight, so far as I was concerned, was the ride on horseback up into the mountains. The whole area was covered in snow and because we were there, out of season, we woke early one morning to catch the horses we were to ride all day. When I say 'catch our horses', I didn't really mean that we were going to catch them. We were driven out a few miles and stopped near a gate where we could see their herd of horses. The Cowboy, I can't recall his name, looked at me and said, "You'd better have TINY". Tiny was, as can be guessed by his name, the biggest horse among the herd.

Catching sufficient horses for us and saddling them up, took quite a long time but eventually, we were all set to go. I think before we set off on our trek into the mountains, we rode them back to the ranch house where we loaded up our saddle bags with goodies etc. so that we could 'eat on the hoof' so to speak. The cowboy and a cowgirl were to chaperone us for the whole day. To say that I was a little nervous was an understatement for, apart from a short ride on holiday in Tunisia with our daughters Lisa and Sarah many years before, horse riding had so far eluded me. I recall thinking that riding all day across country up into those mountains without any real training whatsoever, and oh yes; on the biggest horse they could find, wasn't really the safest thing to do. Where was all that 'health and safety' stuff? I was baffled why we were in fact there, but there I was and I was going to enjoy it. My only comfort was in the knowledge that if I did fall off then the snow would at least, soften the impact.

I was soon to find out that 'TINY' wasn't only the biggest horse in the herd but he was the most cunning. I'm sure that he knew that I couldn't ride properly and what's more, I'm sure that he knew that if he took me under low hanging branches, the disturbance of them would cause me to be showered with snow. He did this many times. I made sure that I wasn't at the front or the rear, in the forlorn hope that as he knew where he was going, he would just walk on, in line.

Our Cowgirl and guide for the day and on the right, she helps catch the mounts and saddles them up.

Unfortunately, the 'show offs' in our team had a little canter or trot here and there and without me giving him any messages or instructions, TINY just took off to keep up with the horse in front of him. 'Woooh boy' I would shout as my torso was yanked backwards as my backside was forced forward as he started to canter. It was only pure luck that I managed to stay on him.

We headed up into the mountains and what with the snow, we came across some marvellous views in such beautiful countryside. I'm sure that if ever I was forced to live in America, then I would be giving the cities a wide berth and would be heading straight for the Wild West where we were. The snow-capped countryside was gorgeous.

We had climbed uphill for several hours when, by popular request and demands from our backsides, we stopped among a clearing in the trees and our expert companions who had obviously done this a thousand times before, got a fire going in no time at all. On the fire went the coffee pot and out came the grub from our saddle bags. This was "Just like the Movies"! All we needed now was Mel Brooks and beans and we would have melted into a set in the film 'Blazing Saddles'.

I shan't go on about it, suffice to say the day was one of those experiences one never forgets.

Tiny and Sheriff Humphreys with our host checking us out before we set off

We eventually arrived back in Tacoma, late evening on 11th December 2001.

From the minute I had landed in Seattle on 5th December until the morning of 12th December, I had not been to our place of work. I say 'place of work' because I was to learn that 'the gang' were going to play a practical joke on me but unbeknown to them, I had been tipped off that whilst I had been back in the UK, they had moved the office from Broadway Plaza (Where SMI were also located) to a much smaller suite of offices, quite a distance away.

Because I had not been there when the move happened, they planned to keep this a secret from me and were hoping that I would go up to the 8th floor of our old Broadway Plaza tower premises, only to find that the place was deserted and empty!! What a joke that would have been! Having been tipped off, however, and with one of the 4 x 4 cars that needed to go back to Budget Car Hire in the morning, I settled into the apartment and then took a ride to find out exactly where the new offices were. It would have been impossible for me to have got there without a car but I found it with no trouble at all.

I made sure that I got up earlier than normal during the following morning so that I would get to the new offices before anyone else. I obviously hadn't been issued with a key to the premises yet, so there I was waiting on the doorstep for them to arrive. It was Karen who arrived first and she would be sure to tell everyone else. I said to her, "Come on then, I've been waiting for ages. Someone's got to come back with me to return my 4 x 4!" I kept absolutely quiet about how I knew that the office had been moved and left them all scratching their heads as to why their practical joke had backfired. Karen also, made no comment about why I had arrived at this new location. It was never mentioned but my informant and I thoroughly enjoyed my prank.

Anyway, back to work in this new office for the next three days and on the 4th day, 15th December, I took an overnight flight back to the UK to commence witness statement taking which would take me up to the Christmas holidays.

2002 saw a few major chapters turn; I continued evidence gathering and paid one more visit to Tacoma to mop up. I ceased working for the AFRC and Hampshire Constabulary in February but as they say, "When one door shuts, another opens".

No sooner had I landed from Tacoma, than ex-Detective Superintendent friend of mine, Barrie Pearce informed me that our old force, The West Mercia Constabulary, were enrolling past Senior Police Officers to mentor junior officers in their crime enquiries and to record witness statements, the latter of which he was engaged in. (It was inevitably tagged as 'Dad's Army')

These people were referred to as REPS. (Retained Experienced Personnel). It was great because members could pick and choose what they became involved in and best of all, could always decline any offer. That was particularly helpful because at the same time, I was asked to work for one day a week at a nearby Industrial Estate to form the 100 or so small businesses on it, into a Business Association. I loved that because it meant that I could spend the day walking around the estate chatting to them and organising a committee. It was eventually named, 'The Sandy Lane Business Association' (SLBA but phonetically, 'Slaba').

Both of these engagements were absolutely fabulous and I have often been quoted as saying that I would have worked at both for free. My short term contracts with the Hampshire County Council concerning the winding up of the AFRC, were to continue and so, the start of the year 2002, saw me continuing to travel around the country recording evidence from ex-employees or others who had some evidence to give.

My final contract with the AFR was to take me up to mid-February but I needed to get all of the statements recorded well before then and to take them to the US on my final visit for discussion.

I was to land at Seatac Airport for the last time on AFRC duty. This was a short five-day visit to tidy things up and I returned to the UK on 6th. February to finalise things there. At least, I had lasted the full term and I believe that I was the last contractor to finish with the whole project.

So that was it! I had spent the last seven and a quarter years being a member of the team who had rolled out the very first Automatic Fingerprint Identification System ever to be deployed in the United Kingdom. My own fingerprints were the first ever to be scanned to the USA for checking against a database. I had travelled to America on numerous occasions and had worked there to set up the second generation system from Tacoma. I had also travelled just about all over the Caribbean where we achieved a total of 22,555 identifications against Scenes of Crime Marks found at the most serious crimes committed. In addition, we identified 1070 criminals operating across borders and of those, 323 had given false identities.

I had worked very hard but had been repaid handsomely, both in financial terms and the experiences I had gained. In short, it had been a great finale to my Police career. Apparently once again, we had won our civil case against SMI but I'm not aware whether it was settled out of court or if it went to trial. The sum awarded was also once again not disclosed, or at least, I wasn't to hear of it.

So now, back at home, I could afford to make up some lost time with my family and that included my mother, who continued to live happily in her care home until she died on 8th July 2007. Life for me had moved on a great deal since my AFRC days and indeed, I managed to retire from all forms of work completely on 31st October 2008, after spending six years as the manager of a large Elgar Technology College which was a mixed senior school in Worcester.

However, right out of the blue, on 19th December 2002, I received an email from a young lady who had worked in the AFRC Project Office. This was a Jackie Cooper and she said that Pat Pitt wanted to ask me whether I was interested in a 'one off' writing job. Why on earth he couldn't have written to me directly, escapes me as he knew my email address but I guess that was Pat. I knew that a company AFRC Associates had been set up years ago when I sent my invoice in respect of the statistical document included in the Interpol proposal. But my knowledge of that was prior to the similar company now available to be searched at Companies House which commenced later, in 2004. Jackie Cooper had been the Company Secretary / PA and the company had been set up by Ron Wright. It had originally been registered as AFRCA (UK) Ltd but later changed its name from that acronym to AFR Consortium Associates (UK) Ltd. All documents of listings, reports and meetings appeared to have been written by the named contact, Ron Wright. Apart from him and Jackie, other directors were Ron's wife, Margaret, Pat Pitt, Peter Linden Jones, a David Peter Loban, the latter not known by me. Ron and Pat held 50% shares each at £100. The company dissolved on 20th July 2010.

It appeared quite likely that Pat and Ron were after all, backing horses both ways and had set themselves up so as to be independent traders to the Consortium as we knew it, should that opportunity ever appear.

```
Subj:      MESSAGE FROM PATRICK PITT
Date:      19/12/02 9:35:59 am GMT Standard Time
From:      jackie.cooper3@btopenworld.com
To:        brianhumphreys0@aol.com
Sent from the Internet (Details)
```

Hi Brian

Hope you are keeping well.

Pat has asked me to contact you to see if you would be interested in five days work (not Consortium work but private work) at $300 per day. Starting just after Christmas for a deliverable by 3rd January. The work is all scribing and it doesn't matter if it is done on weekends or in the evening as long as it is completed by 3rd January.

Look forward to hearing from you.

Regards

Jackie Cooper

One of the many lessons I had learned whilst working with Pat, was to realise that whatever he said or promised, might just turn into some sort of different form. He had that knack of turning a small job into an unnecessary big one and as soon as I saw that he was offering me $1,500 for five days work I instinctively knew that this was a job that stood a very good chance of lasting a lot longer.

I learned that on 2nd July 2002, HM Government had published a consultation paper entitled, 'Entitlement Cards and Identity Fraud – A Government Consultation Paper'. I was aware that the government were doing all they could to soften up the public into accepting a National Identification Card system but, the 'civil liberties' brigade would always be against such a scheme. It appeared to me that this system would not only make the payment of benefits a lot easier but would be the back door through which they could introduce an ID card scheme.

There then followed a mass of e-mail exchanges and I was obviously busy with my fresh ventures with the REP scheme at West Mercia and with SLBA at Sandy Lane, so I wasn't particularly fussed, though even in the knowledge that Pat would get his pound of flesh, I must admit that the $1,500 attracted me. This may sound big headed here, but in addition, I knew that if there was writing to be done, Pat would want me to do it. He was always impressed about my style, which was a mystery to me, in the first place.

Those thoughts were correct because in addition to him wanting me to organise the structure of the submission by taking on, in his words, the role of 'Ringmaster', he wanted me to write the 'Executive Summary' in about 1000 words. The response was required to be submitted to the Home Office by 10th January 2003. (Almost 31 years ago as I write this!)

My old colleagues were to be working on different draft sections and with so many individuals involved, I knew that this was a recipe for a complete shambles unless some administrative discipline was imposed. As 'Ringmaster' I needed a 'work flow' plan that required strict compliance and so I agreed to do the job on condition that I could organise this disciplined approach. In simple terms, any exchanges between writers needed to be disciplined and made through one person only. That was agreed. I think he was pleased that someone had organised a plan however, there was one stipulation from him which was **'Please do not include JCR in it'**. The paper was obviously to be submitted by SMI and JCR – Jean-Claude Richard was still the CEO or Vice President of Sagem, the parent company. I would very much like to bet that Pat was going to get paid a whopping fee which, after paying us, would leave him the lion's share. 'C'est la Vie', so JCR might have said!

For the record, the job was a success but the Government never did introduce the 'Entitlement Card' due to the weight of the civil liberties lobby but many publications since have indicated that the use of fingerprints as a means of checking identity is, by far, the favoured option. So, we did our job well and Pat had kept his promises.

Then on 6th February 2013, I received another mysterious email from Pat himself – Marked URGENT.

The below is an exact copy of the original: -

```
-----Original Message-----
From: Patrick Pitt <PatrickPitt@afrca.org>
To: Brian Humphreys <brianhumphreysO@aol.com>
Sent: Wed, 6 Feb 2013 15:36
Subject: Urgent


Brian

Can you travel to Naples at short notice for a case

You will be away one night

Pat

Sent from my iPhone
```

A batch of emails ensued and the long and short of it was that he had a contract with an American Insurance Company whereby he was investigating dodgy insurance claims. There was an American Air Base in Naples and he wanted me to investigate such a claim by an airman who had already recorded a previous false claim. So, was this email going to again tempt me? I had slowed down a great deal since those earlier days and so, I politely declined.

So, apart from electronic Christmas card receipts now having ceased some eleven years ago, that was the last I heard from Pat. The email I recently sent him had bounced back, perhaps he has now retired his Ringmasters whip. I have no regrets and wow, what a fabulous end to my working life. I have been so lucky.

This experience had once again brought with it a whole string of events by that mysterious factor, fate. Even at this late stage, it can be seen that in the paragraph above, I indicated that my electronic Christmas cards from Pat had ceased some eleven years ago. Wow! I received another, only last evening (New Years Day 2024!) I suspect however, this was due to a leak being received about this book which doesn't get published until 10th January 2024 – eight days' time. I do hope Pat Like it. They were good times.

ABOUT THE AUTHOR & THANKS

Brian Humphreys was raised in Hereford where he married his wife, Josephine in 1966. They have two daughters living nearby and have four grandchildren. Since 1969, they have lived in various locations in Worcestershire and they now reside in a village on the periphery of Worcester.

Brian joined the Herefordshire Constabulary as a Police Cadet in 1960 and retired as a Chief Superintendent in 1994. He had served mainly in CID and Operations roles and when a Chief Superintendent, he was selected to become the Staff Officer to Sir John Woodcock, Her Majesty's Inspector of Constabulary at The Home Office. He also had experience as a Divisional Commander and was trained as a 'Hostage Negotiator'.

It was following his retirement that he commenced work as a self-employed Service Manager with the Automatic Fingerprint Recognition Consortium serving most forces in England and Wales. He developed his own business as a Private Investigator and worked on 'Cold Case' reviews of serious crimes. In addition, he was utilised to review criminal investigations during which he mentored young officers in their crime enquiries.

His last employment was as the manager of a large secondary school and he retained that position for five years before fully retiring in 2008. He has been a prolific author and spends his leisure time in 'Family History' and playing golf, croquet, bowls and table Tennis.

He has constantly promised his wife Jo, that his current book will be his last!

Brian also wished to thank those who have given generously of their time (and patience) in volunteering to provide the many amendments they have caused which at least makes the reading of this book apparently, without any cause for grammatical complaint. Terry Westwood, Craig Nicholl and Jim Jackson are all fellow golfers and bowlers who came rushing to Brian's aid. A very big thank you to you all.

Reflective notes

It was many years ago, when I had been seconded for two years, to one of five HMI's of Constabularies, that provided me with an eye watering experience which should have taught me a lesson.

My 'Pre-Inspections' of many police forces provided me with a real insight into the vagaries of the many mechanisms which made the Home Office tick. Unbeknown to most, the work also included being in the corners of forces who, for example, wished to build on its establishment or maybe build new police stations or even in my case, a new police headquarters. It also led me to tuck under my arm, a senior member of the Police Efficiency Unit who once accompanied me on a two week 'Pre-Inspection' of one force. That too, gave me a unique view of what they were up to.

I was to learn that this section of the Home Office was probably very similar to most others in that they were 'narrow viewed', obstinate, inflexible and very unforgiving and almost totally cost driven. In my view, many times to the cost of efficiency.

I should have known better that the chances of having the Consortium Management Agreement 'bent' so as to allow the AFRC to usurp the decade long procrastinated efforts of PITO to be abandoned in favour of them taking over the very successful re-birth of the Tacoma based project, was little or nowhere near likely to happen. Even more unlikely when its base left these shores.

As it happens, PITO's position has allowed them to influence legislative changes to result in the incorporation of Scotland's fingerprint requirements into that which existed in England and Wales. In addition, the incorporation of the Police National Computer cannot now deny that the complete package has, at long last, been achieved.

Having said that, this does not at all, detract from the efforts of that small team which gave birth to the AFRC's interim solution. Sir John Hoddinott and his feisty lieutenant, Pat Pitt strove with such a small team, to lead the way forward and it is without doubt that I can say that their efforts have managed to drag out of that Home Office, the scheme now existing. They fought through such a bumpy road leading down the paths of two heavyweight litigation processes to a success which at first, was never thought possible.